WORLD EDUCATION FORUM

WORLD EDUCATION FORUM

Editor

Dr. Digumarti Bhaskara Rao
M.A., M.Sc., M.A., M.Ed., Ph.D.
R.V.R. College of Education
D-43, Srinivasa Nagar
Guntur-522006 A.P.

2003

DISCOVERY PUBLISHING HOUSE
NEW DELHI-110002

First Published-2003

ISBN 81-7141-639-X

Published by

DISCOVERY PUBLISHING HOUSE
4831/24, Ansari Road, Prahlad Street,
Darya Ganj, New Delhi-110002 (India)
Phone: 3279245 • Fax: 91-11-3253475
E-mail:dphtemp@indiatimes.com

Printed at: Tarun Offset Printers, Delhi

Contents

Foreword

Education is a fundamental right enshrined in the 1948 Universal Declaration of Human Rights. Yet, today, millions of individuals deprived of basic education are still unaware that this is a right they can demand.

The World Education Forum, held in Dakar from 26 to 28 April 2000, was about making this right a reality. It was the culminating event of the decade of Education for All (EFA) initiated in Jomtien, Thailand, in 1990 and, more specifically, of the EFA 2000 Assessment, the largest evaluation of education ever undertaken. This bottom-up exercise, benefiting from the unprecedented participation of all the EFA partners—governments, aid agencies, non-governmental organisations—brought the meeting solid facts, collected and analysed at country level and subsequently synthesized by region.

The Dakar Framework for Action adopted at the close of the Forum is largely based on the Assessment's invaluable data. The most accurate picture to date of the state of basic education worldwide, the EFA 2000 Assessment highlights the gains and shortfalls in educational provision, pinpoints problem areas and unreached groups, and serves as a blueprint for future action.

Clearly, the message of the World Education Forum is not one of complacency. On the contrary, it is a wake-up call and an invitation to act urgently and effectively. First, the Dakar Framework for Action calls on national governments to take full responsibility for ensuring that its goals and strategies are implemented. Education for all is the obligation and prerogative of the State. In working towards this goal, the Dakar Framework urges governments to establish broad-based partnerships with civil society and to give the ensuing national action plans the strongest political support.

Secondly, it calls on UNESCO to co-ordinate global action. We are, indeed, glad to take up this challenge and to work more closely with countries. Our efforts will be directed towards developing education systems that are authentic, affordable and modern, and accessible to all without exclusion or discrimination and that inspire a universal culture in which all human beings can share.

UNESCO will provide concrete support and guidance to countries in drafting their national action plans and will enhance dialogue between countries, donors and civil society, ensuring that national governments maintain full ownership of their education. The task ahead is enormous and the collaboration of all our partner agencies, non-governmental organisations and civil society will be vital.

Funding too will be of the utmost importance. The resources we allocate to education for all will need to be proportional to the challenge ahead. If governments have to make clear, coherent and courageous choices in this respect, as they will indeed have to do, so too will the donor community. UNESCO is currently engaged in a broad consultation on how to strengthen mechanisms for co-ordinating, reporting and evaluating aid flows and how to deal with debt relief.

UNESCO, for its part, will focus on strategies identified in Dakar as deserving particular attention, such as early childhood development, girl's education, literacy, education in emergencies, HIV/AIDS and health issues, and the role of information and communication technologies in education.

The Organisation's essential asset is the unique multi-disciplinary approach it can bring to bear on all these issues so that education for all becomes a reality by 2015 at the latest, and much sooner if possible.

Koïchiro Matsuura
Director-General of UNESCO

Preface

In April 2000 more than 1,100 participants from 164 countries gathered in Dakar, Senegal, for the World Education Forum. They ranged from teachers to prime ministers, academics to policy-makers, political activists to the heads of major international organisations.

Although the participants in the Forum came from diverse backgrounds, they shared a common vision. They dreamed of a world in which everyone, child and adult alike, would command the basic literacy and numeracy skills needed to function as a citizen, worker, family member and fulfilled individual in the emerging global society. The purpose of the three-day gathering was to agree on a strategy to turn this vision of 'education for all' (EFA) into a reality.

The goal of universal basic education had been vigorously articulated a decade before at the World Conference on Education for All: Meeting Basic Learning Needs, which was held in Jomtien, Thailand, in March 1990. On that occasion, participants from 155 countries and representatives of 160 governmental and non-governmental agencies adopted a World Declaration on Education for All, reaffirming the notion of education as a fundamental human right and urging the nations of the world to intensify their efforts to address the basic learning needs of all. They also approved a Framework for Action to Meet Basic Learning Needs that spelled out targets and strategies for reaching this goal by the year 2000.

The World Education Forum in Dakar was convened to assess progress toward EFA since Jomtien, to analyse where and why the goal has remained elusive, and to renew commitments to turn this vision into a reality. For three days the participants presented data, debated strategies and listened to speakers ranging from students in developing countries to heads of state. In his keynote address, United Nations Secretary-General Kofi Annan announced a major new United Nations initiative to 'demonstrably narrow the gender gap' in primary and secondary education by 2005. Leaders of several major donor organisations and delegates from several large donor countries also announced important new programmes.

Not all of the action took place inside the Forum's meeting rooms. On the opening day hundreds of Senegalese children attired in white T-shirts took part in a Global Campaign for Education rally outside in the main entrance. They displayed placards and banners celebrating EFA and held up yellow cards warning that the nations of the world are failing to provide education to every child. Representatives of non-governmental organisations—some of whom were official participants—kept pressure on delegates by passing out literature, talking to them in the halls and making themselves available to the media.

All the final plenary session on April 28, Forum delegates adopted the Dakar Framework for Action, Education for All: Meeting Our Collective Commitments. The Framework reaffirms the goal of EFA as laid out by Jomtien and other international conferences, commits participants to working toward specific educational goals by 2015 or earlier and affirms that 'no countries seriously committed to education for all will be thwarted in their achievement of this goal by a lack of resources'. It also calls for the developing or strengthening of national action plans and the reinforcing of national, regional and international mechanisms, built on existing national, regional and international structures, to co-ordinate global efforts and to accelerate progress towards EFA.

This book constitutes the final report on the World Education Forum and the pages that follows describe the discussions that took place and record the actions that resulted from participants' conviction that education is, as Kofi Annan put it in his keynote address, 'the key for enabling succeeding generations to succeed.' This book also contains the six regional frameworks for action and the World Declaration on EFA.

The editor is thankful to the UNESCO for using its material in preparing this book to popularise the concept of EFA.

Introduction

The convening of a major international conference on EFA in the year 2000 was anticipated in 1990 by the World Conference for Education for All (Jomtiem, Thailand). In pledging to strive toward primary education for every child and a massive reduction in adult illiteracy by the year 2000, participants in the Jomtien conference were careful to establish mechanisms for assuring that the work was carried on in a systematic manner. They created a Consultative Forum on Education for All with a mandate that called for periodic review of progress towards goals, including a major ten-year appraisal.

In June 1996, 250 participants from 73 countries met in Amman, Jordan, for a four-day Mid-decade Meeting of the Consultative Forum on Education for All to assess progress up to that point. The meeting's final communiqué, adopted as the Amman Affirmation, declared that, in the six years since Jomtien, 'there has been significant progress in basic education, not in all countries nor as much as had been hoped, but progress that is nonetheless real'. Progress was also taken note of by other international conferences that took place during the 1990s.[1]

As a prelude to the ten-year review at the World Education Forum in Dakar, the participating countries took part in the EFA 2000 Assessment, a massive and detailed analysis of the state of basic education around the world. Each country assessed its own progress toward the goals of Jomtien and then reported its findings of six regional meetings in the late 1999 and early 2000. An overall summary was presented at Dakar *(see Chapter I)*. The national assessments were complemented by fourteen thematic studies on educational issues of global concern, twenty case-studies, and sample surveys of learning achievement and conditions of teaching and learning. These data, analyses and observations were then used by the Consultative Forum as a basis for redefining strategies and drawing up the revised Framework for Action to meet basic learning needs for all by 2015.

The World Education Forum was sponsored by five convening agencies: the United Nations Development Programme (UNDP), the United Nations Educational, Scientific and Cultural Organisation (UNESCO), the United Nations Population Fund (UNFPA), the United Nations Children's Fund (UNICEF) and the World Bank. Participants included delegates from 164 nations as well as representatives of the sponsoring agencies, non-governmental organisations, and other agencies and groups with an interest in global education issues.

The Forum opened with a welcoming address by President Abdoulaye Wade of the Republic of Senegal, who stressed the importance of viewing education as a fundamental human right 'rooted in the legal and social environment as well as in the individual's active resolve to enjoy his rights to the full'. Respect for such rights, he said is essential to the functioning of a democratic society. 'Like a building', he said, 'democracy is constructed freedom by freedom, right by right, until the one is reached which tips the balance ... and leads to a changeover'.

In his keynote address, United Nations' Secretary-General Kofi Annan sounded what was to become a leitmotif of the Dakar Forum: whereas much progress has been made toward the goal of EFA, much remains to be accomplished. 'As we open the twenty-first century, we do have some achievements to celebrate', he told the assemblage 'Educational levels in many developing countries have climbed dramatically. The percentage of adult illiterates in the world has declined steadily. An explosive innovation of technology has brought new learning opportunities to millions. We have reached a new level of capacity-building and understanding in our work to attain basic education for all. And yet, at least 800 million adults worldwide are still illiterate, most of them women. A yawning digital divide exists between those who have access to new technology and those who have not. A quarter of a billion children work, in often hazardous or unhealthy conditions. And, according to conservative estimates, more than 110 million school-age children are not attending school.'

The defining mood of the Jomtien Conference had been one of hope and expectancy. Jomtien put the concept of EFA on the global development agenda and raised global consciousness about important strategic issues, most notably the need to focus attention on the education of girls and women. A decade later, the concept of EFA continued to be alive and well.

Whereas Jomtien had looked primarily to the future, participants in the Dakar Forum also had a decade of experience to consider. The optimism of Jomtien was tempered by recognition that, for all of the gains, the overall goal of universal basic education by the year 2000 had not in fact been met. As Koïchiro Matsuura, the Director-General of UNESCO, told participants, 'The broad vision of Education for All proclaimed in Jomtien ten years ago has lost nothing of its wisdom and relevance. What we could not foresee, however, were the sometimes tragic events of the decade affecting all societies and consequently their education systems.'

Much of the discussion at Dakar was thus driven by recognition that the world has changed in ways that could not have anticipated at Jomtien. There are now thirty more countries than there were in 1990. The collapse of Communism in Europe and the resultant end of the Cold War has led to a redrawing of the global map and major shifts in national alliances. There has also been a proliferation of ethnic conflicts and a growing number of refugees and displaced persons. It is now generally accepted that education must be thought in 'global' as well as 'national' terms, and there is far more acceptance of an important role for the private sector in the delivery of 'public' education. Criticism of donor agencies by non-governmental organisations and other representatives of civil society is much stronger than it was in 1990.

Three developments over the last decade were particularly important themes at Dakar. The first was the revolution in communication and information technologies that is transforming virtually all human institutions. There was no such thing as the Internet or the World Wide Web as we now know them at the time of Jomtien. Participants at the Forum struggled to understand how to harness these new technologies as tools for EFA.

The second was the HIV/AIDS pandemic that has had a devastating impact on the teaching force in many countries, especially in sub-Saharan Africa. The final development was what Mr. Matsuura described as 'the ever-increasing rift between rich and poor'. Speaker after speaker reminded the Forum that poverty remains the single most important factor explaining the inability of many governments to meet their goals for EFA. Many called for forgiveness of loans as a requisite first step in addressing the problem.

Such were the challenges as participants in the World Education Forum began their deliberations. 'This conference is a test of all of us who call ourselves the international community', Kofi Annan told them. "Ten years ago, at Jomtien, we set ourselves the goal of basic Education for All. We are still far from achieving it. Let us start this conference by resolving not to rest until we have made it a reality."

REFERENCE

1. The World Summit for Children (1990), the United Nations Conference on Environment and Development (1992), the International Conference on Population and Development (1994), the World Conference on Human Rights (1993) the World Conference on Special Needs Education: Access and Quality (1994), the World Summit for Social Development (1995), the Fourth World Conference on Women (1995), the Fifth International Conference on Adult Education (1997) and the International Conference on Child Labour (1997).

The faith and vision of Dakar

We are optimistic because, for us, universal education does not depend on spending money but is above all a question of political will—the determination to attack head on and to eradicate this vice and injustice by mobilizing all segments of the population. If we are Utopian, we should be left with our Utopias as long as they drive us to act, as long as they motivate us. For it is undeniable that a Utopia that inspires actions is preferable to one that results in inertia and day-dreaming.

Ladies and Gentlemen, if you think our discussions are going to highlight a new approach, if you think that the idea of education should be broadened to encompass the pre-school level and adult education using national languages, and if you think that this challenge concerns not only governments but all levels of the population, why not put a seal on our faith and vision in what we might call the Dakar Declaration on Dakar Appeal?

What this question, I now declare open the World Education Forum.

Abdoulaye Wade, President of the Republic of Senegal, in his welcoming address

1

Progress Since Jomtien

The World Education Forum was preceded by the most in-depth evaluation of basic education ever conducted: the EFA 2000 Assessment. This detailed review examined the current status of basic education in more than 180 countries. Its purposes were to evaluate the progress that each country had made during the 1990s in promoting the goal of education for all and to generate vital information on a wide range of programmes, activities and services that aim to promote basic learning.

Results of the Assessment will help governments and their partners to determine how far they have come towards the realization of EFA goals and to identify effective strategies for future gains. At the international level, the Assessment will provide the basis for dialogue and co-operation for years to come. Denise Lievesley, Director of UNESCO's Institute for Statistics, described the review as 'a vital benchmark to enable us to assess progress in the future and to ensure that any targets we set are realistic and accompanied by appropriate resources.'

The Assessment drew mainly on national assessments of the extent to which governments are meeting the basic learning needs of their people. The project was carried out by thousands of educators and others around the globe who were linked by a network involving ten regional technical advisory groups that were run by regional staff members of the EFA Forum's convening agencies. In each country national co-ordinators, usually from Ministers of Education, were in charge of the

Assessment and produced country reports. Results were reported at six regional meetings in 1999 and 2000 leading up to Dakar.

In addition to individual country reports, the Assessment produced sample surveys of learning achievement and the conditions of teaching and learning in primary schools in more than twenty developing countries, mostly in Africa. These surveys give precise information about the working conditions of teachers, the school environment and the quality of learning. Twenty interested countries also carried out case-studies on the literacy and educational attainment of their young people and adults.

Another feature of the worldwide review was a series of fourteen thematic studies on educational issues of global concern sponsored by a development agency or a major non-governmental organisation. These themes were: adult education, applying new technologies, children in difficult circumstances, decentralization and community participation, demographic transition, donor financing of EFA, early childhood care and development, special needs education, education in economic crises, girls' education, refugees, school health and nutrition, and textbooks and learning materials. Each thematic study gives examples of best practices and describes successful and unsuccessful experiments in policy implementation.

Finally, the EFA 2000 Assessment collected data from participating countries on eighteen Statistical Indicators that quantify progress towards the goal of EFA.

The major findings of the EFA 2000 Assessment were summarized in 'Education for All: Global Synthesis'. At the opening plenary of the World Education Forum, Malcolm Skilbeck, author of this report, presented its highlights. He listed a number of ways in which progress had been made over the past decade toward the various goals of EFA.

More Children in School: A major objective articulated by Jomtien was universal access to and completion of basic education. The number of children enrolled in school rose from an estimated 599 million in 1990 to 681 million in 1998. This means that some 10 million more children have been going to school every year, which is nearly double the average increase during the preceding decade. Eastern Asia and the Pacific, as well as Latin America and the Caribbean are now close to achieving universal primary education *(Figure 1)*. China and India have made impressive progress towards achieving universal primary education, especially with regard to girls. The same countries, along with Bangladesh, register the strongest decrease in population growth rates—a development that has facilitated progress.

Figure 1. Net enrolment ratios (NER) in primary education by region, 1990 and 1998

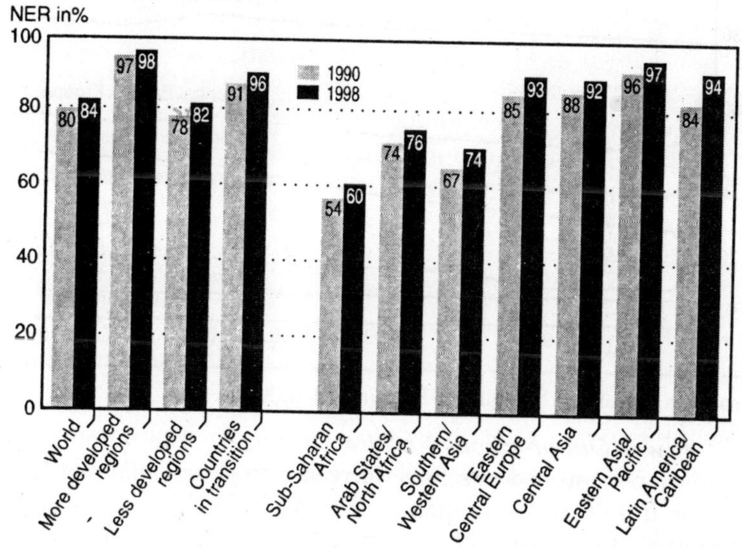

Source: EFA Statistical Document (2000)

Increased Early Childhood Education: Jomtien sought both to increase global awareness of the importance of education and care during the early years and to encourage creation of programmes that foster such development and learning. Understanding of the importance of the early years is now firmly placed on the global agenda and the idea that education begins at birth has taken root in many societies. As a result, the number of children in pre-school education rose by 5 per cent in the past decade. Despite these overall gains, however, the availability of early childhood programmes is erratic, ranging from near-universal in some countries and regions to virtually non-existent in other (*Figure 2*). New acceptance of the value of maternal care, health and nutrition services is not matched in many countries by adequate supply.

Figure 2. Trends in the gross enrolment ratio (GER) in early childhood development programmes by region, 1990-1998

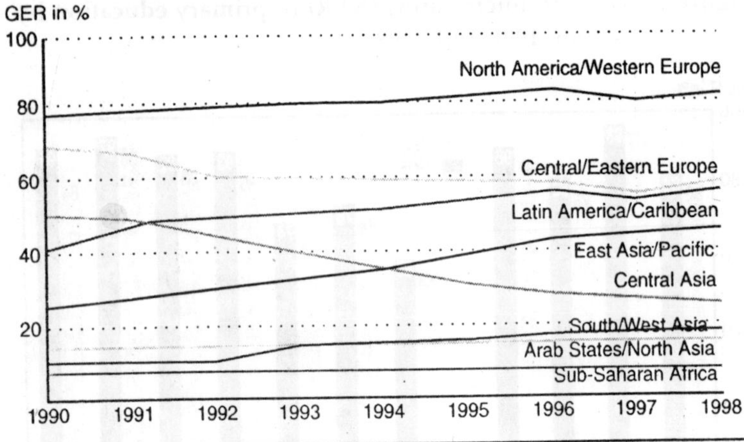

Source : EFA Statistical Document (2000)

Fewer Out-of-school Children (*Figure 3*): The number of children not enrolled in school decreased from an estimated 127 million in 1990 to 113 million in 1998. In Latin America and the Caribbean, for example, the number was more than halved, from 11.4 million in 1990 to 4.8 million in 1998. Countries such as Bangladesh, Brazil and Egypt and leading the way by allocating close to 6 per cent of their gross national product to education. On the other hand, continuing high population growth and other factors make it difficult for many countries in sub-Saharan Africa to make significant reductions in the number of out-of-school children.

Figure 3. Number of primary school-age children in and out of school by region, 1990 and 1998

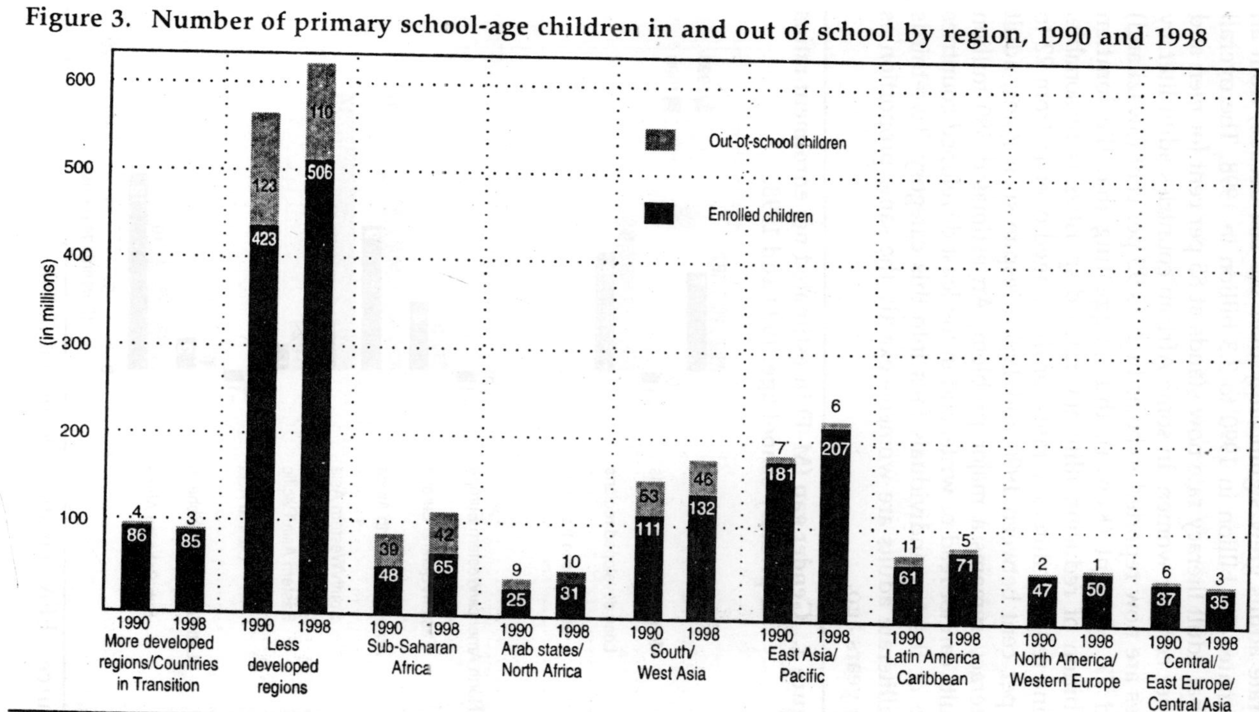

Source : EFA Statistical Document (2000)

Growing Number of Literate Adults: The number of literate adults grew significantly over the last decade, from an estimated 2.7 billion in 1990 to 3.3 billion in 1998. The overall global adult literacy rate now stands at 85 per cent for men and 74 per cent for women. In some African countries adult literacy rates are now reported to be as high as 90 per cent (Swaziland) and 77 per cent (Kenya), thus suggesting that the Jomtien ambition of reducing illiteracy rates disparities is reasonable. China reduced illiteracy rates for those aged over 15 from 22 to 16 per cent between 1990 and 1997. Despite such gains, adult illiteracy remains a major problem. An estimated 880 million adults cannot read or write, and in the least developed countries one of the two individuals falls into this category. Two-thirds of illiterate adults are women—exactly the same proportion as ten years ago.

Figure 4. Gender gap (M–F) in estimated net enrolment ratios of primary school age, 1990 and 1998.

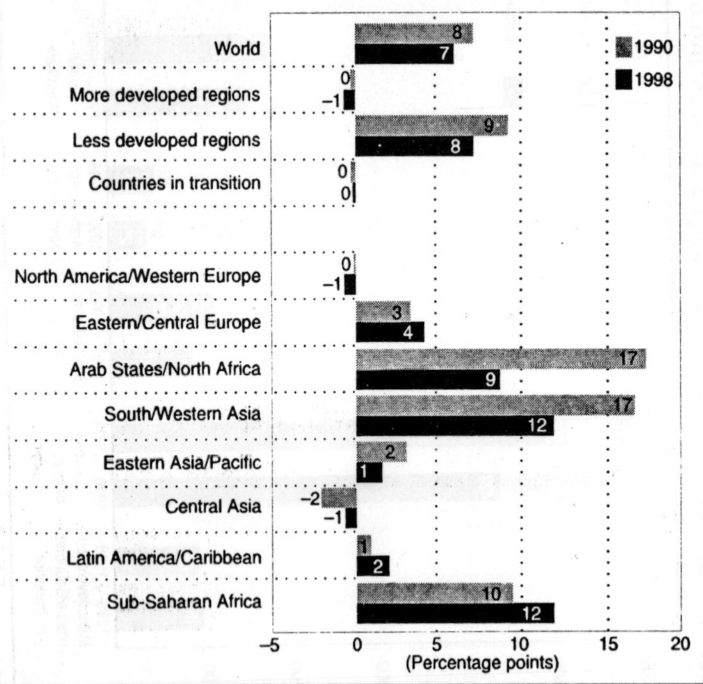

Source: EFA Statistical Document (2000)

Some Reduction in Disparities: In keeping with the appeal of Jomtien, a few countries have made progress in reducing disparities in the distribution of educational opportunity as reflected by gender, disability, ethnicity, urban versus rural location and working children. Nevertheless, positive trends in primary education mask disparity of access both between and within many countries, and disparities in educational quality can remain even when access rates are high *(Figure 4)*.

People in poor, rural and remote communities, as well as ethnic minorities and indigenous, populations, have shown little or no progress over the past decade. In South Asia and sub-Saharan Africa, fewer than three out of four pupils reach Grade 5. In the least developed countries a little over half reach this level, and many drop out after the first or second grade. Low participation rates for girls continue to be a problem in some entire countries and in parts of others, such as rural areas or among low-income families. On the other hand, under-achievement and lack of persistence in school among boys is increasingly being cited as a problem in areas such as the Caribbean and at the secondary level in industrialized countries of Europe and North America, and in Australia and New Zealand.

Other Positive Signs: The EFA 2000 Assessment identified other positive developments that have occurred over the decade since Jomtien. Many countries have adopted new policies, frameworks and legislation aimed at one or more of the EFA targets and backed them up with additional financial and other resources. There is now greater involvement of non-governmental organizations, community groups and parents in making decisions about school policies and in running child care and education facilities than there was in 1990, and there has been a substantial improvement in the capacity of many countries to use national assessments and other forms of evaluation to inform educational policy–making.

In summary, none of the specific EFA targets have been met in their entirety, most notably the fundamental goal of achieving 'universal access to, and completion of basic education by 2000. Nevertheless, there is ample evidence that a large number of countries have taken serious steps to implement the Jomtien agenda, many of which have been successful. Other countries

Education as the Core of a Development Strategy

Since political leaders first came together at Jomtien a new wave of political and economic challenges has swept across our world. But one thing that has not changed over these turbulent ten years is the critical need for education. In anything, the need to priortize Education for All is more morally and economically urgent than ever. Time and again, in study after study and country after country, well-run education programmes have proven themselves to be the best value investment for development dollars. From the Republic of Korea, where a generation of parents allowed the state to plow back the sweat of their labour into their children's education, to my own memories as a first-time visitor to the United States, taking the Greyhound bus across the country and seeing that the oldest building in town after town was always the church or the school—the message is the same: education works.

Ask a parent in a Kenyan village, a young girl in the *alta plano* of Bolivia or a boy in the paddy fields of Thailand: There is no alternative to education. And that is why we at UNDP are very proud to be one of the co-sponsors of the International Consultative Forum on Education for All.

In many parts of the world we have made enormous progress since Jomtien. But even for those countries that have met education targets the goal posts have already shifted; primary education is not enough. Education has moved from being the floor on which a country build its competitive success to being its competitive success. Older measures of competitiveness such as labour costs, resource endowments and infrastructure are being superceded by human capital. The single most important question for economic success is now: How smart are your people? Knowledge does not respect geography or old economies. Ideas have wings, and in the information technology age they fly at the speed of light.

Mark Malloch Brown, Administrator of UNDP, in a plenary address and some regions have experienced major setbacks, including declining enrolment of particular groups of students due to factors ranging from lack of political will to civil unrest.

In presenting the synthesis of the Assessment, the author suggested that the very fact of setting targets by the World Conference on Education for All has had an energizing effect and that these targets, while not fully achieved, are now attainable than they were a decade ago. 'The Jomtien movement cannot be judged a failure simply because targets have not been achieved, although that must be of great concern when little or no progress has been made', he said, 'What is important however, is to reach a conclusion about whether the effort has been worthwhile, whether sufficient commitment, energy and resourcefulness have been present, and whether there is value in taking the next step. The answer yielded by this Global Synthesis is that the effort has been worthwhile, indeed necessary, and that the mission of EFA must again be taken up, with strengthened resolve and renewed energy. Too much is at stake for anything less.'

One that note, participants in the World Education Forum turned their attention to discussing the major themes that would eventually be reflected in the Dakar Framework for Action. The discussions took the form of addresses to plenary sessions, and presentations and debate at a series of smaller sub-plenary and strategy sessions organized around four broad themes: equity and quality, effective use of resources, co-ordination with civil society and promoting education for democracy. These discussions are summarized in the following pages.

2

Improving the Quality and Equity of Education for All

The Jomtien Declaration made it clear that achieving education for all involved the twin goals of attaining universal access and equity while insisting on high standards of teaching and learning. In the early 1990s much of the emphasis was placed on quantitative goals such as increasing the number of pupils enrolled in school. By the middle of the decade, however, political and educational leaders had become increasingly mindful of the fact that enhanced access in the absence of quality instruction is a hollow victory.

In a series of sub-plenary and strategy sessions, participants in the World Education Forum held in-depth discussions of aspects of these twin goals. A common theme, seen most vividly in their analyses of the role of new educational technologies, was the impossibility of separating the issues of access, equity and quality. Following are summaries of the discussions that took place around Theme I: Improving the Quality and Equity of Education for All.

Technology for Basic Education: A Luxury or a Necessity?

One important change that occurred between Jomtien and Dakar was the emergence of new information and communication technologies, most notably the Internet.

Participants in the World Education Forum were well aware that, insofar as it affects the quest for education for all, the information technology (IT) revolution is a potential double-edged sword. On the one hand, the new technologies offer additional tools to extend basic education to underserved geographic regions and groups of students. They have the potential to overcome geographical distances, empower teachers and learners through information, and bring the world into the classroom by the touch of buttons or the glare of a screen. On the other hand, proliferation of technologies exacerbate existing gaps between the educational haves and have-nots.

The Forum examined the impact of technology—both new and traditional—on basic education at a sub–plenary session that began with a discussion whether the use of information technology is a luxury or a necessity. Participants concluded that such technology can only be thought of as a luxury if basic education is defined quite narrowly as literacy, numeracy and rudimentary life skills. We all live in a society where rapid change and growth in knowledge requires constant learning. In such a situation—one where basic education must be conceived of as a learning activity that takes place anytime, anywhere and on the part of everyone—information technology becomes a necessity. In poor countries, and under present conditions, technologies may not be affordable; paradoxically, the new reality is that poor countries cannot afford not to fully use them.

Participants noted the many ways in which the Internet offers an opportunity to reach rural and other communities that have not yet been—and may never be—wired for traditional technologies such as telephones. Affordability is an issue, but countries such as Ghana have successfully addressed this problem through 'community learning centres'. These centres, run by grassroots groups, have served as a cost-effective means to enhance basic education, train teachers, develop local businesses, strengthen governmental and civic organisations, and provide health-care information for populations in small villages. Community radio is another immensely powerful technology whose potential has been enhanced by new technologies such as portable, low-cost FM transmitting stations and digital radio systems that transmit via satellite and through cellular phones.

Speakers emphasized that technology is only a tool and that its success in enhancing the delivery of quality education depends on the quality of prior decisions regarding objectives, methodologies, and educational content. As one speaker emphasized, 'No technology can fix bad educational philosophy and practice, nor can it compensate for a lack of political commitment'. The challenge is to rethink learning objectives and to align decisions regarding appropriate technologies, hardware and content-ware with these educational objectives. Evidence was presented at the session on how Costa Rica has balanced priorities regarding hardware, software and 'human-ware' in 12-year-old programme that has introduced computers to half of primary school pupils and to four out of five junior and high schools.

Another theme that was frequently mentioned during discussion was the importance of lodging new technologies within a sound infrastructure. It is not realistic to expect teachers struggling with new technologies to assume technical responsibility for hardware. Moreover, since integrating new technologies into education is a sophisticated and multifaceted process, it is important to run pilot projects and to make appropriate adjustments before moving to scale.

Speakers emphasized that the new technologies should never be thought of as a panacea for achieving education for all. Nevertheless, with new educational technologies constantly emerging and their costs dropping dramatically, even poor countries must find ways of using these new tools in appropriate manners. For its part, the international community has a significant role in easing regulations that constrain connectivity, in building the necessary infrastructures, in facilitating the sharing both of educational programming and expertise, and in supporting the development of content-ware.

Overcoming Obstacles to Educating Girls

It is widely recognized that devoting resources to quality education for girls is one of the best investments that any society can make. The broad social benefits of girls' education range from increased family income and reduced fertility rates to improvements in family health and nutrition whose significance is magnified through their impact subsequent generations.

Extending basic education to girls and bridging the gender gap were identified as critical priorities at Jomtien, but progress toward these goals over the past decade has been slow for reasons ranging from entrenched discrimination against females to the fact that assistance from countries and inter-governmental organisations of the North has fallen far short of the scale envisaged at Jomtien. In some countries what at first glance seems like progress in narrowing the gender gap is actually a result of decreasing enrolment of boys.

The sub-plenary session on this topic explored the complexities of the gender gap issue with particular reference to the importance of creating learning environments that are supportive of girls' education. Speakers noted that societal attitudes are key to girls' education and that improvements in the quality of education do not inevitably spur parents to enrol their daughters in school. They called for a broader definition of 'quality' that embodies the concepts of 'girl-friendly' or 'gender-sensitive' education. Participants also noted that assuring that schools are physically safe places is particularly important if they are to attract female children.

Speakers at the session agreed on the urgent need to place greater emphasis on the education of girls and to view education as an instrument of women's equality and empowerment. Particular attention was drawn to the need to assure that larger numbers of girls entered science, technology and professional courses as well as higher education in all areas.

The underlying importance of cultural, social and economic factors in causing the gender gap was seen as reason to take a holistic and integrated approach to the problem—one that links in-school improvements with steps to enhance early childhood care and development, reduce child labour, and retrain teachers and school administrators. Discussants also agreed on the importance of gender-sensitive teacher training, improvements in conditions of safety and the provision of separate toilets for female students.

Why Educating Girls must be a Priority

All countries' experience of development shows the economic value of education. Together with primary health care, education is the foundation of development. Experience also shows the importance of concentrating efforts on education for girls. As we have heard, girls are two-thirds of young people not in school, and two-thirds of the world's illiterates are women.

There are many obstacles to closing the continuing gender gap in education, but none of them are insurmountable. Many of these are solely in the mind. Somehow policy-makers, political leaders and even parents still do not see the over-riding need to educate girls. In many societies all the benefits for girls and women from education—such as knowing their rights to protection against violence, protection against diseases and unwanted pregnancy, economic empowerment—are precisely the reasons why these societies/countries consciously or subconsciously have denied girls educational opportunities. In several countries, the content of girls' education is selective and inclusive only of how to be a good wife or mother. Education for girls and young women is still treated as an optional extra—an aim to be pursued when other more urgent needs are satisfied. But there is no more urgent need than to liberate the human potential and the economic contribution of the half of our young people who happen to be female. These are, of course, the reasons why political commitment and leadership will be so important to realizing the goals of education for all, especially of girls.

Poverty is frequently offered as a reason for marrying off young girls, but I think a far more powerful motive is the cultural conservatism that assigns no value to girls except as future wives and mothers. A girl's future is often predetermined and her choices and options pre-empted by cultural norms and practices. Culture that denies choice to women must be changed.

Over the past thirty years, countries which have invested in education for girls as part of their education priorities, and as part of an integrated approach to social development, have seen excellent results. As a group, they have slower population growth, faster economic growth and a higher level of social cohesion. It is time for all countries to put aside their doubts and fears about educating women and give in the highest priority.

Nafis Sadik, Executive Director of UNFPA,
in a plenary address

Finally, speakers emphasized that, while lack of resources is clearly an obstacle to narrowing the gender gap in virtually all developing countries, no country could justify non-action on the basis of resource constraints.

Meeting Special and Diverse Education Needs: Making Inclusive Education a Reality

The concept of 'inclusive education' has emerged in response to a growing consensus that all children have the right to a common education in their locality regardless of their background, attainment or disability. The Framework stressed the goal of meeting the learning needs 'of all young people and adults'.

Concern about inclusion has evolved from a struggle in behalf of children 'having special needs' into one that challenges all exclusionary policies and practices in education as they relate to curriculum, culture and local centres of learning. Instead of focussing on preparing children to fit into existing schools, the new emphasis focuses on preparing schools so that they can deliberately reach out to all children. It also recognizes that gains in access have not always been accompanied by increases in quality.

Discussions at the strategy session on this topic recognized that there are no convincing findings of successful inclusive education on a comprehensive scale and that many teachers do not fully believe that inclusion works. Extending EFA to excluded children and adults demands a holistic approach that seeks to change not only current practices but also values, beliefs and attitudes.

Presenters at the strategy session on this theme called for a 'holistic approach' to inclusion that makes this goal explicit in the design of accountability and funding systems and reinforces it through enabling and protective legislation. Teachers must be trained in pedagogies that accommodate diverse, learning needs through multiple teaching strategies, flexible curricula and continuous assessment. Partnerships must be formed between teachers and administrators, NGOs, parent organisations, unions, business groups and community organisations.

Making Primary Education Universal and Free

Discussion of this theme focused on particular strategies that have shown themselves to be successful in accelerating progress towards universal, compulsory and free primary education in various countries.

A panelist from Uganda presented evidence that a government policy of paying school fees for up to four children per family had led to a sharp increase in school enrolments. A speaker from Brazil reported that the goal of universal access to primary education has nearly been attained in that country, in part because of more defined and focussed funding policies that had a major impact in poorer regions where children, especially boys, are expected to work in order to support their families.

Evidence was also presented from India on how school enrolment was increased through means that included reducing the traditional distance of schools, decentralized planning, community involvement in school mapping and planning, and the use of part-time and alternative schools. A panelist from the International Labour Organisation (ILO) stressed the importance of eliminating the worst forms of child labour in order to promote access to schooling among the most marginalized groups.

Numerous participants called for debt relief as a means of freeing up resources for primary education and emphasized the need for the international community to develop procedures to support capacities at the local as well as the national level. Another recurrent theme was the need to promote demand for schooling on the part of families rather than focus exclusively on supply-side issues.

Expanding Access to Early Childhood Development Programmes

Early childhood care and development (ECCD) emerged at Jomtien as an extension of basic education, one that recognizes that learning begins at birth, not with entrance into primary school. Since then awareness of the importance of the early years has grown in both developed and developing countries, in part because of dramatic new findings from brain research. Recent emphasis has focused on preventing problems rather than on 'compensating' for them once they develop.

Despite growing awareness of these issues, gains in access to ECCD have been erratic. Very few children under age 4 in underdeveloped countries attend organised programmes, and in some areas, such as the countries of the former Soviet Union, enrolments have actually declined. Attention continues to be concentrated on 'pre-schooling' for children about to enter primary school.

Participants in this strategy session emphasized the need for a multi-pronged approach to the task of increasing awareness of the importance of nurturing children during the pre-school years and developing ECCD programmes. By necessity, such an approach must cut across sectoral lines and involve activities and plans of action at the local, regional and national levels. Discussants noted that promoting functional literacy among parents is important to promoting understanding of the importance of the pre-school years, and they emphasized the importance of including handicapped students in ECCD programmes and of directing them equally to girls and boys.

Designing Basic Education Content to Meet the Needs and Values of Society

The economic, social and other changes, sweeping through human society in recent years have forced a reconsideration of what knowledge, skills and values are needed for successful living. The movement toward more open and democratic societies has created a need for learning that goes beyond the academic curriculum and factual knowledge to emphasize problem-solving and open-ended enquiry. The expansion of communication and information technologies necessitates more interactive and exploratory forms of learning and the increased pace of change has put a premium on the need to engage in continuous learning over a lifetime. There is also a new urgency to ensure that education at all levels and in all places reinforces a culture of peace, tolerance and respect for human rights.

Discussants in this strategy session noted that no country can except to function successfully in the future with rigid and closed education systems. There are many types of education, but every form of basic education must be designed specifically to include active citizenship and participation at all levels, in all societies. In order to be relevant, the content of basic education must be geared to exploratory learning, including all learners and encouraging them to take an active role in planning decisions. Culture, art and creativity are essential components of education for all.

Participants suggested that the provision of education might be viewed in terms of an entire 'ecology of learning'. Such an approach would recognize that learning occurs continuously in all activities and throughout people's lifetimes.

Enabling Teachers to Enable Learners

Teachers obviously play a key role in the delivery of education, and the quality of instruction is to a large extent a function of whether classrooms are staffed with competent, well-trained teachers. Unfortunately, there are many barriers to putting competent instructors in classrooms, including low pay, low social status, heavy work-loads, huge class size and lack of professional development.

This strategy session considered ways in which the quality of education can be enhanced by providing greater support to teachers. There was general agreement that in many countries additional resources were necessary—a Southeast Asian country that invests US$ 20 per student per year has no way of competing against industrialized nations that invest more than US$ 5,000—as well as more efficient use of existing ones.

Participants also stressed the importance of ongoing professional development to equip teachers to move beyond lecturing and rote learning. They stressed the need to use supervision as a means of supporting teachers rather than identifying faulty practice. Others cited studies showing that teacher motivation is closely tied to quality of teaching and that the quality of instruction improves when teachers are given a role in making pedagogical decisions and in shaping plans for school improvement.

Assessing Learning Achievement

The World Declaration on Education for All emphasized not only the need to expand access to education but also the importance of assuring that the education offered to children and adults is of high quality. Promoting quality, of course, presumes some way of measuring it. Thus over the past decade there has been a growing awareness of the role that assessment can play in enhancing the quality of basic education.

This strategy session reviewed key findings from recent assessment surveys, including several major projects in developing countries of Africa and Latin America. Discussants noted that achievement differences within the various regions of countries are frequently greater than those between countries. They showed how assessment data have been used as a tool for allocating scarce resources more efficiently by identifying rural and other populations with special needs. Numerous speakers emphasized the need to engage in assessment on a continuous basis and to establish a 'monitoring culture'. Developing a conceptual framework and methodologies for assessing life skills was also put forward as a priority.

Much of the discussion centered on how international support can be used to build local and national capacity for continuous assessment.

Transversal Theme

The Importance of Child-friendly Schools

Achieving universal primary education is not simply a matter of having every child enrolled in school. Once enrolled, the child must stay in school sufficiently long to achieve basic literacy and numbers—a period estimated to be about five years of schooling.

Children drop out of school for a variety of reasons, including perceptions on the part of parents that the school is not effectively meeting the child's needs or operating in the child's best interests. Creating 'child-friendly' schools is thus of critical importance for achieving universal primary education, for increasing educational quality, for promoting educational equity and inclusiveness, and for achieving gender equity in education.

The need for child-friendly schools emerged as a theme that cut across several sessions of the Forum. Discussants identified at least three areas of importance to creating such learning environments: physical plant and infrastructure, policies and services, and curriculum and instruction.

The first requirement of a child-friendly school is that the physical plant and infrastructure be in good repair, with adequate space and furniture for each child, adequate lighting and a general appearance that is bright, welcoming and happy. Providing sanitary washrooms and locating schools close to pupils' homes is important, especially for girls.

In addition to regular teaching programmes, child-friendly schools offer counselling, health and nutrition services as well as opportunities to participate in extra-curricular activities such as sports and clubs. Special policies, such as affirmative action programmes, are needed to address the needs of particular groups of students, such as indigenous peoples or those with special physical or learning needs. In many countries, particularly in parts of South Asia and sub-Saharan Africa, special policies aimed at attracting and retaining girls are needed.

Finally, child-friendly schools use curricula and textbooks that respect local languages, cultures and cognitive styles, and their pedagogical methods and learner-centered rather than teacher-centered.

Participants engaged in vigorous debate over how to achieve child-centered schools. Everyone agreed that teachers need training in order to use more creative and imaginative approaches that unlock the child's own learning potential. Discussants were divided, however, over the issue of community involvement and responsibility. Most felt that communities and parents were a valuable source of information, guidance and support for educators, but others argued that many parents lack the educational expertise to know what is best for their child's education.

Speakers also noted that decentralization of authority can sometimes be a cover for central governments to off-load their own responsibilities to fund and otherwise support education. It is imperative that programmes of decentralization and community empowerment be accompanied by the transfer of resources that will enable communities to assume the responsibility. Locally generated resources should only supplement, not replace, central government financial commitments.

3

Making Effective Use of Resources for Education

Achieving both enhanced access to basic education and improved quality of teaching and learning requires financial, human and other resources. Finding these resources has never been easy, and the task has been further complicated over the past decade by developments such as the HIV/AIDS crisis, military conflicts, natural disasters and the mounting debt levels of many developing nations.

Clearly ways must be found not only to enhance traditional sources of resources but also to target resources more effectively through means such as educational assessments, and to develop new alliances with potential allies such as the business community. Forum participants addressed these issues in a sub-plenary session and a series of strategy sessions. Following is a summary of the discussions carried out under Theme II: Making Effective Use of Resources for Education.

Overcoming the Effects of HIV/AIDS on Basic Education

The fact that the World Education Forum took place in sub-Saharan Africa lent urgency and poignancy to discussions about the impact of the HIV/AIDS pandemic on the work of the Forum. As Peter Piot, Executive Director of UNAIDS, put it in a plenary address 'AIDS constitutes one of the biggest threats to the global education agenda. What HIV/AIDS does to the human body, it also does in institutions. It undermines those institutions that protect us.'

Discussion of HIV/AIDS at a sub-plenary session of the Forum revolved around two interrelated issues: (i) the impact of the pandemic on the education sector and (ii) how HIV/AIDS—specific education can have a salutary impact on the prevalence of infection.

Many speakers, many of them from sub-Saharan Africa, offered disturbing statistics about the impact of HIV/AIDS on the education sector and the capacity of the pandemic to undermine and even negate the progress being made on other fronts toward the goal of education for all. School attendance has declined due to various HIV-related phenomena affecting children. In countries such as Zambia, Swaziland and Zimbabwe the number of children of primary school age will be more than 20 per cent less by 2010 than projected before the epidemic, and a high proportion of these children will be orphans with limited resources and few incentives to enter school. Parents concerned about the early death of their children are likely to be unwilling to spend their limited resources on education.

High morbidity and mortality rates among teachers and administrators have severely affected countries' capacity to deliver teaching and learning. In Zambia, for example, the mortality rate among school teachers in the 15-49-year-old age-group is 70 per cent higher than that cohort in general, and two-thirds of newly trained teachers die of AIDS each year. Shortages of educators lead to erratic teaching schedules and even the closing of schools, and make long-term planning by central authorities difficult. HIV/AIDS is also having an impact on the social climate of schools. Young girls may face increased risk of sexual exploitation when they are assumed to be free from infection and thus 'safe'.

Participants in the sub-plenary session presented evidence that education can be a powerful force—perhaps the most powerful force of all—in combating the spread of HIV/AIDS. A number of studies have shown that, in countries where concerted prevention programmes have been carried out within the education system over time, such as Thailand, Uganda and Senegal, these efforts appear to have helped reduce the incidence of HIV, especially among younger age groups. Successful programmes tend to be those that are targeted, flexible, prolonged intensive and consistent, and operate across sectoral lines. One speaker from Thailand attributed gains in that country in part to the fact that the pandemic was identified as a national crisis early on and that relevant content was introduced into the national curriculum by 1987. A close working relationship was also developed between the Ministries of Education and Health.

A key objective of an international strategy must be to realize the enormous potential that the education system offers as a vehicle to help reduce the incidence of HIV/AIDS and to alleviate its impact on society, thereby also reducing the very constraints that the epidemic is imposing on the quest for education for all. Speakers noted that power structures often resist policies and actions aimed at combating the impact of HIV/AIDS and that legislation and national policies are needed to ensure that children and adults affected by the illness are not denied their rights and excluded from services. They stressed the need to train teachers in HIV/AIDS preventive education and to support them through a healthy and caring learning environment. Education programmes should emphasize life-skills relevant to local communities and adopt a multi-sectoral approach that, among other things, links education with comprehensive health programmes.

Utilizing Debt Relief for Education

The ability of many developing countries to pursue EFA has been severely restricted by the heavy and unsustainable debt burdens that limit their capacities to invest in education. In recent years, however, a series of global partnerships have emerged with the aim of relieving debt burdens and freeing up resources for investment in poverty reduction and other social purposes.

Presenters at this strategy session described how, in keeping with the spread of democratization and the need of governments to respond to challenges with greater agility, precision and capacity, the World Bank and the International Monetary Fund (IMF) and instituting new frameworks to address poverty. These frameworks align education and social sector development closely with macro-economic developments. Because the interaction between education and a nation's economic and social conditions has become so much closer as markets become more open, global communications faster and technological change more rapid, the education sector is necessarily at the centre of these new development initiatives. Among the new efforts is the Heavily Indebted Poor Countries Initiative (HIPC), which has reduced the debt burdens of many of the world's poorest and most heavily indebted nations. In 1999 the World Bank and IMF endorsed proposal linking debt-relief to country-owned poverty reduction strategies.

The discussion showed that international partners and alliances can play important roles in fostering linkages between education sector policy frameworks and macro-economic frameworks. Participants described how a number of countries have already made substantial progress in developing strategies that link social, structural, human, governance, environmental, economic and financial elements not only to progress in education but also to overall national development. Mozambique, for example, has used its relief under HIPC both to increase its budget allocation to education and to mobilize external resources in pursuit of education for all. As a result, it was able to improve the overall quality of teaching and learning. Bolivia is another example of a country that used its debt relief to channel resources into education.

Working with the Business Community to Strengthen Basic Education

Governments bear primary responsibility for organising and funding basic education. Nevertheless, it is becoming increasingly common in developed and developing countries alike that governments seek to build partnerships with the business community in carrying out this task. The private sector is in a position not only to contribute additional financial resources but also to bring diverse approaches, experiences and innovations to the delivery of basic education. A good example of such innovation is the Escuela Nueva project in Colombia.

This strategy session cited contributions that the business community and other partners such as NGOs and development agencies can make in areas such as creating locally designed and produced educational materials. Participants explored ways in which the private financial communities can function as allies of governments in promoting privately financed and even privately run educational programmes. They examined the role of the telecommunications industry in particular in creating networks for teaching and learning, and delivering educational content to schools.

Many speakers at this session, however, expressed concern about the motivation and the agendas of private corporations donating money to education systems. One speaker asked whether, given the fact that ministries of education, agencies and private sector organisations have quite different agendas and constraints, there is the need for some sort of intermediary actor or facilitator to co-ordinate activities. Another suggested that countries must become as creative in the finance field as they are in technology and spoke of the possibility of organising national capital markets, such as the issuing of bonds, to serve the needs of long-term financial needs of education.

Above all, there was general consensus that emphasis must be placed on local models, local resources, local bye-in and local responsibility for finding solutions.

Strategic Choices in the Development and Use of Teaching and Learning Resources

In pursuing the goal of EFA it is important for States to make the most effective and efficient use of their incountry resources, including textbooks and other printed teaching and learning materials. This strategy session examined recent trends in this area, such as a decentralization of textbook selection and procurement that has led to a shift in many countries from single textbooks to choice among textbooks and other media. Other developments include growing privatization in the production and distribution of textbooks and the emergence of large conglomerates that have the clout to challenge the policies of governments.

Speakers described how countries in the Caribbean, the Pacific Islands, Africa and India have developed means of using resources effectively. Pleas were made for 'people-inclusive' strategies to develop books that are written by and about local people, and can be produced locally. Discussants also emphasized the importance of developing materials in local languages, even though such an approach can increase the cost of production. One solution, they said, lies in using local resources to produce the materials. Several speakers called for micro-credit schemes to help develop co-operative publishing ventures at the community level.

Participants stressed the importance of developing national strategies of policies that extend all the way from the jurisdiction of telecommunications to the role of the public, private and non-governmental organisation sectors in ensuring that resources reach schools. Without a strategic view on the part of government it was argued, practice is likely to be driven principally by the interests of the private sector. Policies should include tax structures that encourage rather than discourage local production of materials. Balance must also be struck between print media and other forms of technology.

Providing Basic Education in Situations of Emergency and Crisis

The Jomtien Declaration and Framework made only limited reference to education in emergency situations, but over the past decade conflicts and natural disasters have proved to be a major barrier to the achievement of education for all.

A special study commissioned as part of the EFA 2000 Assessment documented the extent to which displaced populations and other suffering from chronic insecurity lack educational services. In some situations an entire generation of children may miss out on basic schooling. The study stressed the responsibility of the international community to affirm the fundamental human right to education, even under conditions of emergency, and to provide resources. A key recommendation was that education in emergency situations should be built into a country's development process from the outset, not seen as a 'relief' effort.

The strategy session heard first-hand reports from ministers of four countries—Albania, Burundi, Sierra Leone and Sudan—on emergency situations they had faced. Among other things, they stressed the need for co-ordinated efforts between national and international agencies as well as for co-operation among donors. Participants in the session reaffirmed the lead role of UNESCO both in developing strategies and in assisting Member States in putting programmes and projects in place in emergency conditions.

Monitoring the Provision and Outcomes of Basic Education

The establishment of sound statistical systems for monitoring progress is important to the success of education for all. Participants in this strategy session presented evidence of how countries as diverse as Benin, Nicaragua and Uganda have made effective use of such systems and discussed the ways in which co-operation between countries can encourage their development elsewhere.

Speakers emphasized the central role that political will plays in the establishment of sound statistical systems. Statisticians often face political pressure to produce statistics that show the government in the best possible light. Thus it is important for policy-makers to be convinced of the importance of quantitative data and of the need to build robust, sustainable statistical capacity for making evidence-based decisions. In order to achieve this goal, producers of statistics must adjust their operations to the clocks of policy-makers, understand their needs and produce the relevant statistics to help them to take decisions.

Participants in the strategy session stressed that statistics should be collected to serve the needs of particular peoples and government, and designed to allow feedback at the local level. Donors should be aware that the quality of statistics will vary widely, especially in countries that do not have reliable information on population levels. Donors can play an important role in increasing national monitoring and sharing information about successful practices.

Mobilizing New Resources for Basic Education

The volume and management of resources for basic education are insufficient to achieve quality education for all and recent years have seen important changes in the sources of even those resources that are available. External funding has declined and domestic funding relies increasingly on community and family contributions, a situation that leads to regional and social disparities.

This strategy session focused on growing need for partnerships of varying kinds as a means of attracting new resources for basic education. Participants emphasized the need to define 'resources' broadly and to recognize human as well as financial contributions. They spoke of the responsibility of the international community to pressure wealthy nations to shift resources from armaments to education.

Speakers discussed the complexities involved in striking a balance between the responsibility of the State to promote national unity while respecting the rights of communities to devise an education system adapted to their specific needs. They spoke of education as, first and foremost, a community effort and emphasized the critical importance of transparency in the generation of resources. It is essential that democracy and decentralization be accompanied by good governance.

Building Effective Partnerships with Funding Agencies

The last decade has seen a significant shift in thinking about development, moving from preoccupation with structural adjustment to an emphasis on poverty reduction. As a result, the traditional project approach has come under severe criticism and planners have focused attention on sector-wide strategies built around enhanced co-operation among various actors, including donor agencies, governments and non-governmental organisations.

This strategy session heard presentations on successful efforts to implement this new 'co-operation paradigm' in Mozambique and India, and by the Association for the Development of Education in Africa.

Speakers emphasized that the fostering of co-operation between donors and recipients can be problematical, especially in poor countries that lack institutional and technical capacity or in situations where national authorities have little or no commitment to the well-being of their population. They stressed the paramount importance of developing local capacity, implementing reliable systems of monitoring progress and establishing effective financial and procurement mechanisms.

Education is the Key to Relieving Poverty

No country has succeeded without educating its people. Education is key to sustaining growth and reducing poverty. Everywhere I go I see the power of education to improve people's lives.

The World Bank is firmly committed to achieving the goal of Education for All. The Bank has fulfilled its EFA commitments made in Jomtien in 1990 and, subsequently, in Beijing in 1995. We have doubled our lending for education from $918.7 million to an average of $1.9 billion a year. We have increased the percentage of our lending devoted to basic education, from 27 to 44 per cent. We have set up a programme to target 31 countries with populations over 4 million where the gender gap is greatest and have increased lending for girls' education to an average of $860 million per year. Our support, combined with that of other agencies and governments themselves, has helped produce significant progress in raising the number of children in school, especially girls, in many countries.

We have come a long way on EFA, but we still have a long way to go. Too many people are still excluded from education because of poverty, poor policies and corruption. So how do we move forward?

First, we must place education squarely at the core of the global and national development agenda. We pledge to work with renewed vigour with governments and other donors to reach the EFA goals by integrating actions and outcomes across sectors and with macro-economic policies to ensure co-ordinated, coherent strategies.

Second, we need to provide fresh leadership with a very different set of alliances. After Dakar, the EFA movement must move forward at the country, regional and global level. It must be broader, more inclusive, more innovative and more flexible than in the past.

Third, we must intensify our efforts by leveraging stronger partnerships on key interventions that we know make a difference. Of course, we recognize that, in order to help poor countries reach this goal in a sustainable way, we may have to be open in the interim to innovative ways of funding education, including community-based approaches. Clearly we have to work with governments to ensure that the poorest are not further disadvantaged in the process.

Finally, we need to put into place a fast-track action plan for countries that are committed achieving EFA goals sooner than the 2015 timeline. Under such a demand-driven process, we as donors must be ready to respond more quickly and help countries when they are ready to move. We need a truly global plan of action. The time for action is now.

James D. Wolfensohn, President of the World Bank,
in a plenary address

4

Co-operating with Civil Society to Achieve Social Goals Through Education

Schools never exist in a vacuum. As institutions they are powerfully shaped by the economic, social and political contexts in which they operate, but the influence runs both ways. Schools can also have a powerful impact on the societies they serve.

Participants in the Forum examined this symbiotic relation between educational institutions and civil society with an emphasis on how better co-operation can further the cause of education for all. Following is a summary of the discussions at the sub-plenary and strategy sessions relating to Theme III: Co-operating with Civil Society to Achieve Social Goals.

Fighting Poverty and Marginalization Through Basic Education

Extreme poverty and exclusion are significant obstacles to education and the absence of education in turn leads to further marginalization of the poorest individuals and groups. If basic education is to be extended to these populations, it is important to find ways to break this vicious circle through specific, appropriate and innovative actions.

Participants in the sub-plenary session on this theme identified three conditions for using education as a means of fighting and marginalization, starting with the elimination of debt for the poorest countries. They stressed that debt relief will not produce positive effects unless govenments actually allocate the corresponding funds for the education of the poor. It is also imperative that northern countries not view debt forgiveness as a substitute for other assistance to poor nations.

Second, discussants called for redefinition of the roles of the various parties in the education process. Since education cannot be left to the whims of diverse actors, the state has an important responsibility to organise education. At the same time, the role of local communities is fundamental, especially for the poor. Partnerships among the state, communities, organised groups, NGOs and donors thus become the key to the development of education in poverty-stricken regions. Such co-operation can be facilitated by controlled decentralization of authority and by efforts to develop synergy between the formal, non-formal and informal channels of education.

Finally, discussants called for a fundamental rethinking of current concepts of education. The poorest populations, who do not readily relate to traditional educational structures, nevertheless need education in order to better understand modern society, to be able to take informed decisions, in short, to become emancipated and shape their own destinies. Alternative schools, designed and run by communities, often provide solutions that are insufficiently recognized and supported. Conceiving of education within specific contexts also requires a new view of the role of teacher. No longer simply a transmitter of knowledge, teacher must be viewed as facilitators of learning who listen, share and invent forms of education for population groups that society has excluded.

Promoting Population and Reproductive Health, Especially Among Young People, Through Basic Education

The information needs of young people in today's fast-changing world are changing rapidly and it is particularly important that educators in both the formal and non-formal sectors find ways to enhance teaching about life skills and reproductive health.

Speakers at this strategy session included a Senegalese secondary school student who emphasized the extent to which economic and social crises over the past two decades have placed new burdens on schools to equip young people with practical life skills. Representatives of various types of agencies spoke of the need for innovation in dealing with sensitive issues such as reproductive health and HIV/AIDS, and cited examples of successful efforts in countries ranging from India and Burkina Faso to Mexico. Evidence was presented that providing young people with sexuality education actually helps them to delay sexual activity, reduce the number of sexual partners and prevent unplanned pregnancy.

In emphasizing the importance of education in preventing problems such as unwanted pregnancies and sexually transmitted diseases, participants stressed the need for curricula to be flexible and for teachers themselves to be attuned to emerging issues that concern young people.

Building Social Integration Through Bilingual and Mother-tongue Education

Considerable evidence has accumulated over the past four decades that teaching young pupils in a language other than their own is ineffective and contributes to high rates of repeating and dropping out. Nevertheless, instruction in the mother tongue is by no means universal. National languages typically enjoy more prestige than local ones with parents and learners, and education policy-makers argue that practical problems, such as training and deploying teachers in a multiplicity of languages, make mother-tongue instruction expensive and logistically difficult.

Presenters at this strategy session argued that the case for mother tongue instruction is compelling for social as well as pedagogical reasons, including the pride that learning in indigenous languages fosters for children's own culture. They maintained that the practical problems, including cost, could readily be managed if the political will existed to do so. Speakers suggested that decentralization in pedagogical and administrative matters is a prerequisite for the successful use of mother tongue instruction and that community/participation is 'vital for success'. Cameroon was cited as a country where associations have set up local language committees to promote multilingual education. Another example cited was South Africa where multilingual policies have been adopted in the first three years of primary education. In Latin America bilingual intercultural education is progressing in seventeen countries.

Participants also spoke of the importance of maintaining quality in mother-tongue instruction and of paying attention to the importance of official national languages. Mastery of the latter at the end of the basic education cycle, they noted, is critical to the vitality of instruction in local languages and to overcoming resistance to this approach.

A Fresh Start to School Health: Improving Learning and Educational Outcomes by Improving Health, Hygiene and Nutrition

The inter-relationship of health and education is well documented. Nutrition and health have a major impact on the ability of children to learn, and improving the health of students and teachers is a key strategy to achieving education for all. Moreover, effective instruction in these subjects in schools can have significant impact on the health of nations.

This strategy session heard reports about the way in which health education is organised in various countries. Only one-third of countries surveyed by UNESCO/WHO investigators in a 1999 study were found to provide health education as a separate subject in primary and secondary schools. Most include such instruction as part of science or physical education courses. The FRESH Start Partnership (Focused Resources for Effective School Health) was presented as an example of a project in which international agencies can work together in support of national and local initiatives.

Participants agreed that education and health workers, teachers, students parents and community members must work together to implement effective school health and nutrition programmes. Water and sanitation were seen as first steps in the creation of a safe and protective physical and psycho-social environment in schools. Instructional programmes should include skills-based health education focusing on the knowledge, attitudes, values and life skills required for positive health-related decisions. There was also general agreement that teachers are the key to the promotion of health in schools. They must be trained to take care of their own health as well as to understand matter affecting the health of their students.

Promoting Basic Education and Democracy: The Role of the Media

Print and electronic media in all countries are in a powerful position to promote participation in basic education programmes and to monitor progress toward education for all and the spread of democratic values. In recent years the media in many nations have shown a growing willingness to co-operate with education authorities in pursuit of these goals. They recognize that the creation of a literate audience and citizenry is not only essential to their own prosperity and survival, but also for the survival of the democratic societies they serve.

This strategy session focused on different ways that the media, especially newspapers, can contribute to basic education and democracy, including Newspaper in Education programmes that are helping educators teach a full range of subjects ranging from basic maths and reading to higher level analytical skills. Research has shown that children who learn reading and writing skills from newspapers not only often attain greater proficiency than those who experience traditional teaching materials but take a greater interest in the world around them. Using newspapers in classrooms has proved to be an inexpensive but powerful teaching device in developing countries, where textbooks are scarce, as well as in former states of the Soviet Union, where relevant civics textbooks have yet to be developed.

Participants noted that reports who cover education should receive continuing training in both reporting practices and background about education that will offer valuable context and rigour to their stories. They also noted the important role that teachers play in encouraging students to read newspapers and the importance of working both with editors and reporters to improve the coverage of education. Examples were presented from Ireland, Republic of Korea and France of instances in which newspapers had developed materials designed to help children develop greater understanding of themes such as the need for understanding and tolerance of persons for different backgrounds than themselves.

Including the Excluded: Enhancing Educational Access and Quality

While notable progress has been made since Jomtien in improving the quality and scope of education for many children, only marginal progress has been made toward extending education to the millions of excluded children. This strategy session considered ways of addressing this problem, which has implications that extend far beyond the damage done to individual children. The presence of large numbers of uneducated young people in any country makes economic and social development difficult, and is a recipe for civil unrest.

Speakers noted that children are deprived of educational opportunities for a wide range of reasons and that understanding the cause of the problem is a prerequisite for finding solutions. Some children are excluded for circumstantial reasons such as poverty, discrimination or communal violence. Others are pushed out by systematic factors such as unsafe schools, unqualified or unmotivated teachers, inflexible schedules and irrelevant curriculum. Still others are denied access to education because of competing priorities and values within their families.

A first step in addressing the problem, participants suggested, must be to find ways to make excluded children visible. Since excluded children typically have distinctive needs, policy-makers must also change the way traditional education is perceived so as to recognize the diversity and value of non-formal and alternative educational structures. The sessions heard reports on a number of alternative approaches to teaching and learning, including the Bolsa Escola school scholarship programme in Brazil under which poor families are paid a monthly wage to keep their children in school rather than sending them out to work.

Discussants also emphasized that, as in other areas of education for all, solutions to the problem of excluded children will require changes in attitudes both within school systems and in the larger community. People who run the education system must want to include all children in the system.

Literacy for All: A Renewed Vision for a Ten-year Global Action Plan

Jomtien adopted an expanded vision of basic education that encompasses the basic learning needs of all children, youth and adults. Literacy is at the heart of basic education, but with nearly 1 billion illiterate adults and tens of millions of children still out of school, it is painfully obvious that this vision is far from realized.

Given this situation, a movement has developed within the United Nations General Assembly to launch a major worldwide initiative to promote universal literacy under the banner of a United Nations Literacy Decade. This strategy session offered an opportunity for participants to offer comments on a preliminary framework prepared by a group of specialists as a basis for such a ten year plan.

Participants by and large supported the idea of a United Nations Literacy Decade for reasons that included its centrality to cultural, civic and economic success in all countries. Speakers noted that literacy—especially for adults—was not sufficiently addressed during the Jomtien decade and that a decade is a reasonable timeframe to be able to show major gains worldwide.

In backing the idea, participants emphasized that the United Nations initiative should be framed within the EFA global initiative not pursued as a separate and parallel programme, and that quantity must not be pursued apart from quality. Speakers stressed that ownership of the initiative must be country-based and driven from the bottom up rather than the top down within each country. They also emphasized that, inasmuch as illiteracy is a structural problem, it cannot be dealt with effectively if it is not accompanied by serious efforts to address the roots of poverty at the local, national and global levels.

After Primary Education, what?

Abundant evidence exists that secondary education is the 'missing link' in the EFA agenda. All too often the mandate of Jomtien has been interpreted in the narrow sense of achieving universal primary education.

In today's world, however, primary education must be seen as a minimum, not a ceiling. Primary school leavers are too young to start working and, even when they do enter the workforce of the twenty-first century, they need more than mere literacy and numeracy. Democratic participation in social and economic development requires larger numbers of citizens with access to quality secondary-level education. The success of efforts to increase primary enrolment is bringing thousands of qualified adolescents to the doors of secondary schools, and means must be found to accommodate them, including the education of large numbers of teachers.

In addressing these issues, participants in this strategy session emphasized the need to focus on broadly conceived learning rather than on access to traditional forms of education. Young people want solid education, not merely seats in schools were curriculum and teaching methods are out of date. Such education must stress interdisciplinary approaches to solving real problems and more creative linkages between schools, communities and enterprises.

While stressing the need to increase secondary school capacity, speakers also stressed the need to move beyond traditional distinctions between education and training programmes and to make more creative use of a wide range of options, including community polytechnic institutions, evening classes for working youth, non-formal courses and apprenticeship combined with schooling. It was noted that expansion of secondary education opportunities is needed in all countries, including those in the developed world.

5

Promoting Education for Democracy and Citizenship

Democracy has made great strides in recent decades. The number of states where leaders are elected in multi-party and multi-candidate systems increased from 22 in 1950 to 119 in 2000. According to the non-partisan organisation Freedom House, 58 per cent of the world's population now reside in such countries.

This growth of democratic political systems has been paralleled by a dramatic expansion of market economics around the globe. Economic globilization has had a powerful impact on developed and developing countries alike and led to trends such as the predominance of corporate over political power, the weakening of states and national boundaries, and a widening of the gap between haves and have-nots. Even in their most dynamic forms, market economies cannot be expected or relied upon to deal with issues of social justice. They must be supplemented with coherent and realistic social policies. Clearly education must play a central role in the development of such policies. Enlightened political leadership is necessary to ensure that all children receive a good education, not only because it is their right but because pressing social problems such as poverty, inequality, exclusion and disease can best be addressed by informed citizens.

Participants in the World Education Forum took up the consequences of these developments under Theme IV: Promoting Education for Democracy and Citizenship. A plenary session focused on the role of that schools can play in creating and fostering democratic cultures and institutions, and in helping people to shape society and to cope with globilization. Ingemar Gustafsson, the chair, opened the session by affirming the importance of education in promoting democracy and citizenship. He reminded participants of the opening words of the Amman Affirmation: 'Education is empowerment. It is the key to establishing and reinforcing democracy, to development which is both sustainable and humane, and to peace founded upon mutual respect and social justice.'

Discussions at the plenary session centered around two distinct themes. The first concerned what education systems can do to promote democratic values through their instructional activities. Schools bear a primary responsibility for preparing students to become well-informed citizens and active participants in social and political life. They must transmit knowledge to successive generations concerning how democratic institutions are structured and function, the privileges and responsibilities that come with citizenship, and the need for constant vigilance to preserve these institutions.

The most obvious role that schools play in the promotion of democratic institutions is to use their curricula, text-books and pedagogy to convey the knowledge and skills that students need to become productive workers, citizens and individuals. But the obligation of educators extends well beyond the transmission of knowledge and skills to the promoting of much deeper attitude, behaviours and values. As Graça Machel, a former Minister of Education in Mozambique and leader of the Forum for African Women Educationalists, told the plenary session, the challenge is to 'mould persons whose minds and hearts and ready to embrace the principles and practices of a society where solidarity and justice are a daily way of life.' The central question thus becomes 'which values do our school-leavers learn from school'?

Participants noted that while it is important for schools to have curricula that prepare children for democracy and citizenship, the context and manner in which instruction is offered deliver powerful lessons of their own. The way schools are governed, whether teachers and administrators treat students and peers with respect, the extent to which educators not only tolerate but encourage intellectual dissent—all of these characteristics of school life send signals that are just as important as the words that flow from the mouths of teachers or the pages of textbooks.

Corporal punishment was cited as an example of a school-based policy that undermines the transmission of democratic values. In a plenary address, Erica George of Human Rights Watch cited situations in countries as diverse as Kenya, South Africa and the United States where violence in the form of corporal punishment or harassment of students who are seen as 'different' is either condoned or tolerated by school officials. Such a stance, she said, 'sends a message that violence is an effective and legitimate means of controlling and correcting people's behaviour'. By contrast, 'Child-friendly learning environments provide the test lessons in learning for democracy.'

In some cases the messages that schools seek to transmit in support of democratic values are undermined by outside forces beyond the control of schools. Gender disparities are a major problem and in many countries children belonging to ethnic and religious minorities are systematically denied their fundamental right to education. The same can be said of marginalized groups, including children of refugees, street children, children in detention or in institutions such as orphanages, child labourers and children affected by armed conflicts. The exclusion of whole categories of students from school is not lost on those who do have the opportunity to attend, nor are crude efforts by political leaders to control what is taught.

When whole categories of children are unable to attend school because of discriminatory barriers to entry, when violence is endemic in the school environment, and when teachers are arbitrarily arrested or fired for political reasons, any lessons in democracy offered in the classroom, however brilliantly conceived or conveyed, are likely to fall on deaf ears,' Ms George said. 'Actions speak louder than words.'

Why a Free Press is Necessary for Development

Underdeveloped nations are in most, if not all, cases those without free information and a free press. We often hear governments justify their restraint of the right to free expression by the need to develop other rights such as the right to education. In truth, however, freedom of expression is not a luxury which governments can throw in once other problems have been resolved. It is truly the key—an integral part of the solutions to these problems.

A free press and the right to criticize and challenge are absolutely necessary for effective development because they are the real enemies of corruption and waste and mismanagement and the real promoters of honest and sensible governance for the good of the people.

Timothy Balding, Director-General of the World Association of Newspapers, in a plenary address

The second, and closely related, theme related to whether societies themselves are organised so as to promote democratic values. Ms Machel framed this issue when she declared, 'If societies themselves are not organised in a democratic way and access to work is the privilege of so few, how can we expect schools to have an enduring impact on the values of democracy and citizenship? Should we not have the courage to re-examine the model of society itself.'

Ms George also picked up on this theme as it related to the political rights of teachers. In far too many cases, she told the plenary session, 'teachers who are politically active as citizens face reprisals from the state.' She cited a recent example in which thirty-six teachers and a headmaster were fined because they attended a teacher-training programme sponsored by a pro-democracy non-governmental organisation. 'Educational institutions cannot fulfil their mission of strengthening respect for human rights when the basic rights of educators themselves are not respected,' she said. By contrast, governments can foster respect for democratic culture among school children by demonstrating respect for the rights of school personnel. 'Educators who can freely and fully enjoy and exercise their internationally recognized human rights are best placed to encourage independent thought, critical judgement, tolerance of dissenting opinion and creativity in their students.'

The existence of a free press is a prerequisite for the free expression of ideas essential to any democratic society. A free press can also serve as an important ally of schools in supporting basic education and promoting democratic values. In a plenary address, Timothy Balding, Director-General of the World Association of Newspapers, noted that not more than six or seven of the fifty-four African nations have a 'fully free press.' He pointedly added that 'some of the greatest obstacles to the fight against illiteracy, the establishment of educational access for all and indeed human progress as a whole, are crected and maintained in place by scores of governments represented at this conference and in this hall.' Mr. Balding also praised the 'handful of enlightened African leaders who do advocate and encourage a free press' and quoted President Thabo Mbeki of South Africa, who recently told a delegation from his organisation that 'you cannot build a new society if you restrict press freedom and freedom of thought.'

Mr Balding described how a growing number of publishers have developed partnerships with schools whereby newspapers are used in classrooms, sometimes in lieu of expensive textbooks. He cited research showing that children who learn reading and writing from newspapers not only have greater success than those who use traditional teaching materials but, significantly 'take a greater interest in the world around them.' He described examples of countries where newspapers have assisted financially-strapped ministries of education by publishing learning materials. In other places, including Northern Ireland and Kosovo, newspapers have run articles designed to help resolve conflict between sectarian groups. 'There are literally hundreds of examples of this kind where newspapers and education authorities can work together on a permanent basis,' he stated.

Mr. Balding concluded by reiterating that the 'basic condition' for harnessing the influence of the media in support of basic education and democratic values is that 'governments must respect the right of their citizens to enjoy full freedom of information and expression, and that they must respect the freedom of the press.'

Making Education for All a Living Reality

Ten years ago, in Jomtien, the international community proclaimed its commitment to a broad and forward-looking vision: a world where education for all was no longer a cherished dream but a living reality.

A decade later we have moved some steps closer to that world, but we are still far from fulfilling the promise of Jomtien. Too many young children are denied the good care that they need to prepare their minds and bodies to learn. Too many school-age children are still excluded from education, while others are consigned to environments that discourage real learning—environments that are unhealthy, unsafe, ineffective and unfriendly to girls. And too many young people and adults are still denied access to the knowledge and development of skills they need to build a better future.

Education is the right of all children and the obligation of all governments. Education is a key to the fulfilment of other human rights. It is the heart of all development [and] it is the essential prerequisite for equality, dignity and lasting peace. As the late President Julius Nyerere of the United Republic of Tanzania reminded us, education is not a way to escape poverty—it is a way of fighting it. Ensuring the right of education is a matter of morality and of justice. It is also a matter of economic common sense, for in this new and information-driven century, the world simply cannot afford the loss of so much human potential. Mr. President, delay is no longer acceptable. The commitments made at Jomtien must be kept.

There is no single solution to increasing access to education and improving its quality. Rather, there are thousands of proven local and national solutions. And that is why we must continue—in tandem with governments and ministries, schools and communities—to identify the gaps that remain in achieving Education for All, and to design concrete actions to achieve it.

UNICEF strongly endorses the statement in the Framework that 'no country seriously committed to basic education will be thwarted in the achievement of this goal by lack of resources.' We and the whole of the international community must redouble our efforts to ensure that education for all plans and programmes are never again without adequate support.

Ten years after Jomtien, let us see to it that the future begins here and now, in Dakar.

Carol Bellamy, Executive Director of UNICEF, in a plenary address

6

Beyond Dakar

At the final plenary session the World Education Forum adopted a Framework for Action committing their governments to 'the achievement of education for all (EFA) goals and targets for every citizen and for every society'. They characterized the Dakar Framework as 'a collective commitment to action' and specified mechanisms at the national, regional and international levels to co-ordinate the global push for education for all. The participants also committed themselves to finding the financial support necessary to assure that 'no countries seriously committed to education for all will be thwarted in their achievement of this goal by a lack of resources.'

The Commitment

In adopting the Dakar Framework, participants in the Forum reaffirmed the vision of the World Declaration on Education for All that had been adopted ten years earlier at the World Conference on Education for All in Jomtien, Thailand. They also reiterated the conviction that education is a fundamental human right and 'the key to sustainable development and peace and stability within and among countries.'

The Framework cited the significant progress made toward education for all in many countries but added that it is unacceptable that in the year 2000 more than 113 million children have no access to primary education, that 880 million adults are illiterate, that gender discrimination persists, and that many children and adults are denied access to the skills and knowledge necessary to be full participants in their societies. 'Achieving EFA goals should be postponed no longer,' the Forum declared. 'The basic learning needs of all can and must be met as a matter of urgency.'

Goals

The Forum participants collectively committed themselves to attaining six specific goals related to EFA. Running through the goals were the major themes that were repeatedly voiced in the plenary, sub-plenary and strategy sessions, themes such as the need to concentrate on the most vulnerable and excluded children, and the importance of maintaining a focus on the education of girls and women. The goals reflected the growing awareness that access and quality are inter-dependent, and three of them took note of the call by many participants to establish specific target dates.

These goals are:

- Expanding and improving comprehensive early childhood care and education, especially for the most vulnerable and disadvantaged children;
- Ensuring that by 2015 all children, particularly girls, children in difficult circumstances and those belonging to ethnic minorities, have access to and complete free and compulsory primary education of good quality;
- Ensuring that the learning needs of all young people and adults are met through equitable access to appropriate learning and life skills programmes;
- Achieving a 50 per cent improvement in levels of adult literacy by 2015, especially for women, and equitable access to basic and continuing education for all adults;
- Eliminating gender disparities in primary and secondary education by 2005, and achieving gender equality in education by 2015, with a focus on ensuring girls' full and equal access to and achievement in basic education of good quality.

- Improving all aspects of the quality of education and ensuring excellence of all so that recognized and measurable learning outcomes are achieved by all, especially in literacy, numeracy and essential life skills.

Strategies

In order to achieve these six goals, the delegates pledged to collaborate on a dozen broad strategies that had also been shown to have had strong support in forum discussions. The list of strategies began with an over-arching plan to 'mobilize' strong national and international political commitment for education for all, develop national action plans and enhance significantly investment in basic education.' Another broad strategy was to 'create safe, healthy, inclusive and equitably resourced educational environments conducive to excellence in learning, with clearly defined levels of achievement for all.'

Specific strategies agreed upon in the Framework included linking education for all policies to anti-poverty and development efforts, collaboration with institutions of civil society, and the devising of new and improved educational accountability systems. Still others emphasized the need to push for gender equality, to combat the HIV/AIDS pandemic and to address the problems of education systems affected by conflict.

The delegates also pledged to work together on programmes to enhance the status, morale and professionalism of teachers, to harness new information and communication technologies to achieve the goals of education for all and to monitor progress toward these goals in a systematic manner.

National Plans

The Framework for Action emphasized that the heart of EFA activity lies at the country level. It called for the establishment or strengthening in each country of National EFA Forums that would include representatives national civil society organisations. 'They should be transparent and democratic and should constitute a framework for implementation at subnational levels,' it stated.

The Framework calls upon each country to prepare a comprehensive National Educational for All (EFA) Plan by 2002 at the latest. 'These plans should be integrated into a wider poverty reduction and development framework', it says. They should also establish budget priorities reflecting a commitment to achieving EFA goals and targets as soon as possible but no later than 2015. The plans themselves should 'be time-bound and action-oriented' and provide for mid-term assessment of progress.

'Where these processes and a credible plan are in place,' the Framework states, 'partner members of the international community undertake to work in a consistent, co-ordinated and coherent manner. Each partner will contribute according to its comparative advantage in support of the National EFA plans to ensure that resource gaps are filled.'

Regional Support

The Dakar Framework asserts that regional activities in support of national plans and strategies will be based on 'existing regional and subregional organisations, networks and initiatives.' Delegates pledged to help strengthen regional and subregional EFA forums that will be linked with, and accountable to, national EFA forums. Functions of the regional and subregional bodies will include policy co-ordination, technical co-operation, monitoring for accountability and the sharing of best practices and lessons learned.

The Framework adds that the challenge of education for all is greatest in sub-Saharan Africa, in South Asia and in the least developed countries. 'While no country in need should be denied assistance', it said, 'priority should be given to these regions and countries.'

Resources

The Dakar Framework for Action acknowledges that many countries lack the financial resources to achieve such goals within an acceptable time-frame and observes that 'New financial resources, preferably in the form of grants and concessional assistance, must therefore be mobilized by bilateral and multilateral funding agencies.' Such agencies include the World Bank, regional development banks and the private sector.

In order to carry out the pledge that no countries 'seriously committed to education for all' would be kept from achieving this goal because of lack of resources, the Framework calls for 'a global initiative aimed at developing the strategies and mobilizing the resources needed to provide effective support to national efforts.' It listed options to be considered under this initiative ranging for enhanced and more predictable external assistance and better co-ordination among donors to debt relief and more effective monitoring of progress toward EFA.

The Framework emphasizes that 'countries with less developed strategies—including countries in transition, countries affected by conflict, and post-crisis countries—must be given the support they need to achieve more rapid progress towards education for all.'

Co-ordinating Mechanisms

The Dakar Framework says that United Nations Educational, Scientific and Cultural Organization (UNESCO) will continue to perform its role of co-ordinating EFA partners and maintaining their collaborative momentum. It specifies that every year UNESCO's Director-General will convene a small and flexible group of highest-level leaders from governments, civil society and development agencies to serve as 'a lever for political commitment and technical and financial resource mobilization.'

Participants in the Forum also directed UNESCO, in its role as Secretariat, to 'refocus its education programme in order to place the outcomes and priorities of Dakar at the heart of its work.' The Secretariat will work closely with other organisations and may include staff seconded from them.

A $8 Billion Price Tag

The Dakar Framework for Action concludes with the observation that achieving education of all will require 'additional financial support by countries and increased development assistance and debt relief for education by bilateral and multilateral donors.' It estimates the cost at about $8 billion a year.

'It is therefore essential,' the Framework states, 'that new, concrete financial commitments be made by national governments and also by bilateral and multilateral donors, including the World Bank and the regional development banks, by civil society and by foundations.'

UNESCO's Commitment to Education for All

From the first day of my election as the head of UNESCO, I have given a clear and strong undertaking that Education for All will be the foremost priority of this Organization—its most urgent, but also its noblest, challenge. I intend to fight this fight with all the resolve and all the moral and intellectual force that I can muster, with the aid of all UNESCO's partners.

This World Education Forum, with the unprecedented participation of governments, civil society organisations, the private sector, education specialists, bilateral and multilateral development partners and the media, cannot—you will agree—be treated as 'just another major conference'. It must close one chapter in the history of universal literacy and open another. The last day in Dakar must be the first day of a collective and victorious struggle to achieve Education for All.

I call on all States to draw up national plans of action immediately after Dakar. The public and private resources to be allocated to education will need to be proportional to the vital importance we attach to it. Governments will have to make clear, coherent and courageous choices in this respect.

I am also fully aware of the need for a substantial increase in the volume of aid for basic education. The donor community must undertake to grant any country submitting a realistic and practical plan in this field the financial and technical support required to attain its objectives. Special grants—and not simply loans—and an easing of the debt burden must be proposed in exchange for social investment programmes, particularly in basic education.

UNESCO, as the United Nations specialized agency for education, will go on fully assuming its responsibilities in this global and collective bid to achieve Education for All. We have been ensuring the co-ordination of the EFA movement for the past ten years. You can continue to count on UNESCO. Education for all is at the very heart of the mandate entrusted to it within the United Nations system.

Koïchiro Matsuura, Director-General of UNESCO, in a plenary address

Bibliography

The Dakar Framework for Action, Education for All: Meeting our Collective Commitments. Adopted by the World Education Forum, Dakar, Senegal 26-28 April, 2000.

Expanded Commentary on the Dakar Framework for Action. Prepared by the World Education Forum Drafting Committee, Paris, 23 May 2000.

Regional Frameworks for Action

SUB-SAHARAN AFRICA. *Education for All. A Framework for Action in Sub-Saharan Africa: Education for African Renaissance in the Twenty-first Century*. Adopted by the Regional Conference on Education for All for Sub-Saharan Africa. Johannesburg, South Africa, 6-10 December, 1999.

THE AMERICAS. *Education for All in the Americas: Regional Framework of Action*. Adopted by the Regional Meeting on Education for All in the Americas, Santo Domingo, Dominican Republic, 10-12 February 2000.

THE ARAB STATES. *Education for All in the Arab States: Renewing the Commitment, The Arab Framework for Action to Ensure Basic Learning Needs in the Arab States in the Years 2000-2010*. Adopted by the Regional Conference on Education for All for the Arab States. Cairo, Egypt, 24-27 January 2000.

ASIA AND PACIFIC. *Asia and Pacific Regional Framework for Action: Education for All. Guiding Principles, Specific Goals and Targets for 2015*. Adopted by the Asia-Pacific Conference on EFA 2000 Assessment. Bangkok, Thailand, 17-20 January 2000.

EUROPE AND NORTH AMERICA. *Regional Framework for Action. Europe and North America*. Adopted by the Conference on Education for All in Europe and North America Warsaw, Poland, 6-8 February 2000.

THE E-9 COUNTRIES. *Recife Declaration of the E-9 Countries*. Adopted by the E-9 Ministerial Review Meeting, Recife, Brazil, 31 January-2 February 2000.

EFA Regional Reports

Arab States and North Africa

Education for All in the Arab States Assessment 2000. Regional Report, Executive Summary. UNESCO Regional Office for Education in the Arab States, January 2000.

Asia and Pacific

A Synthesis Report of Education for All 2000 Assessment in the South and West Asia Sub-Region. Working Paper No. 4. UNESCO PROAP. UNESCO Principal Regional Office for Asia and the Pacific Bangkok, 2000.

VINE, K., *A Synthesis Report of Education for All 2000 Assessment in the East and South East Asia Sub-Region*. Working Paper No. 2. UNESCO Principal Regional Office for Asia and the Pacific. Bangkok, January 2000.

VINE, K., *A Synthesis Report of Education for All 2000 Assessment in the Trans-Caucasus and Central Asia Sub-Region*. Working Paper No. 1 UNESCO Principal Regional Office for Asia and the Pacific, Bangkok, January 2000.

VINE, K and ORDONEZ, V., *A Synthesis Report of Education for All 2000 Assessment for the Asia-Pacific Region*. Working Paper No. 3. UNESCO Principal Regional Office for Asia and the Pacific. Bangkok, January 2000.

Europe and North America

MOTIVANS A., *Education for All—Central and Eastern Europe Synthesis Report*. UNESCO Institute for Statistics/UNICEF Innocenti Research Centre, Regional Report for the EFA 2000 Assessment.

SKILBECK, M., *Education for All. Trends and Issues from on OECD Perspective. Western Europe and North America*. Regional Report for the EFA 2000 Assessment, 2000.

VAN WASSENHOVE, G. and MOUSNY, C., *Education For All*. Warsaw Regional Conference 6-8 February 2000. Conference working document. EFA Forum.

E9 Countries (Nine high-population countries)

SCHWARTZMAN, S. *Education for All: the Nine Largest Countries.* Regional Report for the EFA 2000 Assessment.

Latin America and the Caribbean: The Americas

BLANCO, R. and TREVINO, E. *Latin America Sub-regional Report, Education for All—the Year 2000 Assessment.* Santiago. UNESCO, 2000.

JULES, V. and PANNEFLEK, A., *Education for All in the Caribbean: Assessment 2000. Subregional Synthesis Report. Vol. 1: Summary,* January 2000.

MILLER, E. *Education in the Caribbean in the 1900s: Retrospect and Prospect.* Education for All in the Caribbean; Assessment 2000 Monograph Series, UNESCO.

Sub-Saharan Africa

Education for All—Report from Spanish, Portuguese and French speaking countries. Assessment during the period 1999-2000.

EFA Thematic Studies

ABLETT, J. and SLENGESOL, I-A. *Education in Crisis: The Impact and Lessons of the East Asian Financial Shock, 1997-1999.* International Consultative Forum on Education for All in association with the World Bank, Paris, UNESCO, 2000, 44 pp.

BENSALAH, K., SINCLAIR, M., NACER, F.H. *Education in Situation of Emergency and Crisis: Challenges for the New Century,* International Consultative Forum on Education for All in association with UNESCO and the Swedish International Development Agency. Paris, UNESCO, 2000. 93 pp.

BENTALL, C., PEART, E. CARR-HILL, R. and COX. A *Funding Agency Contributions to Education for All.* International Consultative Forum on Education for All on association with the Department for International Development (United Kingdom). Paris, UNESCO, 2000, 124 pp.

BERNARD, A.K. *Education for All and Children Who are Excluded.* International Consultative Forum on Education for All in association with UNICEF, Paris, UNESCO, 2000, 79 pp.

BRAY, M. *Community Partnerships in Education: Dimensions, Variations, and Implications.* International Consultative Forum on Education for All on association with the World Bank, Paris, UNESCO, 2000, 57 pp.

HYDE, K.A.L and MISKE, S., *Girl's Education*, International Consultative Forum on Education for All in association with UNICEF, Paris, UNESCO, 2000, 42 pp.

MONTAGNES, I. *Textbooks and Learning Materials 1990-1999: A Global Survey*. International Consultative Forum on Education for All in association with the Department for International Development (United Kingdom), ADEA Working Group on Books Et Learning Materials, and the UNESCO/Danida Basic Learning Materials Initiative, Paris, UNESCO, 2000. 104 pp.

MYERS, R.G. *Early Childhood Care and Development*. Final draft. February 1. International Consultative Forum on Education for All in association with UNICEF. Paris, UNESCO, 2000. 55 pp.

OUEDRAOGO, A and JOMMO, B., *Renewed Hope: NGOs and Civil Society in Education for All*. International Consultative Forum on Education for All in association with the Collective Consultation of NGOs on Literacy and Education for All. Paris, UNESCO, 2000. 68 pp.

PERRATON, H and CREED, C., *Applying New Technologies and Cost-Effective Delivery Systems in Basic Education*. International Consultative Forum on Education for All in association with DFID. Paris, UNESCO, 2000. 93 pp.

SINISCALCO, M. T., *Achieving Education for All: Demographic Challenges*. International Consultative Forum on Education for All in association with UNESCO, Paris, UNESCO, 2000. 61 pp.

WAGNER, D., *Literacy and Adult Education*. International Consultative Forum on Education for All in association with UNESCO, Paris, UNESCO, 2000. 47 pp.

WHITMAN, C.V., LEVINGER, B., ALDINGER, C. and BIRDTHISTLE, I., *School Health and Nutrition*. International Consultative Forum on Education for All in association with WHO, Paris, UNESCO, 2000, 67 pp.

NGO Case-studies

ACTION AID. Civil Society Perspectives on Education for All, Broken Promises, New Hopes. In: The Collective Consultation of NGOs on Literacy and Education for All, *Renewed Hope: NGOs and Civil Society in Education for All*. International Consultative Forum on Education for All in association with UNESCO. Paris, UNESCO, 2000.

DEBOUROU, D., Community Participation: NGO and Civil Society experiences. In: The Collective Consultation of NGOs on Literacy and Education for All, *Renewed Hope: NGOs and Civil Society in Education for All*. International Consultative Forum on Education for All in association with UNESCO. 15 November. Paris, UNESCO, 2000. 33 pp.

FREDERICKSON, U., Education for All: Teachers' Perspectives. In: The Collective Consultation of NGOs on Literacy and Education for All, *Renewed Hope: NGOs and Civil Society in Education for All*. International Consultative Forum on Education for All in association with UNESCO, Paris, UNESCO, 2000.

JOMMO, B., Gender Dimensions in Education for All: NGO and Civil Society Experiences. In: The Collective Consultation of NGOs on Literacy and Education for All, *Renewed Hope: NGOs and Civil Society in Education for All*. International Consultative Forum on Education for All in association with UNESCO, Paris, UNESCO, 2000.

KAHLER, D., Linking Non-Formal Education to Development: NGO Experiences During the Education for All Decade. In: The Collective Consultation of NGOs on Literacy and Education for All, *Renewed Hope: NGOs and Civil Society in Education for All*. International Consultative Forum on Education for All. International Consultative Forum on Education for All in association with UNESCO, Paris, UNESCO, 2000. 15 pp.

PATEL, I. Emerging Trends in Adult Literacy Policies and Practice in Africa and Asia. NGO Perspectives, In: The Collective Consultation of NGOs on Literacy and Education for All, *Renewed Hope: NGOs and Civil society in Education for All*. Draft. International Consultative Forum on Education for All in association with UNESCO, Paris, UNESCO, 2000.

ROBINSON, C., Partnerships in Education for All—NGO and Civil Society Experiences. In: The Collective Consultation of NGOs on Literacy and Education for All, *Renewed Hope: NGOs and Civil Society in Education for All*. International Consultative Forum on Education for All in association with UNESCO. Paris, UNESCO, 2000.

Other Documents

FISKE, E.B., *Status and Trends 2000. Assessing Learning Achievement*. International Consultative Forum on Education for All, Paris, UNESCO, 2000. 72 pp. ISSN 1020-0908.

LITTLE, A. and Miller, E., *The International Consultative Forum on Education for All 1990-2000. An Evaluation. A Report to the EFA Forum Steering Committee.* International Consultative Forum on Education for All. Dakar, UNESCO, 2000. 59 pp.

SKILBECK, M., *Global Synthesis. Education for All 2000 Assessment.* International Consultative Forum on Education for All, Paris, UNESCO, 2000. 71 pp.

Thematic Studies. Executive Summaries. Education for All 2000 Assessment. International Consultative Forum on Education for All, Paris, UNESCO, 2000. 62 pp.

UNESCO INSTITUTE FOR STATISTICS. *Statistical Document. Education for All 2000 Assessment.* International Consultative Forum on Education for All, Paris, UNESCO, 2000. 69 pp.

List of Participants

National Authorities, Institutions, Organisations

Albania

Prof. Dr. Ethem Ruka
Ministre de l'éducation
Ministère de l'éducation
Rruga Durresit 23
Tirana

Dr. Vasil Qano
Chef de cabinet du ministre
Ministére de l'éducation
Rruga Durresit 23
Tirana

Mrs Irma Halimi
Specialist of International Relations
Ministry of Education and Science
Rruga Durresit 23
Tirana

Algeria

M. Boualem Bessaieh
Président de la commission des affaires étrangères du Sénat
Représentant personnel du président
de la République
Sénat Algérie

M. Si Amokrane Arab
Secrétaire général de la commission nationale pour l'UNESCO
14 rue Mohamed Boudjatit
El Annasser
16000 Alger

M. Mohamed Salmi
Directeur de l'Office national de l'alphabétisation
37 Chemin El Bachir Ibrahimi
16000 Alger

M.Ali Seddiki
Député-Président de la commission éducation formation
Assemblée Populaire Nationale
Bvd. Z. Yarcef
Alger

Andorra

Monsieur Josep Areny
Inspecteur de l'éducation
Ministère de l'éducation, de la jeunesse et des sports
C/Bonaventura Armengol 6-8
Andorra La Vella

Angola

M. Antonio Burity da Silva Neto
Ministre de l'éducation nationale et de la culture
Ministére de l'éducation nationale et de la culture
Luanda

M. Pedro Massala
Nsingui-Barro
Chargé d'affaires
Délégation permanente de l'Angola auprès de l'UNESCO
Maison de l'UNESCO
1 rue Miollis
75732 Paris Cedex 15
France

Ms Ana Paula de Silva
Sacramento Neto
National Director
Ministry of Family and Women
CP 6438
Luanda

M. Zivendele Sebastião
Conseiller à l'Education pour tous
du Vice-Ministre chargé
de la reforme éducative
CP 1281 Ministèrio da Educaçao
Luanda

Mme Judite Seabra Martins
Directrice nationale
Coopération internationale
Ministère de l'éducation
et de la culture
Luanda

Mme Adelina Van-Dunem Gamboa
Directrice nationale
Ministère de l'éducation
et de la culture
Luanda

Argentina

Lic Dario Braun
Asesor del Señor Ministro
de Educación
Pizzurno 935 (1020)
Buenos Aires

Sra Cecilia Braslavsky
Profesora, CONICET/Universidad
de Buenos Aires
Melian 3948
1430 Buenos Aires

Ms Roxana Morduchowic
Newspaper in Education Director
ADIRA
Chacabuco 314-4°
1609 Buenos Aires

Ms Rosa Maria Torres
Education Adviser
Lafinur 2932, 6th Floor
Buenos Aires

Mme Zumilda Gonzalez
Enseignante à Bocoya·dans
la pré-cordillère des Andes
Maestra—Bocoya
Salta

Sra Pilar Pozner
Coord. Nacional De Gestión
Institucional
Pizzurno 935 (502) 1020
Buenos Aires

Australia

Ms Susan Pascoe
President of the Australian College
of Education
P.O. Box 3
East Melbourne 3002

Mr Geoff Masters
Executive Director
Australian Council for Education
Research (ACER)
19 Prospect Hill Road
Camberwell 2124/P.O. Box 55
Victoria

Mr Robin Davies
Counsellor (Development
Cooperation)
Australian Delegation to the OECD
4 rue Jean Rey
75724 Paris Cedex 15
France

Professor Malcolm Skilbeck
P.O. Box 278
Drysdale
Victoria 3222

Austria

M. Wilhelm Wolf
Directeur du département éducation
primaire
Ministère fédéral de l'éducation
et des affaires culturelles
1014, Minoritenplatz 5
Vienne

Mme Gabriele Eschig
Secrétaire général
Commission nationale autrichienne
pour l'UNESCO
Mentergass 11
1070 Vienna

M. le professeur Georg Gombos
Université de Klagenfurt
9020 Klagenfurt

Azerbaijan

Mr Iskender Iskenderov
Deputy Minister of Education
Ministry of Education
Government House
Baku 37001

Mr. Sabir Hamidov
Senior Officer of the Ministry of Education
Ministry of Education
Government House
Baku 37001

Mrs Yegana Gafgazli
Sepcialist
Azerbaijani National Commission for UNESCO
Ministry of Foreign Affairs
Baku

Bahamas

Hon. Zhivargo Laing
Minister of State for Education
Ministry of Education and Youth
Shirley Steet, Collins House
P.O. Box N 3913
Nassau

Mrs Iris Pinder
Director of Education
Ministry of Education
P.O. Box N 3913
Nassau

Mr Kingsley Black
President
Bahamas Union of Teachers
P.O. Box N 3482
Nassau

Dr Pandora Johnson
Vice President
Ministry of Education
P.O. Box N 4912
Nassau

Bahrain

H.E. Mr Abdul Aziz M. Al-Fadhel
Minister of Education
Ministry of Education
P.O. Box 43
Manama

H.E. Mr (Dr) Salman R. Al-Zayani
Secretary-General
Bahrain Center for Studies and Research
P.O. Box 496
Manama

Mr (Dr) Ebrahim Y. Al-Abdulla
Assistant Under-Secretary for General and Technical Education
Ministry of Education
P.O. Box 43
Manama

Bangladesh

Mr. Abu Sharaf H.K. Sadique
Minister of Education
Government of Bangladesh
Dhaka 1000

Dr. Saadat Hussain
Permanent Secretary
Government of Bangladesh
Bangladesh Secretariat
Dhaka 1000

Mr Syed Muazzem Ali
Ambassador of Bangladesh in France and Permanent Delegate of Bangladesh in UNESCO
Embassy of Bangladesh
39 rue Erlanger
75016 Paris
France

Mr A.K.M.A. Awal Mazumder
Senior Assistant Secretary
Primary and Mass Education Division
Bangladesh Secretariat
Dhaka

Dr Delwar Hossain
Deputy Chief of Planning
Primary and Mass Education Division
Government of Bangladesh
Bangladesh Secretariat
Dhaka

Mr Kazi Fazlur Rahman
Former Member, Planning Commission
House No. 26, Road No. 4
Dhanmondi Residential Area
Dhaka 1205

Barbados

Senator Cynthia Y. Forde
Parliamentary Secretary
Ministry of Education, Youth Affairs and Culture
Elsie Payne Complex
Constitution Road
St. Michael

Mr Glenroy Cumberbatch
Deputy Chief Education Officer
Elsie Payne Complex
Constitution Road
St Michael

Belarus

M. Vasiliy Strazhev
Ministre de l'éducation
9 vul Savietskaja
Minsk 220010

M. Alaksandr Istomin
Secrétaire général
Commission nationale du Belarus pour l'UNESCO
19 Lenin Street
220030 Minsk

Belgium

S. Exc. M. Hervé Hasquin
Ministre-Président du Gouvernement
de la Communauté française de Belgique, chargé des relations internationales
Place Surlet de Chokier, 15-17
1000 Bruxelles

M. Philippe de Clercq
Ambassadeur de Belgique près la République de Sénégal
Ambassade de Belgique
Route de la Petite corniche Est
BP 524
Dakar
Sénégal

M. Alain Verhaagen
Conseiller pour les relations internationales prés le ministre—Président du Gouvernement de la Communauté française de Belgique;
chargé des relations internationales
Place Surlet de Chokier, 15-17
1000 Bruxelles

Mme Sylvie Van Den Wildenberg
Attaché de presse du Ministre-Président
Place Surlet de Chokier, 15-17
1000 Bruxelles

M. François de Smet
Attaché, Cabinet du Ministre—Président
Place Surlet de Chokier, 15-17
1000 Bruxelles

Mme France Lebon
Directrice du Service
de l'éducation permanente
Ministère de la Communauté francaise
Boulevard Leopold II, 44
1080 Bruxelles

M. Marc Demayer
Conseiller
Ministère de la Communauté Wallonie-Bruxelles
(Listed under 3, Civil Society)

Mme Catherine Stercq
Coordinatrice
Lire et Ecrire—Belgique Place Morichar 42-43
1060 Bruxelles

Belize

Mr Eldrid Roy Cayetano
Permanent Secretary
Ministry of Rural Development and Culture
Vice-President
Belize National Commission for UNESCO
East Block
Belmopan

Mr. K. Mustafa Toure
Director of Planning, Projects and Preformance Measurement
Ministry of Education and Sports
Secretary General
Belize National Commission for UNESCO
West Block
Belmopan

Benin

M. Olabiyi B. Joseph Yaï
Délégué permanent
Ambassadeur du Bénin auprès de l'UNESCO
Maison de l'UNESCO
1 rue Miollis
75732 Paris Cedex 15
France

M. Joseph Ahanhanzo-Glele
Directeur de la programmation et de la prospective
Ministère de l'éducation nationale et de la recherche scientifique
01 BP 348
Cotonou

M. Ange N'Koue
Directeur départmental de l'éducation
BP 06
Natitingou

Mme Agai Berthione née Vitin
Conseiller technique à l'éducation auprès du Président de la République du Bénin
01 BP 3674
Cotonou

Bermuda

Sen. The Hon. L. Minton Scott, J.P.
Minister of Education
Ministry of Education
P.O. Box HM 1185
Hamilton HM EX

Mr Joseph Christopher
Chief Education Officer
P.O. Box HM 1185
Hamilton HM EX

Bhutan

Mr Perna Thinely
Director
Education Department
Ministry of Health and Education
Thimphu

Ms Dechen Zam
Assistant Planning Officer
Education Division
Ministry of Health and Education
Thimphu

Bolivia

Sr Ivan Tavel
Viceministro de Educación Alternativa
Av. Arce No 2147
Lado Radissón Plaza Hotel
La Paz

Sr Carlos Gutierrez F.
Jefe De la Unidad de Información y Análisis VEIPS
Av. Arce No. 2147
Lado Radisson Plaza Hotel
La Paz

Bosnia and Herzegovina

Mr Ramiz Selimovic
External Expert in Education
St Obala Maka Dizdara 2
71000 Sarajevo

Bostwana

Hon. Ponatshego H K Kedikilwe
Minister for Education
Ministry of Education
Private Bag 005
Gaborone

Mr Archibald Sekao Makgothi
Head of Planning, Statistics and Research
Ministry of Education
Private Bag 005
Gaborone

Dr Kathleen Letshabo
Research Fellow
University of Botswana
Private Bag 0022
Gaborone

Mr Jakes Swartland
Secretary, National Council on Education
Ministry of Education
Private Bag 005
Gaborone

Brazil

Mme le Professeur Maria Helena Guimaraes Castro
Présidente de l'Institut national des recherches en éducation (INEP)
Ministére de l'éducation du Brésil
Esplanada dos Ministérios
Anexo 2—4éme
Brasilia D.F.

Mrs Vitoria Alice Cleaver
Head of the Educational Affairs Unit
Ministry of Education
Esplanada dos Ministérios
Bloco "L" sala 824
Brasilia D.F.

Mr Efrem de Aguiar Maranhao
Secretary of Education
Av Vernardo Vieira de Meho
1122/401
Piedade-Jaboatao-PE

British Virgin Islands

Dr Charles Wheatley
President of College
P.O. Box H. Lavity Stoutt Community College
P.O. Box 346, Road Town
Tortola

Mr Angel Smith
Chief Education Officer
P.O. Box 78
Road Town
Tortola

Burkina Faso

M. Julien Daboue
Conseiller technique du Ministre
Ministére de l'enseignement de base
et de l'alphabétisation
03 BP 7032
Ouagadougou

Mme Salimata Sanou
Chargée d'études à la Direction des études et à la planification
Coordonnatrice de l'équipe nationale EPT
Ministére de l'enseignement de base et de l'alphabétisation
01 BP 1308
Ouagadougou

M. Amadé Badini
Directeur général
Ecole Normale Supérieure
BP 376
Koudougou

Ms Maria Kere
Program Representative
Save the Children Burkina Faso
01 BP 642 Ouagadougou 01

Mme Alice Tiendrebeogo
Présidente, Association femmes éducatrices et développement
01 BP 581
Ouagadougou 06

M. Bernard D. Yonli
Secrétaire général de la Commission nationale pour l'UNESCO
03 BP 7046
Ouagadougou

Burundi

M. Prosper Mpawenayo
Ministre de l'éducation nationale
Ministère de l'éducation nationale
BP 1900
Bujumbura

M. Edouard Juma
Inspecteur général de l'enseignement
Ministre de l'éducation nationale
BP 1900
Bujumbura

Cambodia

H.E. Mr Im Sethy
Secretary of State
Ministry of Education, Youth and Sports
Phnom Penh

Mr Nath Bunroeun
Director of Teacher Training Department
Ministry of Education, Youth and Sports
Phnom Penh

Mr Ros Borrom
First Deputy-Director of Personnel Department
Ministry of Economy and Finance
St 92 Sangkat Wat Phnom, Khan Daun Pene
Phnom Penh

Cameroon

Mr Joseph Yunga Teghen
Secretary of State
P.O. Box 16000
Yaounde

M. Yakouba Yaya
Directeur de l'enseignement primaire, maternel et normal
Ministère de l'éducation nationale
BP 1600
Yaounde

Monsieur Pius Njawe
Réseau African des Journalistes pour l'Education de Base (RAJEB)
Directeur
Le Messager
Boulevard de la Liberté
5925 Douala

M. Maurice Tadadjeu
Professeur d'université
BP 2905
Yaounde

Canada

H.E. Ms Maria Minna
Minister for International Co-operation
200 Promenade du Portage
12th floor
Hull, Québec K1A 0G4

Mr Emile Gauvreau
Vice-President
Africa and Middle East Branch
Canadian International Development Agency (CIDA)
200 Promenade du Portage
Hull, Québec K1A 0G4

Mme Marie-France Benes
Directrice régionale de Montréal et Directrice des communautés culturelles et des écoles montréalaises
Ministère de l'éducation de Québec
600 rue Fullum 10e étage
Montréal H2K 4L1
Québec

Ms Marilyn Blaeser
Senior Education Advisor, Policy Branch
Canadian International Development Agency (CIDA)
200, Promenade du Portage
Hull, Québec K1A 0G4

Ms Patricia Miaro
Education Specialist
Africa and Middle East Branch
Canadian International Development Agency (CIDA)
200 Promenade du Portage
Hull, Québec K1A 0G4

(Listed under 3, Civil Society)

Mr Bill Hynd
Campaigns Co-ordinator
OXFAM Canada
Box 1252
St. John's Newfoundland
A1C 5V5

(Listed under 3, Civil Society)

Ms Marilies Rettig
President
Canadian Teacher's Federation (CTF)
110 Argyle Avenue
Ottawa, Ontario
K2P 1B4

Mr Francis Whyte
Canadian Education Expert
Rector, Université du Québec à Hull
283 boulevard Alexandre-Taché
pièce E-2200
Case Postale 1250, Succursale B
Hull, Québec J8X 3X7

Ms Johanna Zumstein
Americas Branch, CIDA
200 Promenade du Portage
Hull, Québec K1A 0G4

Ms Diane Laberge
Programme Officer
Candian Commission for UNESCO
350 Albert Street, CP 1047
Ottawa, Ontario K1P 5V8

Mr Daniel Joly
Director, Policy Coordination,
CIDA
200 Promenade du Portage
Hull, Québec K1A 0G4

Mr John Berry
Education Consultant
60-C Rochester Street
Ottawa, Ontario K1R 7L6

Mr Nick Discepola
Member of Parliament
476 Saint Charles Avenue, Ste. 200
Vaudreuil-Dorion
Québec J7V 2N6

Mr Christopher White
Executive Assistant
Officer of the Minister for
International Cooperation
200, Promenade du Portage
Hull, Québec K1A 0G4

Mr Duncan Fulton
Director of Communication
Canadian International
Development Agency
200, Promenade du Portage
Hull, Québec K1A 0G4

Mme Elizabeth Finney
Conseillére à la Ministre
de la Coopération
200, Promenade du Portage
Hull, Québec K1A 0G4

Cape Verde

Mme Filomena Delgado
Secrétaire d'Etat adjoint
Ministère de l'éducation, des
sciences
de la jeunesse et des sport
Praia

Mme Madaewa Silva
Directeur général de
l'enseignement
Ministère de l'éducation, des
sciences
de la jeunesse et des sports
Praia

Mme Esther Sequeira
Coordinatrice du Projet
"Consolidation et Modernisation
des Bases d'éducation"
(Banque Mondiale)
BP 344
Praia

Central African Republic

M. Elois Anguimate
Ministre de l'éducation nationale
BP 35
Bangui

M. Augustin Yangana Yahote
Coordinateur de l'Education
Pour Tous en l'an 2000
BP 35
Bangui

Mme Alphonsiné Motinoui
Secrétaire général de l'Association
des femmes éducatrices pure le
développement en Centrafrique
(AFEDEC)
BP 116
Bangui

Chad

S. Exc. M. Bireme Hamid
Abderahim
Ministre de l'éducation nationale
BP 743
Nadjamena

M. Dadnadji Djimrangar
Directeur général de l'éducation
Ministére de l'éducation nationale
BP 437
Ndjamena

M. Moussa Wayor
Responsable EPT 2000
Ministère de l'éducation nationale

M. Koko Abderamane
Secrétaire exécutif du CONEFE
BP 777
Ndjamena

Chile

Sr Jose Weinstein
Subsecretario de Educación
y la infrascrita
Simon Gonzales 8121 casa 6
La Reina
Santiago

Sr. Carlos Concha
Coordinator Nacional de la
Comisión
de Evaluación de la Conferencia
Mundial de Educación para Todos
Alameda 1371
Santiago

M. Juan Ruz
Directeur Général d'Education
Almeda 1371
Santaigo

Mr Ernesto Schiefelbein
Rector of Santo Tomas University
Ejercito 146
Santaigo

China

Mr Zhang Chongli
Ambassador and Permanent
Delegate of China to UNESCO
UNESCO House
1 rue Miollis
75732 Paris Cedex 15
France

Mr Jianguo Wang
Deputy Director-General of the
Basic Education
Ministry of Education
Beijing

Mr Yue Du
Division Director of the National
Commission of the People's
Republic of China for UNESCO
37 Damucanghutong
Beijing

Mr Liu Wanliang
Second Secretary of the Chinese
Permanent Delegation to UNESCO
UNESCO House
1 rue Miollis
75732 Paris Cedex 15
France

Mr Wang Hongjin
Deputy Director, Statistics Division
Development and Planning
Department
Ministry of Education
Beijing

Colombia

Dr German Bula Escobar
Minister of Education
Ministry of Education
Apdo 077983
Bogota

H.E. Mr Augusto Galan Sarmiento
Ambassador and Permanent
Delegate of Colombia to UNESCO
UNESCO House
1 rue Miollis
75732 Paris Cedex 15
France

Sra Margarita Peña
Directora, Corpoeducación
Cra 30 # 84-14
Bogotá

Comoros

M. Amroine Darkaoui
Directeur général de l'Organisation
scolaire et de la scolarité
Membre du Comité de
coordination
de l'EPT
Ministère de l'éducation nationale
et de la formation professionnelle
BP 73 Moroni

M Aboubakari Boina
Secrétaire général de la
Commission
nationale des Comores pour
l'UNESCO
Ministère de l'éducation nationale
et de la formation professionnelle
BP 73
Moroni

Monsieur Aby Mze Boina
Administrateur du Programme
Éducation au Bureau de l'UNICEF
à Moroni
Membre du Comité de
Coordination
de l'EPT
Ministère de l'éducation nationale
et de la formation nationale
et de la formation professionalle
Moroni

Congo

M. Pierre Nzila
Ministre de l'enseignement
Ministère de l'enseignement
primaire, secondaire et supérieur
BP 2078 Brazzaville

Mme Aimée Gnali
Ministre de la culture et des arts
Chargée du tourisme
Ministère de la culture et des arts
Brazzaville

M. Joachim Mandano
Directeur de l'Institut national de
recherche et d'action pédagogiques
BP 2128
Brazzaville

M. Léon Voumbo Matoumona
Secrétaire académique à l'ENSP
BP 69 Université Marien
Ngouabi
BP 15405–Brazzaville

M. Ambianzi ltoua-Yoyo
Directeur de l'Alphabétisation et
de l'Education pour Tous
BP 661 Brazzaville

M. Gabriel Bokoumaka
Secrétaire général
Commission nationale congolaise
pour l'UNESCO
Brazzaville

Mme Marie Diamesso
Directrice générale
Education de base

Costa Rica

Mr. Guillermo Vargas Salazar
Minister of Education
Apartado 6617
San Jose 1000

Côte d'Ivoire

M. Michel N'Guessan Amani
Ministre de l'éducation nationale
BP V120
Abidjan

Mme Ana Manouan
Secrétaire générale de la
Commission
nationale pour l'UNESCO
BP V297
Abidjan

Mme Salimata Ble
Coordonnateur national Èducation
pour Tous
BP V120
Abidjan

Mme Marie-Chedez Arkhust
Responsable de plaidoyer
éducation
des filles
Ministère de l'éducation nationale
11 BP 853
Abidjan 11

Mme Constance Yai
Ministre de la solidarité et de
la promotion de la femme
Abidjan

M. N'Diaye Alassane Salif
Ambassadeur
Ambassade de Côte d'lvoire
BP 359
Dakar
Sénégal

M. Raymond Konan
Deuxiéme Secrétaire
Ambassade de Côte d'lvoire
BP 359
Dakar
Sénégal

Croatia

Mr Ivan Vavra
Vice-Minister
Ministry of Education and Sport
Trg Burze 6
10000 Zagreb

Mr Davor Butkovic
Deputy Minister
Ministry of Science and Technology
Strossmayerov trg 4
10000 Zagreb

Cuba

Dr. Luis Ignacio Gomez Gutierrez
Ministro de Educación
Ministerio de Educación
Calle Obispo Esq 17 Vedado
La Habana

Mr. Carlos E. Alfaro Alfaro
Director of International Relations
Ministry of Education
Calle Obispo No 160 Esq entre
Mercaderes y San Ignacio
Habana Vieja
La Habana

M. Pedro Juilo Machado
Hernandez
Ambassadeur de Cuba
Ambassade de Cuba à Conakry

Cyprus

Mr Adonis Constantinides
Director General
Ministry of Education
Kimonos Street
1434 Nicosia

Mr Michael Stavrides
Director, Primary Education
Ministry of Education and Culture
Kimonos Street
1434 Nicosia

Czech Republic

Mr Otto Holubar
Chargé d' affaires a.i.
Embassy of the Czech Republic
Rue Aimé Césaire
Fann Résidence
BP 3253
Dakar,
Sénégal

Democratic People's Republic of Korea

Mr Jae Song Song
Vice-Minister of Education
Ministry of Education
Central District
Pyongyang

Mr. Chang Min Kim
Senior Secretary of National
Commission of DPR Korea to
UNESCO
Ministry of Foreign Affairs
P.O. Box 44
Pyongyang

Mr Tok Hun Choe
Deputy Director
Ministry of Education
Central District
Pyongyang

Democratic Republic of the Congo

M. Augustin Kamara Rwakaikara
Ministre de l'éducation nationale
BP 32
Kinshasa-Gombe

M. Simon Kayoyo Umbela
Conseiller pédagogique du ministre
BP 32
Kinshasa-Gombe

M. Lwamba Lwa Nemba
Secrétaire général à l'enseignement
primaire, secondaire et
professionnel
BP 16.564
Kinshasa-1

M. Baibor André Mukulumanya
Chargé d'affaires p.i
N° 16, rue Léo Fobenius
Fann Résidence
Dakar
Sénégal

Denmark

Mr Gert B. Nielsen
Director
National Education Authority
Ministry of Education
Frederiksholms Kanal 26
1220 Copenhagen K

Mr Finn Ovesen
Head of Section
Ministry of Education
Frederiksholms Kanal 26
1220 Copenhagen K

Mr Knud Mortensen
Chairperson EFA Steering Committee
Senior Technical Adviser, Education
Royal Danish Ministry of Foreign Affairs (DANIDA)
Asiatisk Plads 2
1448 Copenhagen K

Djibouti

M. Abdoul Samad Silah Eddine
Conseiller technique du ministre de l'éducation nationale
BP 107
Djibouti

S. Exc. Mme Hawa Ahmed Youssouf
Ministre de la promotion de la femme, du bien-être familial et des affaires sociales
BP 06
Djibouti

Mme Moussa Saada Abdi
Représentante de l'Union des femmes de Djibouti
BP 1644
Djibouti

M. Ilmi Awaleh Elabeh
Conseiller technique
BP 1504
Djibouti

Dominican Republic

Lic Josefina Pimentel
Sub-Secretaria Docente de la Secretaria de Educatión y Cultura
Av. Maximo Gomez # 10
Santo Domingo

Sr Roberto Reyna, M.A.
Vice-rector Academico de la Universidad Autonoma de Santo Domingo
Cuidad Universitaria
Santo Domingo

Ecuador

Sr Gabriel Pazmino Armijos
Viceministro de Education del Ecuador
Ministerio Educación
Quito

Egypt

H.E. Prof. Hussein Kamal Bahaa Eldin
Minister of Education
Ministry of Education
Silver Tower
12 Waked Street
Z. Code 836 Cairo

Dr Salama Mohamed Shaker
Adjoint au ministre des affaires étrangères
Ministère des Affaires Etrangéres
Corniche El Nil, Maspero
Le Caire

Dr Kowssar Hussein Kougek
Director of Educational Curricula Development Center
Silver Tower 12 Waked Street
Z. Code 836 Cairo

Dr Mrs Nadia Gamal Eldin
Regional Center for Educational Research and Development
Silver Tower 12 Waked Street
Z. Code 836 Cairo

Mr Mohamed El Tayeb
Dean of Faculty of Education
Tanta University
Cairo

Dr Mohamed Amin El-Mofti
Dean
Faculty of Education
Ain Shams University
Cairo

M. Khaled El Mekwad
Deuxième Secrétaire
Ambassade d'Egypte
45 Boulevard de la République
BP 474
Dakar
Sénégal

Mr Osama Mohamed Fattoh
Member of the Cabinet of the Minister of Education
Ministry of Education
Cairo

Ms Laila Zaghoul
Egypt Community Institutional Development
Cairo

Equatorial Guinea

M. Angel Eyene Avine
Vice-Ministre de l'éducation et des sciences
Malabo

M. Santago Bivini Mangue
Directeur général de l'enseignement secondaire
Ministére de l'éducation et des sciences
Malabo

Eritrea

Mr Osman Saleh Mohammed
Minister of Education
Ministry of Education
P.O. Box 1056
Asmara

Mr Tesfamicael Gerahtu
Director General
General Education
Ministry of Education
P.O. Box 1056
Asmara

Mr Berhane Demoz
Director Research Division
Ministry of Education
P.O. Box 1056
Asmara

Estonia

Mr. Tonis Lukas
Minister of Education
Ministry of Education
Tonismagi 9/11
15192 Tallinn

Mr Epp Rebane
Head of the General Education Department
Ministry of Education
Tonismagi 9/11
15192 Tallin

Ethiopia

Mr Tafari Hagos
Head, Planning and Project Deaprtment
Ministry of Education
P.O. Box 11510
Addis Ababa

Mr Mamo Mengesha
Head Department of Teacher Education
Ministry of Education
Addis Ababa

Fiji

Ms Linda S. Crowl
Acting Director
Institute of Pacific Studies
University of the South Pacific
IPS/USP P.O. Box 1168
Suva

Finland

Ms Taina Kiekko
Ambassador
Permanent Delegate of Finland to UNESCO
Ministry of Foreign Affairs
UNESCO House
1 rue Miollis
75732 Paris Cedex 15
France

Mr Simo Juva
Director
General Education Division
Ministry of Education
00170 Helsinki

Ms Zabrina Holmström
Secretary-General of the Finnish National Commission for UNESCO
P.O. Box 293
00171 Helsinki

Mr Heikki Kokkala
Educational Adviser
Department of International Development Cooperation
Ministry of Foreign Affairs of Finland
P.O Box 127
Katajanokanlaituri 3
00161 Helsinki

Mr Hannu Savolainen
Niilo Maki Institute
Executive Director
P.O. Box 35
40351 Jyvaskyla

Ms Hanna Alasuutari
Niilo Maki Institute
P.O. Box 35
40351 Jyvaskyla

France

M. Charles Josselin
Ministre délégué à la coopération et à la francophonie
20 rue Monsieur
75015 Paris 07 SP

M.J. Christophe Deberre
Director adjoint du Cabinet du ministre délégué à la coopération et à la francophonie
Ministère des affaires étrangères
20 rue Monsieur
75015 Paris 07 SP

M Renaud Rhim
Délégué adjoint aux relations internationales et à la coopération
Ministère de l'éducation nationale
173 boulevard Saint Germain
75006 Paris

Mme Claudine Bourrel
Chargée de mission pour la coopération multilatérale
Ministère des affaires étrangéres
20 rue Monsieur
75015 Paris 07 SP

M. Lucien Cousin
Chef de la Division de la coopération éducative
Ministére des affaires étrangères
20 rue Monsieur
75700 Paris 07 SP

Mme Denise Epote-Durand
Directrice Afrique
TV 5
19 rue Cognac Jay
75007 Paris

M. André Guyetant
Délégation aux relations internationales et à la coopération
Ministère de l'éducation nationale
173 boulevard Saint Germain
75006 Paris

Mme Martine D'Halluin
Groupe permanent de lutte contre l'illétrisme (GPLI)
9-11 rue George Pitard
75740 Paris Cedex 15

M. Christian Nique
Directeur
Centre International d'études pédagogiques CIEP
1 avenue Léon-Journault
92318 Sèvres Cedex

M. Claude Pair
Recteur d'Académie
Membre de la Commission française pour l'UNESCO
54 boulevard des Invalides
75700 Paris 07 SP

Mme Valérie Thorin
Le groupe "Jeune Afrique"
57 bis rue d'Auteuil
75016 Paris

Mme Marie-Paule Belmas
Conseillére technique
Commission nationale française pour l'UNESCO
57 boulevard des Invalides
75700 Paris 07 SP

M. Richard Werly
Editeur adjoint, affaires internationales
"La Vie" Weekly
163 boulevard Malesherbes
75017 Paris

Mme Jocelyne de Clausade
Conseiller de Cabinet
Ministéré des affaires étrangères
20 rue Monsieur
75015 Paris

M. Jean de Gliniasty
Ambassadeur, Haut représentant de la France au Sénégal
Ambassade de France au Sénégal
BP 2014
Dakar
Sénégal

Mr. Xavier Roze
Chef du Service de coopération et d'action culturelle
Ambassade de France au Sénégal
BP 2014
Dakar
Sénégal

M. Daniet Boutte
Conseil culturel adjoint
Ambassade de France au Sénégal
BP 2014
Dakar
Sénégal

M Yves Gauffriau
Conseiller pour l'éducation
Ambassade de France au Sénégal
Dakar
Sénégal

Gabon

M. André Mba Obame
Ministre de l'éducation nationale
Ministère de l'éducation nationale
BP 106
Libreville

M. Michel Mboumi
Directeur général des enseignements et de la pédagogie
Mnistère de l'éducation nationale
BP 06
Libreville

Mme Blandine Mefane
Planificateur de l'éducation
Coordinateur EPT
Ministère de l'éducation nationale
BP 06
Libreville

Mme Christiane Bitougha
Secrétaire générale, SEENA
BP 16407
Libreville

Gambia

Ms Anne Therese Ndong-Jatta
Secretary of State for Education
Department of State for Education
Bedford Place Building
Banjul

Dr Pap Sey
Director of Basic Education
Department of State for Education
Banjul

Mr Mohamed Jallow
Director—ITHRU
Deparptment of State for Education
Bedford Place Building
Banjul

Dr Saidou S. Jallow
Permanent Secretary
Minister of Education
Willy Thorpe Building
Banjul

Mr Baboucar Bouy
Director
Department of State for Education
Will Thorpe Building
Banjul

Mr Lawrence Bruce
Porject Manager
Willy Thorpe Building
Banjul

Ms Fatou Njie
Director Standard and Quality Assessment (SQAD)
Department of State for Education
Banjul

Georgia

H.E. Mr. Alexander Kartozia
Minister of Education of Georgia
Ministry of Education of Georgia
52 Uznadze St.
Tbilisi 380002

H.E. Mr. George Matiashvili
Deputy Minister of Education of Georgia
Ministry of Education of Georgia
52 Uznadze St.
Tbilisi 380002

H.E. Mr Tamaz Tatishvili
Vice Minister of Education
National Board Program Deputy Minister
52 Uznadze St.
Tbilisi

Germany

H.E. Mr Erich Stather
Deputy Minister
Ministry of Economic Cooperation and Development
Friedrich-Ebert-Allee 40
53113 Bonn

Mr Christoph Eitner
Director for International Affairs
Ministry of Education
53170 Bonn

Dr Birgitta Ryberg
Secretariat of the Permanent Conference of the Ministers of Culture
Lennestr. 6
53113 Bonn

Dr Herbert Krumbein
Ministry for Economic Cooperation and Development
Friedrich-Ebert-Allee 40
53113 Bonn

Mr Bernd Sandhass
Federal Ministry for Economic Cooperation and Development (BMZ)
Friedrich Ebert-Allee 40
53113 Bonn

Dr Peter Krug
Head of Division for Further and Adult Education and Pedagogical Services
Ministry of Education, Science and Further Education
Thineland-Palatinate
Mittlere Bleiche 61
55116 Mainz

Mr Klaus Heufner
President
German National Commission for UNESCO
Colmontstr. 15
53115 Bonn

Mr Herbert Bergmann
GTZ
P.O. Box 5180
Eschborn

Ms Monika Troester
German Institute for Adult Education (DIE)
Hansaale 150
60320
Frankurt am Main

Ms U.T.G. Ohoven
Special Ambassador for UNESCO
Av. Dreiliudue 5-7
4000 Düsseldorf

Ms Christine M. Merkel
German National Commission for UNESCO
Assistant Secretary General for Education, Sciences, Expo 2000
Colmanstr, 15
53115 Bonn

Ms Susanne Dorasil
Ministry of Economic Cooperation and Development
Friedrich Ebert-Allee 40
53113 Bonn

Ms Anca Welscheid
UNESCO-Botschafterin Ute-H. Ohoven
Heinrichstr. 85
40239 Düsseldorf

Ghana

Hon. Mr Dkwow Spio-Garbrah
Minister for Education
Ministry of Education
Ministry Branch Post Office
P.O. Box M. 45
Accra

Mr Alex Tettey-Enyo
Deputy Director General of Ghana Education Service
Ministry of Education
Ministry Branch Post Office
P.O. Box M. 45
Accra

Mr Frank Briamah
Director, Statistics Research, Information Management and Public Relations
Ministry of Education
Ministry Branch Post Office
P.O. Box M. 45
Accra

Mr Jonnie Akakpo
Community Learning Center (CLC) Coordinator
C/o Center for the Development of People (CEDEP)
Top Floor, BHC Building
Kumasi

Dr Kurt Komarek
Educational Advisor
GTZ Office
P.O. Box 9698
KIA
Accra

Dr Kweko Appiah
Consultant
P.O. Box MB10
Accra

Dr Stephen Ayidiya
Coordinator, DEVP PARTNERS
Ministry of Education
Accra

Greece

Mr John Panaretos
Vice President
Network of National Councils of Education of European Union
Athens University of Economic and Business
76 Patision St.
104 34 Athens

Guatemala

Sr Mario Rolando Torres Marroquin
Ministro de Educatión
Despacho Ministerial
6 Calle 1-87, Zona 10
01010 Guatemala

Mrs Rossana Hegel
Coordinator of the National and International Unit of Cooperation of the Ministry of Education
UCONIME
5a Avenida 17-86, Zona 14
Guatelama

Mr Bienvenido Argueta
Advisor
Ministry of Education
6 Avenida 20-25, Zona 10

Guinea

S. Exc. M. Germain Doualamou
Ministre de l'enseignement Pré-universitaire et de l'éducation civique
BP 2201
Conakry

S. Exc. Mme Bruce Mariama Aribot
Ministre des affaires sociales, de la promotion féminine et de la petite enfance
BP 2201
Conakry

S. Exc. M. Eugène Camara
Ministre de l'enseignement supérieur et de la recherche scientifique
BP 2201
Conakry

M. Bernard Haoumou
Directeur national de l'enseignement secondaire
Ministère de l'enseignement pré-universitaire
BP 2001
Conakry

M. Sekov Kaba
Secrétaire général

Mme Baugoura Famoula Sylla
Chef de cabinet

M. Jean Delacroix Camara
Conseiller

Guinea-Bissau

M. João José Silva Monteiro
Ministre de l'éducation, des sciences
et de la technologie
BP 237
Bissau

Mme Marcelina Santos Ba
Coordonatrice du project EPT 2000
BP 132
Bissau

M. Luis Nancassa
Président de SINAPROF, Syndicat National des Enseignants
BP 765
Bissau

M. Lassana Toure
Ambassadeur
BP 2319
Dakar
Sénégal

Guyana

Mr Hyder Ally
Permanent Secretary
Ministry of Education
26 Brickdam
Georgetown

Ms Evelyn Hamilton
Chief Planning Officer
Ministry of Education
26, Brickdam
Georgetown

Haiti

M. Kénold Moreau
Directeur général
Ministère de l'éducation nationale, de la jeunesse et des sports (MENJS)
5 rue Dr Audain
Port-au-Prince

Dr Gaston Georges Merisier
Directeur général adjoint
Ministère de l'éducation nationale, de le jeunesse et des sports (MENJS)
5 rue Dr Audain
Port-au-Prince

M. Alain Solano Serena
Chef de Projet PAEH
c/o Ministèré de l'éducation nationale, de la jeunesse et des sports (MENJS)
5 rue Dr Audain
Port-au-Prince

M. Miloody Vincent
Bureau de presse du ministére
Ministère de l'éducation nationale, de la jeunesse et des sports (MENJS)
5 rue Dr Audain
Port-au-Prince

Holy See

S. Exc. Monseigneur Jean-Paul Gobel
Nonce apostolique au Sénégal
Nonciature Apostolique
BP 5076
Dakar
Sénégal

Rév. Stefano Sanchirico
Expert
Congrégation pour l'éducation catholique
00120 Cité Vatican

Prof. Léopold Cabral
Expert
c/o Nonciature Apostolique
BP 5076
Dakar
Sénégal

Honduras

S. Exc. M. Jose Ramon Calix Figueroa
Ministre de l'éducation
Tegucigalpa

Monsieur Juan Carlos Bendana-Pinel
Délégué permanent adjoint du Honduras auprés de l'UNESCO
Maison de l'UNESCO
1 rue Miollis
75732 Paris Cedex 15
France

India

Mr Maharj Krishen Kaw
Education Secretary
Ministry of Human Resources Development
Government of India
Shastri Bhavan
New Delhi—110 001

Mr Abhimanyu Singh
Joint Secretary
Ministry of Human Resource Development
Government of India
Shastri Bhavan
New Delhi—110 001

Mr Rangalhar Govinda
Senior Fellow
National Institute of Educational Planning and Administration
17-13, Sri Aurobindo Marg
New Delhi—110 016

Mr Anil Bordia
Former Education Secretary
27 Devi Path
Kanota Bagh
Jaipur—302004

Mr Chander Daswani
Consultant, UNESCO
8 Poorvi Marg, Vasant Vihar
New Delhi—110 057

Indonesia

H.E. Prof. Dr Bambang Soehendro
Ambassador
Permanent Delegate of Indonesia to UNESCO
UNESCO House
1 rue Miollis
75732 Paris Cedex 15
France

Dr Indra Djati Sidi
Director General for Primary and Secondary Edcuation
JLM Sudirman
Jakarta

Mr Endro Sumarjo
Director-General
Out-of-School Education, Youth and Sports
Department of National Education
JLM Sudirman
Jakarta

Iran, Islamic Republic of

H.E. Mr Hossein Mozafar
Minister of Education
Ministry of Education
Tehran

H.E. Mr Ali Asghar Fani
Deputy-Minister of Education
Ministry of Education
Tehran

Mr Javad Safaei
Counsellor
Permanent Delegation of the Islamic Republic of Iran to UNESCO
UNESCO House
1 rue Miollis
75732 Paris Cedex 15
France

Mr Cholumali Heidari Khatehpour
Ambassador of Iran to Senegal
Fann Residence
Dakar 17
Senegal

M. Seyed Farad Eftekhazadeh
Directeur général de la coopération scientifique et internationale
Tehran

Mr Aliasjar Mohammadirad
Director General Department of National Education
Ministry of Education
Tehran

Mr Mohammad Reza Erfani
Headmaster of Education
Ministry of Education
Tehran

Mr Mozaffar Morahedi
Headmaster of Education
Ministry of Education
Tehran

Mr Touraj Jalali
Diplomatic Officer
MFA
Tehran

Iraq

H.E. Fahad Al-Shagra
Minister of Education
Baghdad Post Office
P.O. Box 55309

H.E. Dr Ali Al-Mashat
Ambassador
Permanent Delegation of Iraq to UNESCO
UNESCO House
1 rue Miollis
75732 Paris Cedex 15
France

Dr Kadhim Ghaidan Madhi
Head of the Educational Research and Studies Centre
Ministry of Education
Baghdad

Mr Saihood Shakir Dair
General Director of Education
Ministry of Education
Baghdad

Ireland

Mr Austin Gormley
First Secretary
Development Cooperation Division
Department of Foreign Affairs
76-78 Harcourt Street
Dublin 2

Ms Liz Higgins
Education Advisor
Development Cooperation Division
Department of Foreign Affairs
76-78 Harcourt Street
Dublin 2

Mr Brian Power
Higher Executive Officer
Department of Education and Science
Marlborough Street
Dublin 1

Israel

Prof. Michel Abitbol
President of the Pedagogical Secretariat
Ministry of Education and Culture
Jerusalem 91911

Dr. Yitzhak Tomer
Director of Southern District
Ministry of Education and Culture
Jerusalem 91911

Mr Yitzhak Shapira
Director of the Administration for Values Education
Ministry of Education and Culture
Jerusalem 91911

Italy

M. Giovanni Puglisi
Professor de littérature comparée à l'Université de Milan
Secrétaire général de le commission nationale italienne pour l'UNESCO
Piazza Firenze 27
00186 Rome

M. Paolo Orefice
Professeur
Université de Florence
Viato Scanella 10
50125 Florence

M. Lucio Pusci
Professor
Viale Trastevere 76/A
00153 Rome

Mme Alessandra Rossini
Attaché culturel
Ambassade d'Italie
BP 348 Dakar
Sénégal

Jamaica

Mr Burchell Whiteman
Minister of Education and Culture
P.O. Box 498
Kingston 4

Mrs Valerie Been
Director of Planning and Development
Ministry of Education and Culture
4-6 Richings Ave.
Kingston 6

Mr Lascelles Lewis
Chairman
JAMAL Foundation Ltd
47B South Camp Road
Kingston 4

Mr Errol Miller
Professor of Education
Faculty of Education
University of West Indies
P.O. Box 30
Kingston 7

Mr Ian Randle
Ian Randle Publishers
206 Old Hope Road
P.O. Box 686
Kingston 6

Mr Wesley Barrett
Chief Education Officer
Ministry of Education
2 National Heroes Circle
Kingston

Japan

H.E. Dr Akito Arima
Representative of Japan
Former Minister of Education
Member of the House of Councillors
3-2-2 Kasumigaseki
Chiyoda-ku
Tokyo 1000

Mr Masamitsu Oki
Deputy Director General
Ministry of Education
3-1-8-702 Sendagaya Shibuyaku
Tokyo

Dr Ryo Watanabe
Director, Department of International Education and Cooperation
National Institute for Education Research
6-5-22 Shimomeguro, Meguro-ku
Tokyo

Mr Akira Yoshikawa
Minister—Counsellor
Permanent Delegation of Japan to UNESCO
UNESCO House
1 rue Miollis
75732 Paris Cedex 15
France

Mr Daisuke Machida
First Secretary
Permanent Delegation of Japan to UNESCO
UNESCO House
1 rue Miollis
75732 Paris Cedex 15
France

Jordan

Dr Izzat Jaradat
Minister of Education
Ministry of Education
P.O. Box 1646
Amman

Mr Maher Jewihan
Secretary-General
Jordan National Commission for UNESCO
Ministry of Education
P.O. Box 1646
Amman

Mr Mahmoud Ahmad Al-Massad
Director General of Education
Ministry of Education
P.O. Box 1646
Amman

Kazakhstan

M. Achimzhan Akhmetov
Vice-Ministre
Ministère de l'éducation
et de la science
Av, de la République 26
473000 Astana

Mme Risty Zhoumabekova
Directeur du Départment
de l'enseignement secondaire
et général
Ministère de l'éducation et de la
science
Av. de la République 26
473000 Astana

Mrs Shaizada Tasbulatova
Director
National Observatory
Almaty

Kenya

Mr Erastus Muthuuri Kiugu
Secretary General
The Kenya National Commission
for UNESCO
Commerce House 21
Moi Avenue
P.O. Box 72107
Nairobi

Mr John Lodiaga
Director
Kenya Education Staff Institute
Ministry of Education, Science and
Technology
P.O. Box 62592
Nairobi

Kiribati

Hon. Mr Teambo Keariki
Minister of Education
Ministry of Education
P.O. Box 263
Bikenibeu
Tarawa

Mr Teken Tokataake
Permanent Secretary
Ministry of Education
P.O. Box 263
Bikenibeu
Tarawa

Mr Timau Tira
Chief Education Officer
Ministry of Education
P.O. Box 263
Bikenibeu
Tarawa

Kuwait

H.E. Dr Yusef Hamad Al-Ibraheem
Minister of Education and Higher
Education
Ministry of Education
P.O. Box 3266

H.E. Dr Mussaed Rashed Al-
Haroun
Ambassador and Permanent
Delegate of Kuwait to UNESCO
UNESCO House
1 rue Miollis
75732 Paris Cedex 15
France

Mr Sulaiman Al-Kouh
Educational Director
Al Jahra Region

M. Mbaye Mamadou
Traducteur
Ambassade du Koweit á Dakar
Sénégal

Kyrgyzstan

Mr Tursunbek Bekbolotov
Minister of Education Science and
Culture
Bishkek

Mr Savetbek Toktomyshev
Chairman of the Kyrgyz National
Commission for UNESCO
205 Abdumomunov St
720050 Bishkek

Lao People's Democratic Republic

H.E. Mr Khamatanh Chanthala
Vice-Minister of Education
Ministry of Education
P.O. Box 67
Vientiane

Mr Sikhamtatc Mitaray
Director-General
Department of Planning and International Cooperation
Ministry of Education
P.O. Box 67 Lanex Ang Road
Vientiane

Mr Khamhoung Sacklokham
Director-General
Department of General Education
Ministry of Education
P.O Box 67
Vientiane

Latvia

Mr Maris Vitols
Minister of Education and Science
Valnu Str. 2
Riga

Dr Andrejs Rauhvargers
Deputy of State Secretary of the Ministry of Education and Science
Valņu Str. 2
Riga

Lebanon

S. Exc. M. Mohamad Youssef Beydoun
Ministre de l'éducation nationale, de la jeunesse et des sports
Beyrouth

Mr Nemer Freiha
Head of the Educational Centre
P.O. Box 55264
Sinn Ei-Fil
Beirut

Mme Salwa Saniora Baassiri
Secrétaire générale de la Commission nationale libanaise pour l'UNESCO
Beyrouth

Mr Ghanem Bibi
General Co-ordinator
Arab Resource Collective
P.O. Box 13-5916
Beirut

Lesotho

Mr Lesao Archibald Lehohla
Minister of Education
Ministry of Education
P.O. Box 471
Maseru 100

Mr Paul Khoashame Motholo
Acting Principal Secretary
Minister of Education
P.O. Box 471
Maseru 100

Ms Ntsebe Idlett Kokome
Chief Education Officer—EFA National Coordinator
Ministry of Education
P.O. Box 471
Maseru 100

Liberia

Dr. Evelyn Kandakai
Minister of Education
Ministry of Education
E.G.W King Plaza
Broad Street
P.O. Box 9012
Monrovia

Mr Benjamin Sumo
Director, ISDS and EFA Coordinator
Ministry of Education
P.O. Box 9012
Monrovia

Mr John Sumo
Education Project Officer
UNICEF Liberia
Monrovia

Libyan Arab Jamahiriya

Mr Abdallah Milad Tagiuri
National Coordinator for EFA 2000
National Coordinator
General People's Committee for Education and Vocational Training
Tripoli

Dr Abdalah Abed Abugfar
Head of Committee of the National EFA Report

Mr Asaad Elmasoudi
Head of UNESCO Division
Libyan National Commission for UNESCO
P.O. Box 1091
Tripoli

Lithuania

Mr Kornelijus Platelis
Minister of Education and Science
Ministry of Education and Science
Volano 2/7
2691 Vilnius

Mr Vaiva Vebraite
Vice-Minister of Education and Science
Ministry of Education and Science
Volano 2/7
2691 Vilnius

Mr Arunas Pliksnys
Director of the Department of General Education
Ministry of Education and Science
Valano 2/7
2691 Vilnius

Luxembourg

S.A. Princesse Maria Teresa de Luxembourg
Ambassadeur de bonne volonté pour l'UNESCO
Princesse héritiére
Palais Grand-Ducal

Mr Jean-Pierre Kraemer
Inspector General of Primary Education
President of the Luxembourg National Commission for UNESCO
Ministry of National Education
29 rue Aldringen
2926 Luxembourg

M. Henri Chrisnach
Aide de Camp
Palais Grand-Ducal

Madagascar

M. Jacquit Rosat Simon Nivoson
Ministre de l'enseignement Secondaire et de l'éducation de base, MINESEB
Anosy
Antananarivo 101

M. Boniface Levelo
Ministre de l'enseignement technique et de la formation professionnelle
Ampefiloha
Antananarivo 101

M Albert Rafalimanana
Directeur de la planification de l'éducation
Ministère de l'enseignement secondaire et de l'éducation de base
Anosy
Antananarivo 101

Malawi

Hon. Mosses Dossi M.P.
Deputy Minister of Education, Sports and Culture
Ministry of Education, Sports and Culture
Private Bag 328
Lilongwe 3

Mr Matthew W. Matemba
Principal Secretary for Basic Education
Ministry of Education, Sports and Culture
Private Bag 328
Lilongwe 3

Mr McPherson Jere
Deputy Director Education Planning
Ministry of Education, Sports and Culture
Private Bag 328
Lilongwe 3

Ms Grace Milner
Planning Officer
Ministry of Education
Private Bag 328
Lilongwe 3

Mr Lexon Ndlama
Principal Education Advisor, MOESC
Private Bag 328
Lilongwe 3

Mr David Mulera
Programme Officer
Malawi National Commission for UNESCO
Box 30278
Lilongwe 3

Malaysia

Dr Abdul Shukor
Director General of Education
Ministry of Education
Damai Sara Town Centre
50604 Kuala Lumpur

Dr Ahmad Halim
Principal Assistant Director
Macro Planning Unit
Ministry of Education
Damai Sara Town Centre
50604 Kuala Lumpur

H.E. Jasmi bin Md. Yusoff
Malaysian Ambassador to the Republic of Senegal
Embassy of Malaysia
7 (VDN) Fann Mermow
Dakar
Senegal

Maldives

Dr. Mohamed Latheef
Minister of Education
Ministry of Education
Male

Dr Mahamoodh Shougee
Chief Curriculum Supervisor
Ministry of Education
Male

Mali

M. Mosustapha Dicko
Ministre de l'éducation
BP 71
Bamako

M. Mountaga Lam
Coordinateur de l'équipe de suivi de l'EPT/Mali
BPE 13 29
Bamako

M Maharafa Traore
secrétaire général
Ministére du travail
BP 80
Bamako

M. Paul Diarra
Chef de la Division éducation préscolaire
DNEPS
BP 71
Bamako

M. Salif Samake
Conseiller technique
Ministère of l'éducation
BP 71
Bamako

M. Nouhoum Diakite
Directeur adjoint de l'alphabétisation BP 62
Bamako

Mme Maïmouna Tapo
chef de la Cellule de scolarisation des filles
Direction nationale enseignement fondamental
Bamako

Mme Fatimata Diallo Maiga
chef de section
Division évaluation
Institut pédagogique national
Bamako

Marshall Islands

Mr Falai Taafaki
Special Consultant
Minister of Education, Science and Technology
Ministry of Education
P.O. Box 1628
Majuro 96960

Mauritania

S.Exc. Maitre Sghair Ould M'Bareck
Ministre de l'éducation nationale
Ministère de l'éducation nationale
BP 227
Nouakchott

M. Ely Ould Bouhout
Secrétaire général de la Commission nationale mauritanienne pour l'UNESCO
BP 5115
Nouakchott

M. Mohaméden Ould Bagga
Directeur de la planification et de la coopération
Coordinateur national de l'EPT
Ministère de l'éducation nationale
BP 227
Nouakchott

Mme Mat Mintt Ewnen
Conseiller technique du secrétaire d'état chargé de l'alphabétisation
BP 4963
SEAEO/NKTT
Nouakchott

M. Douahi Ould Mohamed Saleck
Président
Association écoles privées Mauritanie
BP 4892
Nouackhott

M. Abdellah Mounina Mint
Conseiller technique de secrétariat d'Etat à la condition féminine
BP 4472
Nouakchott

Mauritius

Mr Sivallngum Subramanien
Permanent Secretary
Ministry of Education and Scientific Research
1st Level, IVTB House
Phoenix

Mexico

Lic. Miguel Limón Rojas
Secretario de Educación Pública
Argentina 28
México DF

Sra Sofialeticia Morales Garza
Directora General de Asuntos Internacionales
Secretaria de Educación Pública
Argentina 28
México DF

Ms Elisa Bonilla
Director General
Educational Methods and Materials
Obrero Mundial 358
Narvarte, Mexico DF

Ms Lilian Alvarez de Testa
Advisor to the Minister
Argentina 28
Mexico DF

Mr Diego Simancas
Third Secretary
Mexican Mission to UNESCO
UNESCO House
1 rue Miollis
75732 Paris Cedex 15
France

Mongolia

Mr Avirmed Battur
Minister of Education, Science and Culture
Ministry of Education
Government House III
Bagatoiruu 44
Ulaanbaatar

Mr Davaasuren Munkhjargal
Director of Department
Ministry of Education
Government House II
Bagatoiruu 44
Ulaanbaatar

Morocco

Mrs Aïcha Belarbi
Secretary of State for Cooperation
Ministry of Foreign Affairs and Cooperation
Rabat

M. Ali Ben Bachir Hassani
Chargé de mission auprès du premier ministre chargé de l'éducation et de la formation
Primature
Rabat

Mr Ahmed Lamrini
Secretary General
Ministery of National Education
Bab Rouah
Rabat

M. El Mostafa Hddigui
Directeur de l'administration-centrale
Ministère de l'éducation nationale
32 rue Saadiyine (Hassane)
10000 Rabat

M. Hassan Hassan El Iklil
Conseiller au cabinet de
Mme la Secrétaire d'Etat chargée de la coopération
Rabat

Mozambique

Dr Alcido N'guenha
Minister of Education
Ministry of Education
Av 24 de Julho 167
C.P. 34
Maputo

Mr Virgilio Juvane
Director of Planning
Ministry of Education
Av 24 de Julho 167
C.P. 34
Maputo

Mr Anisio Matangala
Advisor of the Minister of Education
Ministry of Education
Av 24 de Julho N 167
C.P. 34
Maputo

Dr. Graça Machel
Ex-Minister of Education of Mozambique
c/o Private Bag 152
Pretoria
South Africa

Namibia

Hon. John Mutorwa
Minister of Basic Education and Culture
Ministry of Basic Education and Culture
Private Bag 13186
Windhoek

Mr Robert West
Director of Planning and Development
Ministry of Basic Education and Culture
Private Bag 13186
Windhoek

Ms Sylvia Bonisile Valashiya
Professional Nurse
Programme Coordinator (HIV/AIDS) Youth
Ministry of Youth and Sport
P.O. Box 22617
Windhoek

Mr Justin Ellis
Under Secretary, Culture and Lifelong Learning
Ministry of Basic Education, Sports and Culture
Private Bag 13186
Windhoek

Nepal

Hon. Prasad Upadhyaya
Minister of Education and Sports
Ministry of Education and Sports
Kathmandu

Hon. Member Dr Nirmal Prasad Pandey
National Planning Commission
Singh Durbar
Kathmandu

Mr Chuman Singh Basnyat
Joint Secretary
Ministry of Education and Sports
Kathmandu

Netherlands

Ms Eveline Herfkens
Minister of Development Cooperation
Ministry of Foreign Affairs
P.O. Box 20061
2500 EB The Hague

Mr Dick Lageweg
Deputy Secretary General
National UNESCO Commission of the Netherlands
Kortenaerkade 11

Mr Arriën Lekkerkerker
Spokesperson for the Minister
Ministry of Foreign Affairs, D.V.L.
P.O. Box 20061
2500 EB The Hague

Ms Hanke Koopman
Basic Education Adviser
Ministry of Foreign Affairs, DCO
P.O. Box 20061

Mr Ronald Siebes
Sector Expert Basic Education, DCO
Ministry of Foreign Affairs
P.O. Box 20061
2500 EB The Hague

Mr Gabriel Rugalema
Anthropology of Health and HIV Risk
Department of Technology and Agrarian Development
Wageningen University

Netherlands Antilles

Mr Stanley Lamp
Minister of Education
Fort Amsterdam 17
Curaçao

Mr Humphery Senior
Head of Advisory Bureau for Research Planning
Planning Department
Department of Education
Boerhaavestraat 16
Curaçao

Ms Sarah Wescott-Williams
Commissioner of Education
Philipsburg
Saint Maarten

New Zealand

Hon. Matt Robson, M.P.
Minister of Corrections
Minister for Courts
Associate Minister of Foreign Affairs and Trade
Parliament Buildings
Wellington

Mr Lester Taylor
Chief Executive Officer Education
Education New Zealand Trust
P.O. Box 10-500
Wellington

Me Roger King
Senior Private Secretary to Associate
Minister of Foreign Affairs
Parliament Buildings
Wellington

Nicaragua

Sr Francisco Chavarria Valenzuela
Vice Ministro de Educación, Cultura y Déportes
Ministerio de Educación, Cultura y Deportes
Centro Civico
Modedo J. Planta alta

Licenciada Ana Luisa Sanchez Narvaez
Directora General de Educación
Ministerio de Educación
Cultura y Deportes
Centro Civico
Modedo J. Planta alta

Niger

M. Ibrahim Ary
Ministre de l'éducation nationale
BP 557
Niamey

M. Hamissou Oumarou
Directeur plantification
Coordonnateur EFA 2000
Ministére de l'éducation
Secrétariat général
BP 557
Niamey

M. Morou Moumouni
Direction de I'ordonnancement au Ministére des finances
223 Niamey

M. Maman Mallam-Garba
Projet éducation de base
Conseiller technique
GTZ-Niger

Mme Thérèse Keita Mai Manga
Coordonnatrice de la Cellule technique pour la promotion de la scolarisation des filles au Niger
BP 10798
Naimey

Nigeria

Prof Tunde Adeniran
Honourable Minister of Education
Federal Ministry of Education
Shehu Shagari Way
Maitama
Abuja

H.E. Prof. Michael Omolewa
Ambassador and Permanent Delegate of Nigeria to UNESCO
UNESCO House
1 rue Miollis
75732 Paris Cedex 15
France

Prof. Pai Obanya
Chief Executive, Universal Basic Education (UBE) Commission
c/o Federal Ministry of Education
Box 6806, Wuse Zone 4
Abuja

Dr Peter Shehu Abdu
Director
Educational Support Services Department
Federal Ministry of Education Headquarters
Shehu Shagari Way
Maitama
Abuja

Mr Young Nwafor
Secretary General
Nigerian National Comission for UNESCO
Federal Ministry of Education
PMB 476 Garki
Abuja

Mr Obododimma Oha
(University of Ibadan, Nigeria)
UFR des Lettres et Sciences Humaines
Gaston Berger Université de Saint-Louis
BP 234
Saint-Louis
Sénégal

Mr Uche Aloy Ewechukwu
Head, Nigeria Bureau
West Africa Magazine
P.O. Box 7189, Wuse
Abuja

Mr Remi Solape Longe
Department of Education
University of Ibadan

Mr Tunji Olaopa
Assistant Director
Federal Ministry of Education
Hon. Minister's Office
New Federal Secretariat
3rd Annex, Maitama
Abuja

Mr Lami Amodu
Chief Education Officer
Nigeria Federal Ministry of Education
Abuja

Mr Mobolaji Olurunfunmi
Deputy Director
Inter. Educ. Coop
6 Gimbiya Street
Abuja

Mr Abosede Akande
Retired Principal
P.O. Box 5
Ikere, Ekipi

Norway

Ms Torild Skard
Senior Advisor
Ministry of Foreign Affairs
7 Juni Plass 1
Post-box 8114 Dep
0032 Oslo

Ms Hanna Marit Jahr
Director General
Ministry of Education, Research and Church Affairs
Akersgt, 44 (block Y)
Post-box 8119 Dep
0032 Oslo

Ms Birgitta Naess
President of the Norwegian
National Commission for UNESCO
Rute 510
1765 Halden

Ms Sissel Volan
Senior Education Advisor
NORAD, P.O. Box 8034 DEP
0030 Oslo

Oman

Dr Fawzia Al-Farsi
Under Secretary for Education
Ministry of Education
P.O. Box 3
Muscat 113

Dr Hamed Al-Hammami
Director General of Curricula and Training
Ministry of Education
P.O. Box 3
Muscat 113

Mr Mohamed bin Saleem Al-Yacoubi
Deputy Director General
National Coordinator of the EFA 2000 Assessment
Ministry of Education
P.O. Box 3
Muscat 113

Pakistan

Ms Zobaida Jalal
Federal Minister for Education
Minister of Education
Government of Pakistan
Pakistan Secretariat
Block D
Islamabad

Ms Shaheen Attiqur Rehman
Minister of Literacy
Government of Punjab
226 Munir Road
Lahore

Prof. Anita Ghulam Ali
Provincial Minister of Education
Education Department
Tuahlar House
Government of Sindh
Karachi

Mr Syed Imtiaz Hussain Gillani
Education Minister
Government of NWFP
Peshawar

Prof. Dr Razia Babar
Education Minister
Government of Balochistan
Babar Manzil
Tola Ram Road
Quetta
Balo

Palestine

Dr Naim Abu Hommos
Deputy Minister of Education
Ministry of Education
P.O. Box 576
Ramallah
West Bank

Mrs Lamis Alami
Chief, Field Education Programme
UNRWA
West Bank Field Office
P.O. Box 19149 Jerusalem
Via Israel

Mr Hasan Abu-Libdeh
President
Palestinian Central Bureau of Statistics
P.O. Box 1647
Ramallah

Mr Nabil Soblabu
General Programme Coordinator
P.O. Box 25222
Jerusalem

Panama

Sra Doris Mata
Ministra de Educación
Ministerio de Educación
Apdo. 2440 Zona 3
Panama

Sra Adela Abad
Directora General de Educación
Ministerio de Educación
Apartado 2440 Zona 3
Panama

Papua New Guinea

Dr John Waiko
Minister for Education
National Parliament
P.O. Waifani

Mr Pala Wari
Advisor
Ministry of Education
P.O. Box 446
Waigwi

Paraguay

Licenciada Blanca Ovelar de Duarte
Viceministra de Educación
Chile 849
Asunción

Sr Ramón Rodas Duarte
Docente
Tte J. Martinez N° 1140
c/ Dr Sosa
Asunción

Sra Mirta Vera
Jefe—Viceministerio de Educación
Ministerio de Educación
Chile 849
Asunción

Peru

Dra Susana Seto Miyamoto
Vice Minista de Gestión Institucional
Van de Velde 160
San Borja
Lima 41

Ing Tula Luna Moncayo
Secretaria General de la Comisión Nacional Peruana de cooperacion con la UNESCO
Van de Velde 160
San Borja
Lima 41

Sr Wolfgang Küper
c/o Agencia de la GTZ en Lima
Prolongación Arenales 801
Casilla 18—1335
Agencia de la GTZ
Lima 18

Philippines

Mr Ramon Bacani
Assistant Secretary
Department of Education, Culture and Sports
UL Complex
Meralco Avenue
Pasig City

Mr Ruperto Alonzo
Deputy Director General
National Economic Development Authority
NEDA sa Pasig
Amber Avenue
Pasig City

Ms Lourdes Balanon
Assistant Secretary
Department of Social Welfare and Development
Constitutional Hill
Batasang Pambansa Complex
Quezon City

Ms Feny de Los Angeles-Bautista
Executive Director
Community of Learners Foundation
1 Castilla Street
Quezon City
Metro Manila

Poland

Mr Ryszard Mosakowski
Personal Representative of the Minister of National Education
Ministry of National Education
Department of European Integration and International Cooperation
ai. Szucha 25
00-918 Warsaw

Portugal

Mme Ana Benavente
Secrétaire d'état à l'éducation
Av. 5 Outubro 107-9
Lisboa

Mme Marcia Trigo
Président de la commission de l'agence nationale de l'éducation et de la formation des adultes
Rua Vale de Pereiro No. 16-1
1250-271
Lisboa

Mme Maria Eduarda Boal
Directeur général
Ministère de l'éducation
Av. 5 Outubro 107-7
Lisboa

M. Manuel Silva
Secrétaire d'Ambassade
Ambassade du Portugal à Dakar
Dakar
Sénégal

Qatar

H.E. Dr Mohammed Abdul Rahim Kafood
Minister of Education and Higher Education
P.O. Box 80
Doha

Dr Abdul Aziz Abdul Rahman Kamal
Head of Educational Research Centre
P.O. Box 9760
Doha

Mr Salem Rashid Al-Azbeh
Director of Minister's Office
P.O. Box 80
Doha

Repubic of Korea

Mr Sang-sik OH
Deputy Permanent Delegate
Permanent Delegation of the Republic of Korea to UNESCO
UNESCO House
1 rue Miollis
75732 Paris Cedex 15
France

Mr Gul-woo Lee
First Secretary for Education
Permanent Delegation of the Republic of Korea to UNESCO
UNESCO House
1 rue Miollis
75732 Paris Cedex 15
France

Mr Zun-sang Han
Professor
Deaprtment of Education
Yonsei University
134 Shinchon
Seodaemoonku
Seoul 120-749

Mr Jong-hung Kim
Programme Officer Education Unit
Korean National Commission for UNESCO
P.O. Box Central 64
Seoul

Republic of Moldova

Ms Lidia Gutu
Deputy Prime Minister
The Government of Moldova
Government House
Piata Marii Adunari Nationale 1
2033 Chisinau

M. Nicolae Bucun
Ministre adjoint au ministére
Ministére de l'éducation et des sciences
Government House
Piata Marii Adunari Nationale 1
2033 Chisinau

Prof. D.Sc. Vladimir Gutu
Chief of the Department of pre-school, primary and secondary general education
Ministry of Education and Sciences
Government House
Piata Marii Adunari Nationale 1
2033 Chisinau

Romania

M. Mihai Korka
Conseiller du ministre
Ministére de l'éducation nationale
Str Sen Berthelot 28-30
Bucarest 70738

Mme Anca Butuca
Conseiller du ministre
Ministére de l'éducation nationale
Str Sen Berthelot 28-30
Bucarest 70738

M. Cătălin Baba
Conseiller du ministre
Ministére de l'éducation nationale
Str Sen Berthelot 28-30
Bucarest 70738

Russian Federation

M. Vladimir Filippov
Ministre de l'éducation
de la Fédération de Russie
51 Lussinbovskay
Moscou

Mr Alexander Kondakov
Deputy-Minister of Education
Shabalovke, 33
Moscow

M. Nikolaï Dmitriev
Directeur, Départment
des relations internationales
Ministère de l'éducation
33 Shabolovka
Moscou

Mme Olga Ivanova
Conseiller principal
Commission nationale russe
pure l'UNESCO
Smolenskaya-Sennaya Pl, 32/34
Moscou

Rwanda

M. Emmanuel Mudidi
Ministre de l'éducation
BP 622
Kigali

M. Narcisse Musabeyezu
Directeur de l'enseignement
préscolaire, primaire et éducation
spéciale
Ministére de l'éducation
BP 622
Kigali

M. Faustin Habineza
Directeur de la gestion et du
développement du personnel
Enseignant au ministére de
l'éducation
BP 622
Kigali

Saint Lucia

Hon. Mario Michel
Deputy Prime Minister and
Minister of Education, Human
Resourrce Development, Youth and
Sports
New NIS Building
Waterfront
Castries

Dr. Didacus Jules
Permanent Secretary
Ministry of Education,
Human Resource
Development, Youth and Sports
New NIS Building
Waterfront
Castries

San Marino

Mme Marina Freschi
Secretario Particolare Ministro
Pubblica Istruzione e cultura
Secretaria Di Stato Pubblica
Istruzione e cultura
Contrada Omerelli
San Marino

Sao Tome and Principe

Mme Anna Maria Vera Cruz Costa
Coordinatrice de l'E.P.T
Ministére de l'éducation
Direction du dévelopment
curriculaire
BP 41
Sao Tomé

Saudi Arabia

Dr Mohammed Ahmed Rasheed
Minister of Education
Ministry of Education
Riyadh

Dr Ibrahim Al Shaddi
Deputy Minister for Cultural
Affairs
Ministry of Education
Riyadh

Dr Ali Al-Khabti
Director of Schol Evaluation
Ministry of Education
P.O. Box 108903
Jeddah 21351

Dr Saudi Al Dohian
Director of Research Dep
Ministry of Education
Riyadh

Dr. Ali Al Hakami
Director of Department of
Measurement and Evaluation
Ministry of Education
Riyadh

Dr Ali Al-Karni
Secretary General
Higher Educational Policy
Committee
Ministry of Education
Riyadh

Professor Mr Ibrahim Al-Wadi
Chief of Secretariat and Relations
Unit
Minister Office
Ministry of Education
Riyadh

Senegal

M. Kasoumbaly Ndiaye
Ministre de l'éducation nationale

M. Madier Diouf
Ministre de l'enseignement
supérieur
et de la recherche scientifique

M. Bécaye Diop
Ministre délégué chargé de
l'éducation de base et des langues
nationales

M. André Sonko
Ancien ministre de l'éducation
nationale

M. Kéba Birane Cisse
Ambassadeur, Délégué permanent
du Sénégal auprés de l'UNESCO

M. Ousmane Blondin Diop
Délégué permanent adjoint du
Sénégal auprès de l'UNESCO

M. Alexandre Mbaye Diop
Présidence de la République

M. Elhadji Tamsir Mbaye
Primature

M. Assane Hane
Comité préparatoire

Mr Pape Momar Sow
Director of Planning
Ministry of Education

M. Mohamadou Aly Sall
Comité préparatoire

M. Seigne Tacko Ndaw
Comité préparatoire

M. Bala Dia
Comité préparatoire

M. Cheikh Alassane Mbaye
Comité préparatoire

M. Mafakha Touré
Comité préparatoire

M. Pape Madiop Fall
Comité préparatoire

M. Magatte Sow
Comité préparatoire

M. Cheikh Aw
Comité préparatoire

M. Cheikh Ndiaye
IA/AISEN

M. Alioune Ndoye
ENS/UCAD

M. Mamadou Badiane
Association des Parents d'éléves

M. About Sy
Enseignants retraités

M. Mamdou Diop
Syndicat

M. Iba Ndiaye Diadji
Syndicat

M. Ibrahima Niokhobaye Diouf
Syndicat

M. Bakhao Ndiogue
Répresentant du SNEEL
Syndicat

M. Seydou Sall
CONGAD

M. Yves Richard
ONG

M. Tay
ONG

M. Serge Mareil
ONG

Mme Mame Bousso Samb
SCOFI

Mme Awa Diagne
Enseignement Privé

M. Michel Tokopuku
ONG

M. Mamadou Lamine Gassama
Comité préparatoire

M. Ka Ibra Deguene
Ambassadeur du Sénégal à l'ONU
238 68th Street
New York, New York 10021
Unites States

M. Malick Sembene
Directeur
Division de la santé scolaire
Ministére de l'éducation nationale
BP 5252
Dakar Fann

Ms Yaye Astou Cissé
1999 Miss Senegal
c/o UNFPA Field Office Dakar

Mlle Dibou Faye
Equipe Jeunesse Action ENDA
TM/MAEJT
BP 3370
Dakar

Seycheiles

H.E. Mr Dany Rollen Antoine Faure
Minister of Education
P.O. Box 1098
Victoria
Mahe

Mr Jones Belmont
Director Resource Planning and Project Development
Ministry of Education
P.O. Box 48
Victoria
Mahe

Sierra Leone

Hon. Dr Alpha Tejan Wurie
Minister of Education, Youths and Sports
Ministry of Education, Youth and Sports
New England
Freetown

Dr Albert C.T. Dupigny
Head—A and E, National EFA Coordinator
Ministry of Education, Youth and Sports
New England
Freetown

Slovakia

Mr Milan Ftácnik
Minister of Education
Stromova 1
83103 Bratislava

Mrs Ludmila Simcáková
Institute of Information and Prognosis
Stromova 1
831 03 Bratislava

Solomon Islands

Hon. Japhet Waipora
Minister for Education and Training
Department of Education and Training
P.O. Box 525
Honiara

Mr Joseph Ma'Ahanua
Counsellor
Embassy of Solomon Islands
Bd. St. Michel 28
1040 Brussels
Belgium

South Africa

Mr Smangaliso Mkhatshwa
Deputy-Minister of Education
Private Bag X895
Pretoria 0001

Dr (Ms) Nomso Myijima
Chief Director, Quality Assurance
Department of Education
Private Bag X895
Pretoria 0001

Mr Bobby Soobrayan
Chief Director, Planning
Department of Education
Private Bag X895
Pretoria 0001

Dr (Mrs) Nithi Muthukrishna
8 Keens—Meave Place
Malverm 4093
Durban

Dr Anil Kanjee
Human Sciences Research Council
134 Pretoria 0001

Prof. Neville Alexander
P.O. Box 13338
Mowbray 7705

Mr Ghaleeb Jeepie
Director International Relations
Private Bag X895
Pretoria 0001

Mr Mauritz Lindeque
Chargé d'affaires
South African Embassy
Dakar
Senegal

Dayanidhie Pillay
Personal Assistant to Mme Garça
Machel Mandela
Sohth African Embassy
Dakar
Senegal

N.S. Kunene
South African Embassy
Dakar
Senegal

Spain

Sr Luis Antonio Buñuel Salcedo
Subdirector General de
Cooperatión
Internacional
Ministerio de Educación y Cultura
Paseo del Prado 28
28014 Madrid

Sra Mcdolores Lopez-Aranguen
Consejera Técnica de Relaciones
Multilaterales
Subdirección General de
Cooperation Internacional
Ministerio de Educación y Cultura
Paseo del Prado 28
28014 Madrid

Sra Clara Barreiro
Consejera Embajada UNESCO
Delegación Permanente de España
en la UNESCO
UNESCO House
1 rue Miollis
75732 Paris Cedex 15
France

Sra Maria Noguerol Alvarez
Consejera Técnica
Agencia Española de Cooperación
Internacional
Avda. Reyes Católicos Nº 4
28040 Madrid

Mireia Montané
Subdirector Forum 2004 Barcelone
C. Maina 16-18, planta 29
08005 Barcelona

Mr Ferran Ferrer
Expert
Gran Via 488 2º2º
08015 Barcelona

Sri Lanka

Hon. Prof. Viswa Warnapala
Deputy Minister of Education
Ministry of Education
Isurupaya
Battaramulla

Prof. Lal Senaka Perera
Additional Secretary
Ministry of Education
Isurupaya
Battaramulla

Ms Sunila Mendis
Kumarapatabemoige
Senior Assistant Secretary
President's Office
Isurupaya
Battaramulla

Ms Kamala Peiris
Member, National Educational
Commission and President
Siyath Foundation
14 A, Charles Drive
Colombo

Sudan

Mr Abdel Basit Abdel Magid
Minister of Education
Ministry of Education
Khartoum

Mr Ibrahim Suleman El-Dasis
Director General of Planning
Ministry of Education
Khartoum

Mr Abdel Gadir Mohd El Haq
Secretary General of the Sudanese
National Commission for UNESCO
Khartoum

Swaziland

Mr Magwagwa Mdluli
Minister of Public Service
and Information
P.O. Box 170
Mbabane

Ms Adelaide P. Mkhonza
Principal Secretary
Ministry of Education
P.O. Box 39
Mbabane

Ms Faith Mazibuko
Planning Officer
Ministry of Economic Planning
and Development
P.O. Box 602
Mbabane

Sweden

Mr Carl Lindberg
Deputy State Secretary
Ministry of Education and Science
10333 Stockholm

Mr Torgny Danielsson
Member of the Parliament
Member of the Swedish National
Commission to UNESCO
Riksdagen
10012 Stockholm

Dr Ingemar Gustafsson
Deputy Director
Swedish International
Development
Cooperation Agency (SIDA)
10525 Stockholm

Ms Agneta Lind
Head of Education Division
Swedish International
Development
Cooperation Agency (SIDA)
10525 Stockholm

Prof. Ingemar Fagerlind
Director
Institute of International Education
Stockholm University
10691 Stockholm
Sweden

Mr Kaviraj Appadu
Senior Programme Officer,
Eduacation Division
Division for Democracy and Social
Development
Swedish International
Development
Cooperation Agency (SIDA)
Sveavägen 20
10525 Stockholm

Ms Ulla-Stina Ryking
Senior Administrative Officer
Ministry of Education and Science
10333 Stockholm

Switzerland

M. Pierre Luisoni
Responsable des affairs internationales
Secrétariat de la Conférence suisse des Directeurs de l'instruction publique (CDIP)
Zaehringerstrasse 25
3001 Berne

M. Ahlin Byll-Cataria
Adjoint scientifique de service sectoriel ressources humanies
Swiss Agency for Development and Cooperation (SDC)
Federal Department of Foreign Affairs
Freiburgstrasse 130
3003 Berne

M. Pier-Angelo Neri
Président du Comité suisse de lutte contre l'illettrisme de la Commission
nationale suisse pour l'UNESCO
Avenue de la Grenade 24
1207 Genéve

Syrian Arab Republic

Prof. Mahmoud Al Sayeed
Minister of Education
Ministry of Education
Damascus

Ms Ghada Al Jabi
Director of illiteracy Elimination
Ministry of Culture
Chair-Person of the Executive Council of the Arab Network of Literacy and Adult Education
Vice President of International Council for Adult Education
Damascus

Mr Issam Diab
Senior Inspector of Curicula and Research
Ministry of Education
Damascus

Tajikistan

Ms Lola Dodkhoudoeva
Secretary General
Tajikistan National Commission for UNESCO
Rudaki Str 37
Dushanbe

Thailand

Dr Thongkoon Hongpan
Deputy Permanent Secretary
Office of the Permanent Secretary
Ministry of Education
Bangkok 10300

Dr Kasama Varavarn
Secretary General, National Primary Education Commission
Ministry of Education
Bangkok 10300

Dr Duangtip Surintatip
Deputy Permanent Delegate of Thailand to UNESCO
Office of the Permanent Secretary
Ministry of Education
Bangkok 10300

Dr Athipat Cleesuntorn
Director
Bureau of Policy and Planning
Office of the Permanent Secretary
Ministry of Education
Ratchadammoen-Nok Avenue
Bangkok 10300

Togo

Mr Oteth Adji Ayassor
Secretary-General of the Ministry of National Education and Research
P.O. Box 398
Lome

M. Yao K. B. Babnabana
Coordonnateur national EPT
Secrétaire permanent du Conseil supérieur de l'éducation nationale
BP 4830
Lome

Trinidad and Tobago

Ms Vena Jules
(Co-writer of the Caribbean Synthesis Report of EFA)
The University of West Indies
Saint Augustin Campus
Trinidad
West Indies

Tunisia

M. Houcine El Oued
Secrétaire général de la commission nationale tunisienne pour l'éducation, la science et la culture
Ministère de l'éducation
22 rue d'Angleterre
1000 Tunis

M. Mohamned Knani Gsouma
Directeur du programme national tunisien d'alphabétisation et d'éducation des adultes
Ministère des affairs sociales
Bab B'Nat
1000 Tunis

Mme Fatma Tarhouni
Inspectrice générale de l'éducation
Coordinatrice nationale pour l'EPT
Ministère de l'éducation
Bab B'Nat
1000 Tunis

Turkey

H.E. Mr Metin Bostancioğlu
Minister of National Education
Ministry of National Education
Milli Egitim Bakanligi
Bakanliklar
Ankara

Assistant Prof. Dr Ata Tezbasaran
Director-General for Primary Education
Ministry of National Education
Milli Egitim Bakanligi
Bikanliklar
Ankara

Mrs Zühal Gökçesu
Head of Department
General Directorate for External Affairs
Ministry of National Education
Milli Egitim Bakanligi
Bakanliklar
Ankara

Mr Senbir Tümay
Ambassadeur de la République de Turquie à Dakar
Ambassade de Turquie
Dakar
Sénégal

Turkmenistan

Mr Saparbay Gunbarbayen
Head of Education Department
Dasoguz Mir
S5/1 f.0
Ashgabat

Mr Nowruz Kurbanmuradow
Vice Minister of Education
Ministry of Education
Gonoglu N 2
Ashgabat

Uganda

Hon. Dr Edward Khiddu Makubuya
Minister of Education and Sports
Ministry of Education and Sports
Embassy House
Kampala

Mr Francis Xavier K. Lubanga
Permanent Secretary
Ministry of Education and Sports
Box 7063
Crested Towers
Kampala

Mr Sam Servy Onek
Acting Director of Education
Ministry of Education
P.O. Box 7063
Crested Towers
Kampala

Ukraine

Mr Victor Ogneviuk
Vice Minister of Education and Science
10 Prospect Peremogy
01135 Kiev

Mr Yevhel Polishchuk
Director of the Institute of International Cooperation
Ministry of Education and Sciences
27a T Shevchenko Blvd
01001 Kiev

United Arab Emirates

Mr Ali Meihad Al Suwadi
Assistant Under Secretary for Private and Specific Education
Ministry of Education
P.O. Box 295
Abu Dhabi

Mr Awad Ali Saleh
Secretary General of the National Commission for UNESCO
Ministry of Education and Youth
P.O. Box 295
Abu Dhabi

United Kingdom of Great Britain and Northern Ireland

Ms Clare Short
Secretary of State for International Development
Department for International Development (DFID)
94 Victoria Street
London SW1E 5JL

Mr Chris Austin
Private Secretary to the Secretary of State

Mr Barrie Ireton
Director General (Programmes)
DFID

Ms Myra Harrison
Chief Education Advisor
DFID

Mr Steve Packer
Deputy Head of Education Department
(Policy and Programme Development DFID

Dr Carew Treffgarne
Senior Education Adviser DFID
Leader ADEA Books Working Group
DFID

(Listed under 3, Civil Society)

Ms Anne Jellema
ActionAid UK
Hamlyn House
MacDonald House
Archway
London N19 5PG

Mr Owen Barder
Imfundo Project Manager
Prime Minister's Initiative
DFID

Dr Hilary Perraton
Director, International Research Foundation of Open Learning (IRFOL)
Cintra House
12 Hills Road
Cambridge CB2 1PF

Prof. Keith Lewin
Director
Centre for International Education
Institute of Education
University of Education
University of Sussex
Farmer, Brighton, Sussex BN1 9RG

Prof. Tony Booth
Centre for Educational Research
Canterbury Christ Church University College
North Holmes Road
Canterbury
Kent CT1 1QU

Prof. Angela Little
Institute of Education
University of London
20 Bedford Way
London WC1H OAL

(Listed under 3, Civil Society)

Mr Kevin Watkins
Senior Policy Adviser
OXFAM GB
274 Banbury Road
Oxford, OX2 7DZ

Prof. Roy Carr-Hill
Institute of Education
University of London

Mr Sylvain Semilinko
Head French Africa Department
BBC
Bush House
London WC2B 4PH

Mr Clinton Robinson
Summer Institute of Linguistics (SIL)
Horsleys Green
High Wycombe Bucks, HIP 14 3XL

Ms Sue Torr
Director, Project Leader
151 Pembroke Street
Devonport

United Republic of Tanzania

Hon. Alhaj Juma Kapuya MP
Minister for Education and Culture
P.O. Box 9121
Dar es Salaam

Ms Mary Mushi
Permanent Secretary
Ministry of Education and Culture
P.O. Box 9121
Dar es Salaam

Dr Said Gharib Bilal
Deputy Permanent Secretary
Ministry of Science, Technology and Higher Education
P.O. Box 394
Zanzibar

Mr Salum R. Mnjagila
National EFA Coordinator
Ministry of Education and Culture
P.O. Box 9121
Dar es Salaam

United States of America

Dr Thomas Fox
Assistant Administrator
Bureau for Policy and Programme Coordination
US Agency for International Development
Ronald Reagan Building,
Room 6.08—113
1300 Pennsylvania Avenue, N.W.
Washington, DC 20523-6802

Mr Gene Sperling
Head of Delegation (for Friday 28th)
Assistant to the President for Economic Policy and Director
National Economic Council

Ms Norma Cantu
Assistant Secretary
Office of Civil Rights
US Department of Education
330 C Street, S.W.
Washington, DC 20202—1100

Dr Gordon Ambach
Executive Director
Council of Chief State School Officers
2715 31st PL N.W.
Washington, DC 20008

Ms Emily Vargas-Baron
Deputy Assistant Administrator
Director, Center for Human Capacity Development, USAID
Ronald Reagan Building
1300 Pennsylvania Avenue, N.W.
Room 3.09—036
Washington, DC 20523-3901

Mr Richard M. Samans
Assistant to the President for International Economic Policy
National Economic Council

Ms Kathy Byrne
Senior Assistant to Gene Sperling
National Economic Council

Ms Melissa Green
Senior Assistant to Gene Sperling
National Economic Council

Mr Donald Foster-Gross
Team Leader for Basic Education
Center for Human Capacity Development
USAID
1300 Pennsylvania Avenue, N.W.
Washington, DC 20523-3901

Ms Julia Owen-Rea
Education Specialist,
Bureau for Africa USAID
Ronald Reagan Building
1300 Pennsylvania Avenue, N.W.
AFR/SD 4.8
Washington, DC 20523

Ms Maureen McClure
Director, GINIE Project Global Information Networks in Education
University Professor
115E University of Pittsburgh
5K38 Forbes Quad
Pittsburgh, PA 15260

Dr Phyllis Magrab
Professor, Paediatrics
Georgetown University Child Development Center
3307 M Street N.W.—Suite 401
Washington, DC 20007–3935

(Listed under 3, Civil Society)

Mr Stephen F. Moseley
President and Chief Executive Officer
Academy for Educational Development (AED)
1825 Connecticut Avenue, N.W.
Washington, DC 20009-5721

(Listed under 3, Civil Society)

Mr Alfred W. Wood
Director of Education
Save the Children USA
54 Wilton Road
Westport, CT 06880

(Listed under 3, Civil Society)

Ms Janet Robb
Director
Education, Mobilization and Communication Division
Creative Associates International, Inc
5301 Wisconsin Avenue, N.W
Suite 700
Washington, DC 20015

(Listed under 3, Civil Society)

Ms Vivian Toro
Education Assistant Specialist
Academy for Educational Development (AED)
1825 Connecticut Avenue, N.W.
Washington, DC 20009–5721

Mr Ash Hartwell
Education Advisor
USAID Africa Bureau
130 Red Gate Lane
Amherst, MA 01002

(Listed under 3, Civil Society)

Ms Susan Malone
International Literacy Consultant
Summer Institute of Linguistics (SIL)
41/5 Soi Sailom
Phahol Yothin Road
Samsennai, Phyayathai
Bangkok 10400

(Listed under 3, Civil Society)

Ms Erika George
Human Rights Watch
Fellow Academic Freedom Committee
350 Fifth Avenue, 34th Floor
New York, NY 10118–3299

Mr Robert Berg
International Development Conference
Suite 720
1875 Connecticut Avenue, N.W.
Washington, DC 200009–5728

Dr Hassana Alidou N'game
Fondation Allemande DES
2910 Jennifer Drive
College Station
Texas 77845

Ms Lynne Murphy
Stanford University
School of Education
Stanford, CA 94305

Vanuatu

M. Jacques Sese
Ministre de l'éducation
Ministére de l'éducation
PMB No. 028
Port Vila

Venezuela

H.E. Mr Hiram Gaviria
Ambassador
Permanent Delegate of Venezuela to UNESCO
28 rue Galilée
75016 Paris
France

Licenciada Yanet Ramirez
Coordinadora de Relaciones Multilaterales de la Ofcina de Relaciones Institucionales
9091
Caracas

Viet Nam

Prof. Dr Pham Minh Hac
Former Minister of Education
Chairman of the National Committee for Literacy of Viet Nam
7 Nguyen Canh Chan
Hanoi

Mr Le Vu Hung
Vice Minister of Education and Training
Ministry of Education and Training
49 Dai Co Viet
Hanoi

Mr Pham Quang Tho
Deputy Secretary General of the Viet Nam National Commission for UNESCO
8 Khuc Hao Street
Hanoi

Mr Chi Nguyen Quoc
National Consultant for EFA
Ministry of Education and Training
49 Dai Co Viet
Hanoi

Yemen

Dr Abu Baker Al-Qirbi
Professor
University of Sana'a
P.O. Box 11351
Sana'a

Prof. Abdul-Karim Al Gindari
Deputy of Minister of Education
Ministry of Education
P.O. Box 95
Sana'a

Prof. Abdullah Al-Hamam
Coordinator of the EFA 2000 Assessment
P.O. Box 11115
Sana'a

Zambia

Mr Godfrey Miyanda MP
Minister of Education
Mogadishu Road
P.O. Box 50093
Lusaka

Dr Elizabeth Mumba
Deputy Vice Chancellor
University of Zambia
P.O. Box 32379
Lusaka

Mr Emmanuel Silanda
Director Planning and Information
Ministry of Education
Mogadishu Road
P.O. Box 50093
Lusaka

Mr Michael Kelly
Professor
Luwisha House
5880 Great East Road
P.O. Box 35391
Lusaka

Prof. Geoffrey Lungwangwa
Director, Drirectorate of Research and
Post Graduate Studies
University of Zambia
P.O. 32379
Lusaka

Ms Marian Leaf
Project–Coordinator
Zambia Open Community Schools (ZOCS)
P.O. 50429
Lusaka

Zimbabwe

Hon Dr Ignatius M.C. Chombo
Minister of Higher Education and Technology
P.O. Box UA275
Union Avenue
Harare

Mr Gabriel Machinga
Minister of Education, Sport and Culture
P.O. Box UA275
Union Avenue
Harare

Mr Menias S. Machawira
Acting Secretary General
Zimbabwe National Commission for UNESCO
P.O. Box UA275
Union Avenue
Harare

Mr Chipo Olga Zindoga
Chargée d'affaires
Zimbabwe Embassy
Dakar
Senegal

Dr Patrick Pfukani
Interim Co-ordinator
SACMEO
UNESCO Harare Sub-Regional Office
P.O. Box No. HG425
Highlands
Harare

Ms Glory J.T. Makawati
Regional Director, Education
P.Bag 5824
Gwanda

International Organisations and Groups

A. UNITED NATIONS SYSTEM

United Nations

Mr Kofi Annan
Secretary-General of the United Nations
United Nations Headquarters
New York, NY 10017
United States

Mr John Langmore
Director, Division for Social Policy and Development, Department of Economic and Social Affairs
Room DC2—1370

M. Ibrahima Fall
Sous-Secrétaire général
Nations Unies

Mme Elizabeth Lindenmayer
Assitante du Secrétaire-Général

Mr James Setterlin
Assistant

M. Fred Eckhard
Porte-Parole du Secrétaire Général

Mme Hawa Bunti Diéye
Administrateur hors classe

M. Lamlin Sise
Administrateur

M. Edward Mortimer
Administrateur

Mme Anne Marie Ibanez
Secrétaire

M. Mamadi Touré
Rédacteur

Mme Danielle Loff-Fernandez
Rédactrice

M. William Shawcross
Journaliste

M. Americo Canepa
Responsable des télécommunications

M. Evan Schneider
Photographe

M. Arnulfo Fareux
Agent de sécurité

M Bryant
Agent de sécurité

M. Bernard Robinson
Agent de Sécurité

Mrs Nane Annan
c/o The Secretary-General of the United Nations

M Mohamed Sahnoun
Conseiller spécial du Secrétaire Général des Nations Unies
1 rue Miollis
75732 Paris CEDEX 15
France

Food and Agriculture Organisation of the United Nations (FAO)

Ms Vera Boerger
Agricultural Education and Extension Officer
Sub-Regional Office for Southern and Eastern Africa
FAO
Box 3730
Harare
Zimbabwe

Mr Daniel Gregoire
Expert Information Education
Communication
FAO—Mali
BP 1820
Bamako
Mali

International Labour Organisation (ILO)

M. Carlos Castro-Almeida
Directeur, BIT/EMAS
BP 414
Dakar
Sénégal

M. Frans Roselaers
Directeur du programme IPEC
ILO
4 route des Morillons
1211 Geneva 22
Switzerland

M. Geir Myrstad
Charge de l'éducation IPEC
ILO
4 route des Morillons
1211 Geneva 22
Switzerland

Mme Fatou Kiné Sall
Coordinatrice nationale du programme IPEC
BIT/ILO Dakar
BP 414
Dakar
Sénégal

Mme Maria Koulouris
BIT/ILO Dakar
BP 414
Dakar
Sénégal

Mme Corinne Vargha
NIT/ILO Dakar
BP 414
Dakar
Sénégal

M. Abdoulaye Ndour
Chargé d'information
BIT/ILO Dakar
BP 414
Dakar
Sénégal

Mme Elisabeth Venn
Assistante au programme
BIT/ILO Dakar
BP 414
Dakar
Sénégal

International Monetary Fund (IMF)

M. Koffi Yao
Représentant résident
FMI
8 Rue Docteur Guillet
Dakar
Sénégal

United Nations African Institute for Economic Development and Planning (IDEP)

Mr Samuel Ochola
Acting, Director, IDEP
P.O. Box 3186
Dakar
Senegal

United Nations Development Programme (UNDP)

(All Addresses at UNDP HQ unless otherwise noted)

Mr Mark Malloch Brown
Administrator
UNDP
DC1-2128
1 UN Plaza
New York, NY 10017
United States

Mr Abdoulie Janneh
Acting Director
UNDP Africa
DC1-2418

Mr Dijibril Diallo
Director COA
(Official Spokesperson for the EFA Forum)
DC1–1918

Mr Ahmed Rhazaoui
Resident Representative Senegal
UNDP
P.O. Box 154
Dakar
Senegal

Mr Abdoulaye Mar Dieye
Chief Economist
(Alternate to Mr Janneh)
DC1–2424

Mr Naresh Singh
Principal Poverty Advisor
DC1–2048

Ms Hilda Paqui
Chief Social Mobilisation and Operations Branch (COA)
DC1–1920

Mr Mamadou Bah
Information Officer (COA)
DC2–2609

Mr Mark Suzman
Advisor to the Administrator
DC1–2148

Gulden Turkoz–Cosslett
Programme Specialist to the Administrator
DC1–2141

Ms Anjimile Mtila Doka
Senior Advisor, Social Analysis and Policy (Education)
DC1–2050

Mr John Lawrence
Senior Adviser to UNDP's Social Development Division

M. Albert Tevodedjre
Coordonnateur
Projet International
"Millénaire pour l'Afrique"
PNUD
BP 506
Cotonue
Bénin

Mr Assad Ahamadi
Deputy Resident Representative
UNDP Dakar
P.O. Box 154
Dakar
Senegal

Ms Khady Diaw
Programme Assistant
UNDP Dakar
P.O. Box 154
Dakar
Senegal

Mr Mamdou Guéye
Principal Administrative Assistant and Protocol Officer
UNDP Dakar
P.O. Box 154
Dakar
Senegal

Ms Danielle Hayes
Photographer

Mrs Gifty Mbow
Secretary
UNDP Dakar
P.O. Box 154
Dakar
Senegal

Ms Aminata Ndiaye
UNV/Administrative Assistant
UNDP Dakar
P.O. 154
Dakar
Senegal

Mrs Louise Page
PSU and Programme Assistant
UNDP Dakar
P.O. Box 154
Dakar
Senegal

Mr Yves Sassenrath
Programme Officer
UNDP Dakar
P.O. Box 154
Dakar
Senegal

Mrs Seynabou Guéye Tall
Programme Officer, UNIFEM/PNUD
UNDP Dakar
P.O. Box 154
Dakar
Senegal

Ms Yasmine Thiam
Advisor, UNIFEM/PUND
UNDP Dakar
P.O. Box 154
Dakar
Senegal

Mrs Assitan Diarra Thioune
National Economist
UNDP Dakar
P.O. Box 154
Dakar
Senegal

Mr Laba Touré
Assistant Resident Respresentative
UNDP Dakar
P.O. Box 154
Dakar
Senegal

M. Bernard Verschueren
Chargé de l'information
UNDP Dakar
P.O. Box 154
Dakar
Sénégal

United Nations Economic Community for Africa (UN AEC/CEA)

Mr Joseph Ngu
Economic Affairs Officer
United Nations Economic Community for Africa (UN AEC/CEA)
P.O. Box 3001
Addis Ababa
Ethiopia

UNESCO Executive Board

H.E. Mrs Sonia Mendieta de Badaroux
Chairwoman of the Executive Board of UNESCO
7 place de Fontenoy
75352 Paris 07 SP
France

United Nations Educational, Scientific and Cultural Organisation

(All Addresses at UNESCO HQ unless otherwise noted)

Mr Koïchiro Matsuura
Director-General
7 place de Fontenoy
75352 Paris 07 SP
France

Mr Colin N. Power
Deputy Director-General for Education

Mr Jacques Hallak
Assistant Director-General
International Bureau of Education (IBE)
15 route des Morillons
1218 Grand Saconnex
Switzerland

Mr Noureini Tidjani-Serpos
Assistant Director-General, Africa

Mr Alain Modoux
Assistant Director-General
CII/FED
1 rue Miollis
75732 Paris CEDEX 15
France

Mr Dieter Berstecher
Director
Global Action Plan on Education for all

Ms Aicha Bah Diallo
Director
Basic Education Division

Ms Denise Lievesley
Director
UNESCO Institute of Statistics

Mr Victor Billeh
Director
Regional Office for the Arab States
P.O. Box 5244
Cité Sportive Av
Beirut
Lebanon

Mr Victor Ordoñez
Director
Regional Office for Asia and the Pacific
920 Sukhumvit Road
Bangkok
Thailand

Ms Ana Luiza Machado
Director, Regional Office for Latin America and the Caribbean
Calle Enrique Delpiano 2058
Providencia
3187 Santiago
Chile

Mr Armoogum Parsuramen
Director
UNESCO Dakar
12 avenue L.S. Senghor
Dakar
Senegal

Mr Helene Gosselin
Director
Office of Public Information

Mr Adama Ouane
Director
UNESCO Institute of Education (UIE)
Feldrunnenstrasse 58
2000 Hamburg 13
Germany

Mr Gudmund Hernes
Director, International Institute of Educational Planning (IIEP)
7-9 rue Eugène Delacroix
75116 Paris
France

Mr Gene Seiti
Executive Officer
Office of the Director Genéral

Mr Richard Sack
Association for the Development of Education in Africa (ADEA)
7-9 rue Eugéne Delacroix
75116 Paris
France

Ms Anna-Maria Barthés
Programme Specialist
SVE/STE

Mr Kacem Bensalah
Director
Emergency Educational Assistance Unit

Ms Rosa Blanco
Programme Specialist
UNESCO
Calle Enrique Delpiano 2058
Providencia
3187 Santiago
Chile

Mr Diomansi Bombote
Regional Information Officer
OPI/REG

Ms Françoise Caillods
International Working Group on Education
Senior Programme Coordinator, IIEP
7-9 rue Eugéne Delacroix
75116 Paris
France

Mr Vinayuagum Chinapah
Head of Project
Monitoring Learning Achievement and Quality Indicators Project
ED/MIP

Ms Camilla Gidlof
Associate Expert
ED/MIP

Mr Marc Gilmer
Director Literacy
ED/BAS

Mrs Winsome Gordon
Director Primary Education Section

Ms Linda King de Jardon
Deputy Director
UNESCO Institute of Education (UIE)
Feldbrunnenstrasse 58
2000 Hamburg 13
Germany

Dr Malika Ladjali
Senior Programme Sepcialist
EPD

Mr Frank Method
Director
UNESCO Washington
1775 K Street NW
Washington, D.C. 20006
United States

Mr Toshio Ohsako
Senior Research Specialist
UNESCO Institute of Education (UIE)
Fledbrunnenstrasse 58
2000 Hamburg 13
Germany

Ms Ulrika Peppler-Barry
Programme Specialist
EFA/FOR

Ms Nureldin Satti
Director
UNESCO Regional Programme for Emergency
P.O. Box 30592
Nairobi
Kenya

Ms Sai Vayrynen
UNESCO Liaison to the 'Working Group on Disability and Development' (IWGDD)
Division of Basic Education (ED/BAS/SNE)

Ms Claudia Harvey
Director UNESCO Kingston
P.O. Box 8203
Kingston 5
Jamaica

Mr Moegiadi
Director UNESCO New Delhi
8 Poorvi Marg, Vasant Vihar
New Delhi
India

Mr Jorge Sequeira
Head of Office
UNESCO Alamty
G7-Tole-gi-Street
Almaty 408100
Kazakhstan

Mrs Nour Dajani Shehabi
Programme Specialist Literacy
UNESCO Beirut
P.O. Box 5244
Cité Sportive Av
Beirut
Lebanon

Ms Edna Tait
Director UNESCO Apia
P.O. Box 5766
Matautu-uta Post Office
Apia
Samoa

Mr Ko-Chin Tung
Chair, EFA Sub-Saharan Africa RTAGs
UNESCO Harare
P.O. Box HG 435
Highlands, Harare
Zimbabwe

Mr Warren Mellor
Senior Programme Sepcialist
ED/EFA

Mr Emmanuel Apea
Director UNESCO Nigeria
Plot 77
Bouake Street, Zone 6
Wuse, Abuja
Nigeria

Ms Fay Chung
Director UNESCO International Institute for Capacity-Building in Africa (IICBA)
P.O. Box 2305
Addis Ababa
Ethiopia

Mudiappasamy Devadoss
Programme Coordinator
UNESCO PEER
P.O. Box 30592
Nairobi
Kenya

Lucette Diawara
Representative UNESCO Côte d'voire
01 BP 1747
Abidjan 01
Côte d'Ivoire

Mr J. Hironaka
Web Editor, Press Edition
OPI/PSS

Mr Hubert Charles
Representative
UNESCO Mozambique
515 Frederick Engles Avenue
Maputo
Mozambique

Ms Koto Kanno
Programme Specialist
BER/FIT

Ms Aigull Khalafova
Education Specialist
UNESCO Almaty
67, Tole Bi Street
408891 Almaty
Kazakhstan

Mr Jones Kyazze
Director Africa Section
BRX/AFR

Ms Ushio Miura
Associate Expert
ED/BAS/LIT

Mme Elke Sales Rossenbach
Chef du Service de Presse
OPI/PSS

Mr Ken Vine
Consultant
UNESCO Bangkok
920 Sukhumvit Road
Bangkok
Thailand

Int'l Cons. NGO

Mme Fatoumata Marega
Chargée de liaison, Division des relations avec les organisations internationales
BRX/RIO

Int'l Cons. NGO

Ms Claire Mollard
Consultant, NGO Program
Basic Education Division

Int'l Cons. NGO

Ms Susanne Schnuttgen
Programme Specialist, NGO
ED/BAS

United Nations Information Centre (UNIC)

M. Toussaint Kong-Doudou
Directeur
CINU Ouagadougou (c/o UNDP)
BP 135
Ouagadougou
Burkina Faso

Alioune Loum
Chargé de l'information
CINU-Dakar
12 avenue Léopold Sédar Senghor
BP 154
Dakar
Sénégal

United Nations Population Fund (UNFPA)
(All Addresses at UNFPA HQ unless otherwise noted)

Dr Nafis Sadik
Executive Director
220 East 42nd Street, 19th Floor
New York, NY 10017–5880
United States

Mr Ali Ugur Tuncer
Chief, Coordination Branch
Technical and Policy Division

Ms Delia Barcelona
Senior Technical Officer
Technical and Policy Division

Mr Niangoran Essan
Representative
UNFPA Field Office
Boîte Postale 154
Dakar
Senegal

Ms Bintou Sanogoh
Regional Director
UNFPA Country Support Team, Dakar
Boîte Postale 154
Dakar
Senegal

Mr Makane Kane
Regional Adviser on Population and IEC
UNFPA Country Support Team, Dakar Boîte Postale 154
Dakar
Senegal

Mr Claude George
Regional Adviser
UNFPA Country Support Team, Dakar
Boîte Postale 154
Dakar
Senegal

Mr Ismaila M'bengue
UNFPA Country Support Team, Dakar
Boîte Postale 154
Dakar
Sénégal

Dr Fatou Sarr Diop
Chargé de programme au FNUAP
Boîte Postale 154
Dakar
Senegal

M. Cheikh Tidiane Cisse
Chargé de programme au FNUAP
Boîte Postale 154
Dakar
Sénégal

Mme Thérése Eleazar
Secrétaire au FNUAP
Boîte Postale 154
Dakar
Sénégal

Mme Ténéba Badiane
Secrétaire à l'équip d'appui technique de FNUAP
Boîte Postale 154
Dakar
Sénégal

United Nations Children's Fund (UNICEF)

(All Addresses at UNICEF HQ unless otherwise noted)

Ms Carol Bellamy
Executive Director
UNICEF House
3 United Nations Plaza
New York, NY 10017
United States

Mr Andre Roberfroid
Deputy Executive Director for Programmes

Ms Rima Salah
Regional Director
West and Central Africa Regional Office
UNICEF WCARO
Boîte Postale 443
Abidjan 04
Côte d'Ivoire

Mr Ian Hopwood
Representative
UNICEF Senegal
2 rue Carnot X Salva
Dakar
Saengal

Mr David Pulkol
Deputy Regional Director
Eastern and Southern Africa
UNICEF ESARO
P.O. Box 44145
Nairobi
Kenya

Ms Leila Bisharat
Representative
UNICEF Egypt
7 Lazoughly Street
Garden City
Cairo
Egypt

Mr Edwin Judd
Representative
UNICEF China
12 Sanlitun LU
Beijing 100600
China

Mr Louis-Georges Arsenault
Representative
UNICEF Afghanistan
GPO Box 3117
Islamabad
Pakistan

Mr Rodney Hatfield
Representative East Timor
UNICEF
17 West Lane Arcade
Darwin NT 0800
Australia

Mr Franscisco Basili Dominguez
Education Programme Officer
UNICEF
P. Meliton Porras # 350
Lima 18
Peru

Ms Cecilia Baldeh
Education Programme Officer
UNICEF Eritrea
5 Andinet Street
Asmara
Eritrea

Mr Sheldon Shaeffer
Chief Education Section
Programme Division

Ms Mary Pigozzi
Senior Education Advisor
Programme Division

Ms Aline Bory-Adams
Regional Education Adviser
West Africa and Central Africa
UNICEF WCARO
Boîte Postale 443
Abidjan 04
Côte d'Ivoire

Mr Robert Fuderich
Regional Education Adviser
Europe and Tokyo Offices
UNICEF
Palais des Nations
1211 Geneva 10
Switzerland

Mr Frank Dall
Regional Education Adviser
Middle East and North Africa
UNICEF MENA
AI Dahak Bin Soufian Street
P.O. Box 1551
11821 Amman
Jordan

Mr Garren Lumpkin
Regional Education Adviser
Latin America and Caribbean
UNICEF TACRO
Transversal 38
100025 Bogota
Colombia

Ms Shamse Hasan
Regional Education Adviser
South Asia
UNICEF ROSA
P.O. Box 5815
Lethmandu Marg
Kathmandu
Nepal

Ms Elaine Furniss
Senior Education Adviser, East Asia

Mr Kadayapreth Ramachandran
Senior Education Programme Officer
Eastern and Southern Africa
UNICEF ESARO
P.O. Box 1169
Africa Hall
Addis Ababa
Ethopia

Mr Peter Buckland
Senior Education Officer
Emergencies

Ms Eveline Pressoire-Lofficial
Regional Education Officer
West and Central Africa
UNICEF WCARO
Boîte Postale 443
Abidjan 04
Côte d'Ivoire

Ms Aster Haregot
Education Programme Officer

Dr Amaya Gillespie
Senior Adviser, AIDS and Life Skills
Education Section

Mr Nicolas Pron
Programme Coordinator
UNICEF Benin
Rue du Collége Aupiais
01 BP 2289
Cotonou
Benin

Mme Henriette Alavo
Chargée de l'information
UNICEF Dakar
2 rue Carnot X Salva
BP 429
Dakar
Sénégal

Ms Margherita Amodeo
Communication Officer
UNICEF Geneva
Switzerland

M. Mamdou Bagayoko
Chief, Basic Education Child Protection and Development Unit
UNICEF Kenya
P.O. Box 44145
Nirobi
Kenya

Mme Nathalie Biagui
Secrétaire
UNICEF Dakar
2 rue Carnot X Salva
BP 429
Dakar
Sénégal

Ms Sally Burnheim
Communications Officer

Ms Aurora Bushati
Project Officer Education
UNICEF Albania
Rruga Arben Broci, No. 6
Tirana
Albania

Professeur Jean-Marie De Ketele
Titulaire de la Chaire UNESCO en sciences de l'éducation (UCAD-ENS
Dakar depuis 1994)
Consultant permanent de l'UNICEF
Professeur ordinaire au département
des sciences de l'éducation de l'Université catholique de Louvain
Place du Cardinal Mercier, 10
1348 Louvain-la-Neuve
Belgique

Mme Aissatou Dia
Assistante au programme
UNICEF Dakar
2 rue Carnot X Salva
BP 429
Dakar
Sénégal

M. Sidy K. Diagne
Assistant administratif
UNICEF Dakar
2 rue Carnot X Salva
BP 429
Dakar
Sénégal

Mme Madeleine Diatta
Secrétaire
UNICEF Dakar
2 rue Carnot X Salva
BP 429
Dakar
Sénégal

M. Marc Dieng
Informaticien
UNICEF Dakar
2 rue Carnot X Salva
BP 429
Dakar
Sénégal

M. Mohamed Fall
Assistant chargé de projet éducation
UNICEF Dakar
2 rue Carnot X Salva
BP 429
Dakar
Sénégal

Mr Andres Guerrero
Education Adviser

Mme Noreen Hamiltion
Administrateur chargé des opérations
UNICEF Dakar
2 rue Carnot X Salva
BP 429
Dakar
Sénégal

M Amadou Mbodj
Documentaliste
UNICEF Dakar
2 rue Carnot X Salva
BP 429
Dakar
Sénégal

M Jean-Baptiste Ndikudana
Chargé de l'éducation
UNICEF Dakar
2 rue Carnot X Salva
BP 429
Dakar
Sénégal

Mr Kris Oswalt
Child Info Coordinator
C/o UNICEF ICO-SPME
73 Lodi Estate
New Delhi
India

Mme Teresa Pinilla
Coordinatrice des programmes
UNICEF Dakar
2 rue Carnot X Slava
BP 429
Dakar
Sénégal

Ms Jehane Sedky-Levandero
Communication Officer

Mr Maman Sidikov
Chief of Education Section
UNICEF Nigeria
30A Oyinkan Aboyomi Drive
Ikoyi
Nigeria

Mme Maimouna Sy
Secrétaire
UNICEF Dakar
2 rue Carnot X Salva
BP 429
Dakar
Sénégal

NCO Committee on UNICEF

Dr Nancy Brown
NGO Committee on UNICEF
12 West 72 Street, Apt, 3D
New York, NY 10023
United States

Unites Nations Industrial Development Organisation (UNIDO)

M. François d'Adesky
Représentant reésident
Bureau de l'ONUDI pour le Sénégal,

Le Cap-Vert, la Guinée-Bissau et la Mauritanie
19 rue Parchappe
BP 154 Dakar
Sénégal

Joint United Nations Programme on HIV/AIDS (UNAIDS)

M. Peter Piot
Directeur exécutif
20 avenue Appia
1211 Genéva 27
Suisse

Mme Awa Marie Coll-Seck
Directeur de dépaprtement
20 avenue Appia
1211 Genéve 27
Suisse

United Nations High Commissioner for Refugees (UNHCR)

M. Dillah Doumaye
Délégué régional ad interim
Représentant UNHCR
BP 3125
Dakar
Sénégal

Mr Christopher Talbot
Senior Education Officer
UNHCR
CP 2500
1211 Genéva 2 Depot
Suisse

United Nations International Drug Control Programme (UNDCP)

Mme Christiane D'Almeida
Représentante
UNDCP/PNUCID
BP 455
Dakar
Sénégal

Aliare Sall
UNDCP/PNUCID
BP 455
Dakar
Sénégal

The World Bank
(All Addresses at World Bank HQ unless otherwise noted)

Mr James D. Wolfensohn
President
The World Bank
MC12—745
1818 H Street N.W
Washington, D.C 20433
United States
(care of Jane Holden Executive Assistant to the President)

Mr Eduardo Doryan
Vice President, Human Development Network
G8-005

Mr Bassary Toure
Executive Director for West Africa
Mc 13-335

Ms Maris O'Rourke
Director, Education
Human Development Network
G8-072

Ms Marlaine Lockheed
Sector Manager
Middle East and North Africa
H9-269

Mr Birger Fredriksen
Sector Director
Human Development Africa
J8-089

Ms Ruth Kagia
Director
Strategy and Operations
Human Development Network
G8-015

Mr Mamadou Ndoye
Senior Education Specialist, Africa
J9-077

Mr Ayub Mahmood
Country Director, Senegal, Africa
J9-153

Mr Adriaan Verspoor
Lead Specialist Education, Africa
J8-107

Mr Donald A.P. Bundy
Knowledge Coordinator
Human Development Network
G8-105

Ms Carolyn Winter
Knowledge Coordinator
Human Development Network
G8-049

Mrs Elaine Wolfensohn
c/o The President
The World Bank

Mr James Richard Prietsch
President's Security Operations Officer
MC1-627

Mr Robert Floyd
President's Trip Assistant
J5-005

Mr Akintola Fatoyinbo (Press)
Senior Public Affairs Specialist, Africa
The World Bank
Corner of Bocker
Washington and Jacques Aka Streets
Cocody
Abidjan
Côte d'Ivoire

Ms Carolyn Reynolds (Press)
Communications Officer
External Affairs
U11-217

Mr Cadman Atta Mills
Resident Representative
Senegal Country Office
3 place de l'Indépendence
Dakar
Senegal

Mr Sam Carlson
Manager
World Links For Development Program

Mr Alassane Diawara
World Bank Office
3 place de l'Indépendence
Dakar
Senegal

Ms Vivian Jackson
Administrative Coordinator
G8-150

Ms Vivien Stewart
Consultant
8 Locust Ridge Road
Larchmont, NY 10538
United States

Mr Christopher M. Walsh (Press)
Junior Communications Associate
U11-133

World Food Programme (WFP)
(All Addresses at WFP HQ unless otherwise noted)

Mr Jean-Jacques Graisse
Assistant Executive Director
Director of Operations
World Food Programme
Via Cesare Guilio Viola, 68/70
00148 Rome
Italy

Mr Jamie Wickens
Director of the WFP Regional Office
for the Sahel

Ms Gretchen Bloom
Senior Programme Adviser

M. Mahamat Kasser Badaouri
Représentant du PAM au Sénégal
BP 154
Dakar
Sénégal

World Health Organisation (WHO)

Dr Kadri Tankari
Représentant résident
OMs Sénégal
BP 4039
Dakar
Sénégal

Ms Isolde Birdthistle
Technical Officer
6051 HPS 1211 Geneva 27
Switzerland

Mr Jack Jones
Health Education Specialist
Department of Health Promotion
20 Avenue Appia
1211 Geneva 27
Switzeland

Dr Inon Schenker
HIV/AIDS Coordinator
20 Avenue Appia
1211 Geneva 27
Switzerland

B. OTHER INTERGOVERNMENTAL ORGANISATIONS

African Development Bank

Mr Gabriel Bayemi
Education Analyst
African Development Bank
01 BP 1387
Abidjan 01
Côte d'Ivoire

Agence intergouvernementale de la Francophonie

M. Hamidou Arouna Sidikou
Directeur de l'éducation et
de la formation technique et professionnelle
Agence intergouvernementale
de la Francophonie
13 quai André Citröen
75015 Paris
France

Arab Educational, Cultural and Scientific Organisation (ALECSO)

Dr Abdul Aziz Al Sunbul
Deputy Director General
Arab Educational, Cultural and
Scientific Organisation (ALECSO)
P.O. Box 1120
Tunis
Tunisia

Mr Hassan Kamal
Adult Education Coordinator
Arab Educational, Cultural and Scientific Organisation (ALECSO)
P.O. Box 1120
Tunis
Tunisia

Arab Gulf Programme for United Nations Development Organisations (AGFUND)

Mr Nasser Al-Kahtani
Executive Director
Arab Gulf Programme for United Nations Development Organisations (AGFUND)
P.O. Box 18371
Riyadh
Kingdom of Saudi Arabia

Dr Mohamed Hamdan
Rector, Arab Open University
Arab Gulf Programme for United Nations Development Organisations (AGFUND)
P.O. Box 18371
Riyadh
Kingdom of Saudi Arabia

Asian Development Bank (ADB)

Mr Edward M. Haugh, Jr. Manager
Education, Health and Population (West) Division
Agriculture and Social Sectors (West) Department
Asian Development Bank (ADB)
P.O. Box 789
0980 Manila
Philippines

Mr Yasushi Hirosato
Education Specialist
Education, Health and Population (West) Division
Agriculture and Social Sectors (West) Department
Asian Development Bank (ADB)
P.O. Box 789
0980 Manila
Philippines

Caribbean Community Secretariat (CARICOM)

Dr Carole Maison Bishop
Programme Manager, Human Resources Development
Caribbean Community Secretariat (CARICOM)
Bank of Guyana Bldg.
P.O. Box 10827
Georgetown
Guyana

Commission économique pour l'Afrique

Mme Lala Ben Barka
Secrétaire exécutive adjointe
Commission économique pour l'Afrique
P.O. Box 3001
Addis Ababa
Ethiopia

The Commonwealth of Learning

Dr Gajaraj Dhanarajan
President and CEO
The Commonwealth of Learning
1285 West Broadway, Suite 600
Vancouver, BC V6H 3X8
Canada

Mr David Walker
Education Specialist, Educational Technology
The Commonwealth of Learning
1285 West Broadway, Suite 600
Vancouver, BC V6H 3X8
Canada

Commonwealth Secretariat

Professor Stephen Matlin
Director
Human Resource Development Division (HRDD)
Commonwealth Secretariat
Marelborough House
Pall Mall
London SW1Y 5HX
United Kingdom

Dr Cream A.H. Wright
Sepcial Adviser
Head of Education Dept.
Commonwealth Secretariat
Marlborough House
Pall Mall
London SW1Y 5HX
United Kingdom

Ms Alison Girdwood
Human Resource Development
Division (HRDD)
Commonwealth Secretariat
Harborough House
Pall Mall
London SW1Y 5HX
United Kingdom

Dr Henry Kaluba
Commonwealth Secretariat
Marborough House
Pall Mall
London SW1Y 5HX
United Kingdom

Dr Ved Goel
Chief Programme Officer
Commonwealth Secretariat
Marborough House
Pall Mall
London SW1Y 5HX
United Kingdom

Conférence des ministers de l'éducation des pays ayant le français en partage (CONFEMEN)

M. Bougouma Ngom
Secrétaire général
Conférence des ministres de
l'éducation des pays ayant le
français en partage (CONFEMEN)
Immeuble Kebe
Extension -3e étage
BP 3220
Dakar
Sénégal

European Commission

M. Philip Lowe
Directeur général du Dvpt
Commission européenne
200 Rue de la Loi
1049 Bruxelles
Belgique

Mr José-Javier Paniagua
Principal Administrator
European Commission
Development Directorate-General
A-2 Unit
Rue de Genéva N° 12
1140 Brussels
Belgium

Ms Louise Hilditch
Policy Adviser
European Commission
70-72 rue du Commerce
1040 Brussels
Belgium

Islamic Educational, Scientific and Cultural Organisation (ISESCO)

H.E. Dr. Abdulaziz Othman
Altwaijri
Director General
Islamic Educational, Scientific and
Cultural Organisation (ISESCO)
BP-2275-10104
Rabat
Morocco

H.E. Mr Omar Saad Touré
Deputy Director General
Islamic Educational, Scientific and
Cultural Organisation (ISESCO)
BP 2275-10104
Rabat
Morocco

Mr Mohammed Ghemari
Director of External Relations
and Cooperation
Islamic Educational, Scientific and
Cultural Organisation (ISESCO)
BP 2275-10104
Rabat
Morocco

Mr Mamadou Lamrana Bah
Expert
Islamic Educational, Scientific and
Cultural Organisation (ISESCO)
BP 2275-10104
Rabat
Morocco

Mr Seydou Cisse
Expert
Islamic Educational, Scientific and Cultural Organisation (ISESCO)
BP 2275-10104
Rabat
Morocco

Organisation of African Unity (OAU)

Ambassadeur Mahamat Habia Doutour
Secrétaire général adjoint
Chargé de l'ESAS
Organisation de l'Unité Africaine
P.O. Box 3243
Addis Ababa
Ethiopia

M. Marcel Diouf
Chef, Division Education et Culture
Organisation of African Unity
P.O. Box 3243
Addis Ababa
Ethiopia

Organisation for Economic Co-operation and Development (OECD)

(All Addresses at OECD HQ unless otherwise noted)

Mr Jean-Claude Faure
President, Development Assistance Committee (DAC)
Organisation for Economic Co-operation and Development (OECD)
2 rue André-Pascal
75775 Paris Cedex 16
France

Mr Peter Evans
Professor (CERI)

Mr Hans Lundgren
Adviser on Aid Effectiveness
Development Co-operation Directorate

Organisation of Eastern Caribbean States (OECS)

Ms Lorna Callender
Representative of the Organisation of Eastern Caribbean States
Educational Reform Unit (OERU)
Organisation of Eastern Caribbean States
P.O. Box 179
Morne Future
Castries, Saint Lucia
West Indies

Organización de Estados Iberoamericanos para la Educación, la, Ciencia y la Cultura (OEI)

Sra Maria Del Rosario Fernandez Santamaria
Secretaria Assistente General
Organización de Estados Iberoamericanos para la Educación, la Ciencia y la Cultura (OEI)
Bravo Murillo, 38
28015 Madrid
Spain

Sr Daniel Gonzalez
Director de la Comisión, de Planificación
Organización de Estados Iberoamericanos para la Educación la Ciencia y la Cultura (OEI)
Bravo Murillo, 38
28015 Madrid
Spain

Civil Society: Non-Governmental Organisations, Foundations and Others

(Listed under 1. National Authorities)

Academy for Educational Development (AED)

Mr Stephen F. Moseley
President and Chief Executive Officer
Academy for Educational Development (AED)
1825 Connecticut Avenue, N.W.
Washington, DC 20009-5721
United States

Ms Barbara O'Grady
Academy for Educational Development (AED)
1825 Connecticut, Avenue, N.W.
Washington, DC 20009-5721
United States

Mr Edward B Fiske
Academy for Educational Development (AED)
1723 Jisdale Street
Durham, NC 27705
United States

Mr Albert Byamugisha
Academy for Educational Development (AED)
P.O. Box 7063
Kampala
Uganda

(Listed under 1. National Authorities)

Ms Vivian Toro
Education Assistant Specialist
Academy for Educational Depelopment (AED)
1825 Connecticut Avenue, N.W.
Washington, DC 20009-5721
United States

ACCU-Asia/Pacific Cultural Centre for UNESCO

Mr Shigeru Aoyagi
Director, Literacy Promotion Division
ACCU-Asia/Pacific Cultural Centre
for UNESCO
Japan Publishers Building
No. 6 Fukuromachi, Shinjuko-ku
Tokyo 162-8484
Japan

Action Aid Alliance

Mr David Archer
International Education Unit
ActionAid UK
Hamlyn House
MacDonald House
Archway
London N19 5PG
United Kingdom

(Listed under 1. National Authorities)

Ms Anne Jellema
ActionAid UK
Hamlyn House
MacDonald House
Archway
London N19 5PG
United Kingdom

Ms Maggie Burns
International NGO Coordinator for Education
ActionAid UK
Hamlyn House
MacDonald House
Archway
London N19 5PG
United Kingdom

Ms Louise Hilditch
ActionAid Alliance
70-72 rye du Commece
1040 Brussels
Belgium

Ms Jacqueline Bataringaya
ActionAid Africa Regional Office
6 Natal Road, Belgravia
P.O. Box CY2451
Causeway, Harare
Zimbabwe

Mogre Salifu
Africa Elimu Coordinator
ActionAid Ghana
P.O. Box 190 83
Accra North
Ghana

Adu-Gyamfi Juliana
Reflect Coordinator
ActionAid Ghana
P.O. Box 190 83
Accra North
Ghana

Ms Tasqeen Macchiwalla
Citizens' Initiative on Elementary Education
ActionAid India
3 Rest House Road
P.O. Box 5406
Bangalore 560 001
India

Ms Mary Rose Warue Kariuki
Education Co-ordinator
ActionAid Kenya
Nairobi Kenya
Nairobi
Kenya

Dr Sarah Hasan Tirmazi
Country Director
ActionAid Pakistan
House 4B, Street 34, Sector F-8/1
Islamabad
Pakistan

Moussa Faye
Programme Manager
ActionAid Senegal
Mermoz BP 412
Fann, Dakar
Senegal

Ms Debe Bruku
Gender Coordinator
ActionAid Regional Office (Zimbabwe)
Harare
Zimbabwe

M. Gorgui Sow
Responsable Pédagogique
Aide et Action Sénégal
BP 412
Dakar
Sénégal

M. Yves Richard
Responsable Pédagogique
Aide et Action Sénégal
BP 412
Dakar
Sénégal

Mme Claire Calosci
Directeur
Aide et Action
53 boulevard de Charonne
75545 Paris Cedex 11
France

Mme Sheela Pimpare
Aide et Action
53 boulevard de Charonne
75545 Paris Cedex 11
France

Mr Joel Bedos
Aide et Action
53 boulevard de Charonne
75545 Paris Cedex 11
France

M. Andrianantenaina Rafetiarison
Chargé du mission
Aide et Action Madagascar
BP 4182
Madagascar

African Community Education Network

Ms Berewa Jommo
Member of the Collective Consultation of NGOs
African Community Education Network
Bureau for the Arfican Region
4C Adalyn Flats, Ngong Road
P.O. Box 29214
Nairobi
Kenya

Aga Khan Foundation

Ms Kathy Bartlett
Co-director of Secretariat for the Consultative Group in Early Childhood Care and Development
Education Programme Officer
Aga Khan Foundation
P.O. Box 2369
1211 Geneva 2
Switzerland

Albania Education Development Project (AEDP)

Ms Snezhi Bedalli
Albania Education Development Project
Ruga, the germenji N3/1
Tirana
Albania

Amnesty International

Cheikh Tidiane Camara
Amnesty international
1, Easton Street
London WC1X 8DJ
United Kingdom

Arab Network for Literacy and Adult Education

(Listed under 1. National Authorities)

Ms Ghada Al Jabi
Chairperson Arab Network for Literacy and Adult Education
Vice President, International Council
for Adult Education—Arab Region
Ministry of Culture
Rawda Street
Damascus
Syrian Arab Republic

Asian-South Pacific Bureau of Adult Education (ASPBAE)

Ms Nitya Rao
Programme Officer
Asian-south Pacific Bureau
of Adult Education (ASPBAE)
C/o H. Bhargava
First Floor, Shroff Chambers
259/261 Perin Nariman Street
Fort, Mumbai 400 001
India

Asociación Brasileria de ONGs (ABONG)

Mr Sergio Haddad
Asociación Brasileria de ONGs (ABONG)
Açao Educativa
Rua, Itapicura, 305
05463-050 Sao Paulo SP
Brazil

Ms Camilla Croso Silva
Asociación Brasileria de ONGs (ABONG)
Açao Educativa
Av Higienopolis 901
Brazil

Association Algérienne d'Alphabétisation

Mme Aïcha Barki
Présidente
Association Algérienne d'Alphabétisation
Réseau des ONGs Arabes d'Alphabétisation
4 Rue Wargnier
Ben Aknoun
BP 377
16030 Alger
Algérie

Association Islamique de secours à l'enfant déshérité (AISE)

Mme Fatimatou Gaye Lo AISE
BP 10518
Dakar
Sénégal

Association du Sahel d' Aide à la Femme et à l'Enfance (ASSAFE)

M. Sékou Traore
Président
Association du Sahel d'Aide à la Femme et à l'Enfance (ASSAFE)
BP 6049 Bamako
Mali

M. Zoumana Kone
Chargé de Programme Education
Association du Sahel d'Aide à la Femme et à l'Enfance (ASSAFE)
BP 6049 Bamako
Mali

Association for the Development of Education in Africa (ADEA)

Listed under 1, National Authorities

Mr Richard Sack
Association for the Development of Education in Africa (ADEA)
7-9 rue Eugéne-Delacroix
75116 Paris
France

Thanh-Hoa Desruelles
Information and Communication Officer
Association for the Development of Education in Africa (ADEA)
7-9 rue Eugéne Delacroix
75016 Paris
France

Mr Hamidou Boukray
Programme Officer
Association for the Development of Education in Africa (ADEA)
7-9 rue Eugéne Delacroix
75016 Paris
France

Association Nationale pour l'Alphabétisation et la Formation des Adults (ANAFA)

M. Ibrahima Fall
Coordinateur Réseau
Association Nationale pour l'Alphabétisation et la Formation des Adultes (ANAFA)
BP 10 358
Dakar
Sénégal

Barefoot College

Mr Sanjit (Bunker) Roy
Director, Barefoot College
Tilonia 305816, Madanganj
District Ajmer
Rajasthan
India

Bernard Van Leer Foundation

Mr Peter Laugharn
Bernard Van Leer Foundation
P.O. Box 82334
Eisonhowerlann 156
2566 KH, The Hague
The Netherlands

Bokk Jang Bokk Jee (2BL-SN)

Mamadou Lamine Bangoura
Secrétaire général
Bokk Jang Bokk Jee
22 rue Guillet et Pasteur
Dakar
Sénégal

Cadre de Concertation en Education de Base (CCEB)

M. Christophe Zoungrana
Coordonnateur
Cadre de concentration en Education
de Base
01 BP 642
Ouagadougou 01
Burkina Faso

Campaign for Popular Education (CAMPE)

Ms Rasheda Choudhury
Director (CEO)
Campaign for Popular Education (CAMPE)
5/14 Humayun Road
Mohammadpur
Dhaka 1207
Bangladesh

Canadian Council for International Cooperation (CCIC)

Mr Bill Hynd
Canadian Council for International Cooperation
See OXFAM Canada

Canadian Teachers' Federation (CTF)

Listed under 1. National Authorities

Ms Marilies Rettig
President
Canadian Teachers' Federation (CTF)
110 Argyle Avenue
Ottawa, Ontario
K2P 1B4
Canada

CARE International

Aben Ngay
Programme Director, CARE zambia
P.O. Box 36 238
Lusaka
Zambia

Caribbean Regional Council for Adult Education (CARCAE)

Ms Vilma McClenan
Chairman, Caribbean Regional Council for Adult Education (CARCAE)
C/o University of the West Indies
Distance Education Centre (UWIDEC)
Mona Campus, Kingston 7
Jamaica

Caritas Internationalis (Caritas)

M. Michel Deyglun
Caritas Internationalis (France)
c/o Secours Catholique
106 rue du Bac
75341 Paris Cedex 07
France

Elise Ways
Caritas Internationalis (Ile Maurice)

CCSVI

M. Paco Garcia
CCSVI
BP 19 092
Dakar
Sénégal

International Development Research Centre (IDRC) Canada

M. Sibry Tapsoba
Directeur Régional
Afrique de l'Ouest et du Centre
CRDI—IDRC
BP 11007
Dakar
Sénégal

Christian Children's Fund

M. Michel Toko-Puku
Directeur Régional
Christian Children's Fund
BP 1608
Dakar
Sénégal

CIVICUS—world Alliance for Citizen Participation

Mr Thierno Kane
Vice-Chair, Board of Directors
CIVICUS-World Alliance for Citizen
Participation
9191 18th Street, N.W. Third Floor
Washington, DC 20006

Civil Society Action Committee on EFA (CSAEFA)

Ms Iréne Ogbogu
Civil Society Action Committee on EFA (CSAEFA)
P.O. Box 14 903
Kano State
Women's Health Education (WHED)
Nigeria

Ms Stella Iwuactwu
Representative
Civil Society Action Committee on EFA (CSAEFA)
P.O. Box 72944
Victoria Island
Lagos
Nigeria

Mr Tom Maiyashi
Civil Society Action Committee of EFA (CSAEFA)
10 Shehu Laminu St
P.O. Box 442
Kaduna
Nigeria

Kiru Aisha
Civil Society Action Committee on EFA (CSAEFA)
Baiero University
Kano
Nigeria

Chike Anyanwu
Programme Officer Literacy
Civil Society Action Committee on EFA (CSAEFA)
P.O. Box 1827
Garki, Abuja
Nigeria

Community and Institutional Development (CID)

Ms Laïla Kamel Rashed Iskandar
Community and Institutional Development (CID)
11, Al-Gabalaya Street
Zamalek 11211
3rd Floor, Suite (9)
Cairo
Egypt

Confédération Syndicale Mondiale de l'Enseignement (CSME)

M. Gaston de la Haye
Secrétaire général
Confédération Syndicale Mondiale de l'Enseignement (CSME)
33 rue de Tréves
1040 Bruxelles
Belgique

Conseil des ONGs d'Appui au Développement (CONGAD)

M. Moustapha Sane
Conseil des ONGs d'Appui au Développement (CONGAD)
Sicap Amike III
Dakar
Sénégal

Conseil National des O.N.G.D. (CNONGD)

M. Félicien Malanda
Secrétaire exécutif
Conseil National des O.N.G.D. (CNONGD)
Avenue Katanga n°2
Kinshasa
République Démocratique du Congo

Consultative Group on Early Childhood Care and Development (CGECCD)

Ms Kathy Bartlett
Co-director of Secretariat for the Consultative Group in Early Childhood Care and Development
See Aga Khan Foundation

Convenio Andrés Bello

Sr Eduardo Fabara Garzon
Convenio Andrés Bello
Coordinator Del Area de Educación
Avenida 13 No. 85-60
Santafé de Bogotá
Colombia

Cooperation Technique Belge

M. Olivier Cogels
Représentant résident
Coopération Technique Belge
5 rue Victor Hugo, 5e Etage D
Dakar
Sénégal

Creative Associates International

(Listed under 1. National Authorities)

Ms Janet Robb
Director
Education, Mobilization and Communication Division
Creative Associates International
5301 Wisconsin Ave, N.W. Suite 700
Washington, DC 20015
United States

Dhaka Ahsania Mission

Mr Kazi Rafiqul Alam
Executive Director Dhaka Ahsania Mission
House # 19 Road # 12 (New)
Dhanmondi R.A. Dhaka—1209
Bangladesh

Disabled People International (DPI)

Ms Venus Ilagan (Mr. Rodolfo Ilgan)
Area Chair—Asia Pacific Council
Unit 701
Disabled People International (DPI)
Merchants Square Condominium
1386 E. Rodriquez Avenue cor. Mabolo St
Quezon City
Philippines

Education Enfants de la Reu-Développement

M. Abdoulaye Ball
Président
Education Enfants de la Rue—Développement
BP 1033
Nouakchott
Mauritanie

Education International (EI)

Mr Elie Jouen
Deputy General Secretary
Education International (EI)
5 bld du Roi Albert II
1210 Brussels
Belgium

Mr Ulf Fredriksson
Coordinator Education
Education International (EI)
5 bld du Roi Albert II
1210 Brussels
Belgium

M. Rudy Dejaeghere
Secrétaire Général
Education International (EI)
C. Plantijnstraat 34
8510 Kortryk
Belgique

Mr Thomas Bediako
Chief Coordinator Africa
Education International (EI)
BP 14058
Lome
Togo

Mr Richard Langlois
Economist
Education International (EI)
5 bld du Roi Albert II
1210 Brussels
Belgium

Education Network Nepal

Mr Manvi Shrivastav
Education Network Nepal
P.O. Box 6257
Lazinpat, Kathmandu
Nepal

Education Watch Network-Gambia

Lamin Nyangado
Adovcacy Officer
Education Watch Network-Gambia
ActionAid Gambia
PMB 450 Sera Kuna
Gambia

Elimu Education Campaign-Gambia

Lamin K Sise
Education Advocacy Officer
Elimu Education Campaign
c/o AAIG
Bajul
Gambia

Environment et Développement Tiers Monde (ENDA International)

M. Jacques Bugnicourt
Secrétaire exécutif
Environment et Développement
Tiers Monde (ENDA International)
54 rue Carnot
BP 3370
Dakar
Sénégal

M. Raphaël Ndiaye
Coordination de la Communication
Environnement et Développement
Tiers Monde (ENDA International)
54 rue Carnot
BP 3370
Dakar
Sénégal

Prof. M. Cheik Kamara
Environnement et Développement
Tiers Monde (ENDA Mauritanie)
BP 512
Nouakchott
Mauritanie

Fédération Africaine des Parents d'Eléves (FAPE)

M. Martin Itoua
Président, Fédération Africaine
des Parents d'Éléves (FAPE)
BP 1113
Brazzaville
Congo

Fédération Africaine des Parents d'Éléves et des Etudiants (APEEC)

M. Anatole Milandou
Directeur exécutif
Fédération Africaine des Parents
d'Elèves et des Etudiants (APEEC)
BP 1113
Brazzaville
Congo

Fédération des Universitiés Catholiques

Mme Odile Moreau
Fédération des Universitiés
Catholiques
21 rue d'Assas
75270 Paris Cedex 06
France

Fédération internationale des Centres d'Entrainement aux Méthodes d'Education Active (FICEMEA)

M. Claude Vercoutere
Secrétaire général
FICEMEA
24 rue Marc Séguin
75883 Paris Cedex 18
France

Fédération Internationale des Femmes Diplômées d'Universitiés (FIFDU)

Mme Madeleine Deves Senghor
Fédération Internationale des Femmes Diplômées d'Universitiés (FIFDU)
BP 1348
Dakar
Sénégal

Mme Mama Sakho
Fédération Internationale des Femmes Diplômées d'Universitiés (FIFDU)
BP 5085
Dakar
Sénégal

Fédération Internationale Syndicale de l'Enseignement (FISE)

M. Jean-Pierre Adami
Fédération Internationale Syndicale de l'Enseignement (FISE)
78 rue du Faubourg St Denis
75010 Paris
France

Fédération Mondiale des Associations, Centres et Clubs UNESCO (FMACU/WFUCA)

M. Saku Diarra
Vice-Président, Région Afrique
Fédération Mondiale des Associations, Centres et Clubs UNESCO (FMACU/WFUCA)
BP 119
Bamako
Mali

Fédération Syndicale des Enseignants de l'Education Nationale (FESEENA)

Damil Kombe Lekambo
Secrétaire général
Fédération Syndicale des Enseignants de l'Education Nationale (FESEENA)
BP 10533
Libreville
Gabon

Fondation Paul Gérin Lajoie

M. Serge Marcil
Président directeur général
Foundation Paul Gérin Lajoie
465 rue Saint-Jean, bureau 900
Montréal QC H2Y2R
Canada

M Paul Gérin Lojoie
Président
Foundation Paul Gérin Lajoie
465 rue Saint-Jean, bureau 900
Montreal QC H2Y2R
Canada

Forum for African Women Educationalist (FAWE)

Prof. Mme Bouli Ali Diallo
Présidente, FAWE
BP 237
Niamey
Niger

Mme Marie Bwirana
FAWE Burundi
BP 6382
Bujumbura
Burundi

Dr Mariana Sarr-Ceesay
Director of Planning and Programme Administration
FAWE Kenya
P.O. Box 53168
Nairobi
Kenya

Dr Eddah Gachukia
FAWE Kenya
P.O. Box 53168
Nairobi
Kenya

Mr Francisco Assis Joao
FAWE Mozambique
Av. Eduardo Mondlame 1170
Maputo
Mozambique

Ms Clara Antunes
FAWE Mozambique
AV. Eduardo Mondlame 1170
Maputo
Mozambique

Ms Juliana Osei
FAWE Ghana
P.O. Box C1217
Cantoments, Accra
Ghana

Ms Yeboah Vida
FAWE Ghana
P.O. Box C1217
Cantoments, Accra
Ghana

Ms Regina Musokotwane
FAWE Zambia
Box 51028
Kusaka
Zambia

Gambia Teachers' Union

Bakary Badijie
Regional Coordinator
Gambia Teachers' Union

Ghana Education Network (EDN)

Mr William Ahadzie
Coordinator
Ghana Education Network
P.O. Box CT 48 52
Cantoments
Ghana

Global Campaign for Education

Mr Richard Langlois
Co-ordinator Global Campaign
for Education
See Education International

Global March Against Child Labour

Mr Kailash Satyarthi
Global March Against Child
Labour
L6 Kalkagi
New Delhi 19
India

GNECC

Dr Robert Aboagye-Mensah
General Secretary GNECC
CCG P.O. Box 919
Accra
Ghana

Group d'Etude sur l'Éducation en Afrique (GRETAF International)

M. Cheikhe Tidiane Dem
Président
Groupe d'Étude sur l'Éducation
en Afrique
(GRETAF International)
29 avenue Georges Mandel
75116 Paris
France

Groupe Pivot Éducation de Base du Mali (GP/EB)

Mariam Naamogo
Président du Groupe Pivot
Éducation
de Base du Mali (GP/EB)
BP E 1309
Bamako
Mali

M. Moussa Traore
Coordinateur, Groupe Pivot
Éducation de Base du Mali (GP/
EB)
BP E 1309
Bamako
Mali

Groupe pour l'Étude et l'Enseignement de la Population (GEEP)

M. Babacar Fall
Coordinnateur
Group pour l'Étude et
l'Enseignement
de la Population (GEEP)
BP 5036
Dakar
Sénégal

Human Rights Watch

(Listed under 1. National Authorities)

Ms Erika George
Human Rights Watch
Fellow Academic Freedom
Committee
350 Fifth Avenue, 34th Floor
New York, NY 10118-3299
United States

Idara Taleem-O-Angahi (Center of Education and Consciousness)

Ms Baela Jamil
Coordinator Programmes
Idara Taleem-O-Angahi
43 Gulberg V
Justice Iqbal Road
Lahore
Pakistan

Inclusion International

Mr Gordon Porter
Inclusion International
13 D chemin du Levant
02 12 10 Ferney Voltaire
France

Institute for Inernational Cooperation of the German Adult Education Association (IIZ/DVV)

Prof. Dr Heribert Hinzen
Director
Institute for International Cooperation of the German Adult Education Association (IIZ/DVV)
Obere Wilhemstr, 32
53225 Bonn
Germany

International Committee of the Red Cross

Mr Sobhi Tawil
Exploring Humanitarian Law Education Unit (DC/COM/EDUC)
International Committee of the Red Cross
19 avenue de la Paix
1202 Geneva
Switzerland

International Council for Adult Education (ICAE)

Mr Maria Lourdes Almazan-Khan
Vice President, ICAE Executive Board
Secretary General
South-Asian Pacific Center of Adult Education (ASPBAE)
C/o H. Bhargava
First Floor, Shroff Chambers
259/261 Perin Nariman Street
Fort. Mumbai 400 001
India

Ms Ghada Al Jabi
Vice-President, International Council
for Adult Education—Arab Region
See Arab Network for Literacy and Adult Education

International Council for Distance Education (ICDE)

Mr Bernard Loing
General Delegate of ICDE at UNESCO
International Council for Distance Education
5 rue Jean-Carries
75007 Paris
France

International Literacy Institute (ILI)

Mr Dan Wagner
Director and Professor of Education
International Literacy Institute (ILI)
University of Pennsylvania
3910 Chestnut Street
Philadelphia, PA 10104-3111
United States

Mr Mohamed Maamouri
Associate Director
International Literacy Institute (ILI)
University of Pennsylvania
3910 Chestnut Street
Philadelphia, PA 10104-3111
Unites States

International Telecommunication Union (ITU)

Mr Yapi Bancouli
International Telecommunication Union (ITU)
P.O. Box 154
Dakar
Senegal

Internationale Culturelle de la Jeunesse (ICF)

Ibra Fall
Président, Internationale Culturelle de la Jeunesse
Las Palmas N° 862

Fall Codou
Internationale Culturelle
de la Jeunesse
Las Palmas N° 862

Jesuit Refugee Service

Mr Lolin Menendez
Education Coordinator
Jesuit Refugee Service
P.O. Box 76 490
Nairobi
Kenya

Knowledge Enterprise

Dr Wadi D. Haddad
President
Knowledge Enterprise, Inc.
9926 Courthuse Woods Court
Vienna, VA 22181
Unites States

LABAYI

Lata Maimanchi Tombai
President/Director
LABAYI
Box 90 94
Kaduna
Nigeria

Laboratoire d'Études Politiques et d'Analyses Cartographiques (LEPAC)

M. Jean-Christophe Victor
Laboratoire d'Études Politiques et d'Analyses Cartographiques (LEPAC)
47 avenue de Maréchal Fayolle
75016 Paris
France

Lar Fabiano de Christo (LFC)

Mme Claudia Bonmartin LFC
12 rue Ledru Rollin
92220 Bagneux
France

LINK NGO Forum

Ms Else Lichtenberg
Project Leader, ADPP
Link NGO Forum
CP 489
Maputo
Mozambique

Lire et Ecrire—Belgique

(Listed under 1. National Authorities)

Mme Catherine Stercq
Coordinatrice
Lire et Ecrire—Belgique
42-43 place Morichar
1060 Bruxelles
Belgique

Literacy and Adult Basic Education (LABE)

Mr Patrick Delba Kiirya
Director
Literacy and Adult Basic Education (LABE)
P.O. Box 16176
Kampala
Uganda

Missao Crianca

Mr Cristovam Buarque
President
Missao Crianca
SCN, Edificio Liberty Mall
Torre A. Sala 391
CEP 71710–500
Brasilia
D.F. Brazil

Mouvement International ATD Quart Monde (ATD)

Mr Philippe Hamel
Mouvement International ATD
Quart
Monde
107 avenue de Général Leclerc
95480 Pierrelaye
France

National Adult Education Association of Tanzania

Ms Hlima Zinga
Secretary General
National Adult Education
Association of Tanzania
Box 7484
Dar Es Salaam
United Republic of Tanzania

National Education Association

Ms Jill Christianson
Senior Professional Associate
International Relations
National Education Association
1201 Sixteenth Street N.W.
Washington, DC 200 36
United States

National Union of Disabled Persons of Uganda

Macline Twimukye .
Executive Director
National Union of Disabled
Persons of Uganda
P.O. Box 8567
Kampala
Uganda

Nederlands Organisatie voor Internationale Ontwikkelingssa-men-werking (NOVIB)

Ms Greetje Lubbi
Director
NOVIB
P.O. Box 30919
2500 GX The Hague
The Netherlands

Nigerian Education Non-Governmental Organisation (NENGO)

Dr Rashid A. Aderinoye
Nigerian Education
Non-Governmental Organisation
c/o University Village Association
(UNIVA)
Deaprtment of Adult Education
University of Ibadan
Ibadan
Nigeria

Notre Dame Foundation for Charitable Activities, Inc.

Ms Myrna B. Lim
Executive Director
Notre Dame Foundation for
Charitable Activities, Inc.
Cotabato City
Philippines

Office International de l'Enseignement Catholique (OIEC)

M. Fulgence Kone
Représentation permanente de
l'OIEC auprés de l'UNESCO
Office International de
l'Enseignement Catholique (OIEC)
227 rue Saint-Jacques
75005 Paris
France

Olinga Foundation for Human Development

Mme Lesile De Casely-Hayford
Director
Olinga Foundation for Human
Development
Box 7726
Accra North
Ghana

ORGENS—Sénégal

Mme Awa Fall Diop
ORGENS—Sénégal
Coordinatrice de Programme
Dakar
Sénégal

OXFAM

(Listed under 1. National Authorities)

Mr Kevin Watkins
Senior Policy Adviser
OXFAM GB
274 Banbury Road
Oxford, OX2 7DZ
United Kingdom

Frances Rudd
Campaign Manager
OXFAM GB
274 Banbury Road
Oxford, OX2 7DZ
United Kingdom

Mr Twyford Phil
Director of Advocacy
OXFAM International
733 15th St N.W.
Washington, DC
United States

(Listed under 1. National Authorities)

Mr Bill Hynd
Campaigns Co-ordinator
OXFAM Canada
Box 1252
St. John's Newfoundland
A1C 5V5
Canada

Mr Anne Sikwibele
Programme Coordinator
OXFAM Zambia
P.O. Box 211323
Kitwe
Zambia

P.A.U. Education

Sr Paul Fenton
Coordinator Proyectos Internacionales
P.A.U. Educación
Avenida Diagonal 441, 3°
08036 Barcelona
Spain

PAX ROMANA/C.P.N. Nairobi

M. Etienne Triaille
Pax Romana/C.P.N. Nairobi
Aumonier Panafricain
P.O. Box 62102
Nairobi
Kenya

People's Action Forum

Ms Jennifer M. Chiwela
Executive Director
People's Action Forum
P.O. Box N° 33709
Lusaka 10101
Zambia

PLAN International

Mr Varghese Sathyabalan
Learning Adviser
PLAN International UK
Chobham House
Christchurch Way
Working, Surrey GU21 1JG
United Kingdom

Mr Winnie Tay
Country Director
Plan International Senegal
P.O. Box 15042
Fann, Dakar
Senegal

Platforme des ONG de Madagascar

M. Armand Andriamampiomona
Plateforme des ONG de Madagascar
BP 3044
Tana 101
Madagascar

Poder Ciudadano

Sra Cécilia Ponteville ép. Gostuski
Directora de Programa
Poder Ciudadano
Murature 583
1642 San Isidro
República Argentina

Réseau Alpha Collectif des ONG d'Education des Adults

M. Dieudonné Mparara
Secrétaire exécutif
Réseau Alpha
Collectif des ONG d'Education des Adultes
BP 3
Cyangugre Rwanda
Bukavu
République Démocratique du Congo

Réseau Education pour Tous

M. Jean Blaise Bilombo
Vice Président
Réseau Education pour Tous—Congo
BP 13341
Brazzaville
Congo

Mme Yvette Mbeto
Réseau Education pour Tous—Congo
BP 13341
Brazzaville
Congo

M. Abdoua Mainassara
Coordonnateur National
Réseau Education pour Tous—Niger
BP 708 Niamey
Niger

Réseau des ONG Education pour Tous

M. Gabriel Zie Zeeri
Réseau des ONG Education pour Tous
01 BP 446
Abidjan
Côte d'Ivoire

Rotary International

Mr Alain Bambara
Past District Governor
Rotary International—Africa
Fann Residence
Dakar
Senegal

SADTU

M. Aubrey Patrick Matlole
SADTU
P.O. Box 6401
Johannesburg 2000
South Africa

SAEG (Gabon)

M. Simon Ndong Edzo
Président du Syndicat
SAEG (Gabon)
5573 Libreville
Gabon

Save the Children Alliance

Mr David Norman
Education Advocacy Adviser
Save the Children UK
17 Grove Lane
London SE5 8RD
United Kingdom

(Listed under 1. National Authorities)

Mr Alfred W. Wood
Director of Education
Save the Children U.S.A.
54 Wilton Road
Westport, CT 06880
Unites States

Mr Fawad Usman Khan
Director, SUDHAAR
Save the Children Pakistan
Lahore
Pakistan

Deepika Nair
Regional Education Adviser
Office of South and Central Asia Region
Save the Children Nepal
Kupendo, Kathmandu
Nepal

Usha Acharya
Save the Children Nepal
Chakupat
Kathmandu
Nepal

Ms Tove Nagel
Education Adviser
Save the Children Norway
Hammersborg torg 3
Postboks 6902 St. Olavs Plass
0130 Oslo
Norway

M. Oumer Mohammed Sado
Education Project Officer
Save the Children U.S.A., Ethiopia Field Office
P.O. Box 387
Addis Ababa
Ethiopia

Mr Kedir Ali Kediro
Education Project Manager
Save the Children U.S.A., Ethiopia Field Office
P.O. Box 387
Addis Ababa
Ethiopia

Sebenta National Institute

Ms Thulisile Dladla
Director
Sebenta National Institute
P.O. Box 64
Mbabane
Swaziland

Shikshantar

Mr Manish Jain
Shikshantar
21 Fatchpura
Rajasthan
India

Shoma Education Foundation

Ms Claire Brown
Director
Shoma Education Foundation
P.O. Box 1502
Randburg 2125
South Africa

Soroptimist International

Mme Marie Louise Sow
Directrice Ecole Président
Soroptimist Sénégal
Nolivé Liberté VI
Dakar
Sénégal

South Africa NGO Coalition (SANGOCO)

Ms Bothale Nong
South Africa NGO Coalition (SANGOCO)
P.O. Box 31 471
Braamfontein 2017
South Africa

SYNERGIE—Femmes

Mme Serigne Nbaye Gaye
Responsible Programme EFA
Synergie—Femmes
BP 18215
Ouagadougou
Burkino Faso

SYPROS Senegal

Seckel Gning
SYPROS Senegal
7 avenue Lamine Gueye
Bourse de Travail CNTS
BP 937
Dakar
Sénégal

Summer Institute of Linguistics (SIL)

(Listed under 1. National Authorities)

Ms Susan Malone
International Literacy Consultant
Summer Institute of Linguistics (SIL)
41/5 Soi Sailom
Phahol Yothin Road
Samsennai, Phyayathai
Bangkok 10400
Thailand

TANGO

M. Mamsamba Joof
Education Officer
TANGO
P.O. Box 828
Gambia

Tanzania Education Network

Leoncia Salakana
Representative
Tanzania Education Network
P.O. Box 15102
Arusha
United Republic of Tanzania

Cairo Mwaitete
Tanzania Education Network
P.O. Box 15102
Arusha
United Republic of Tanzania

The Lebanese Down Syndrome Association

Ms Fadia Farah
The Lebanese Down Syndrome Association
P.O. Box 113–7345
Beirut
Lebanon

Union pour la Solidarité et l'Entraide (USE)

Mme Aby Sarr
Chargée de mission
Union pour la solidarité et l'Entraide (USE)
Centre Ahmadou M. Gaye
BP 5070
Dakar
Sénégal

Ndeye Maty Ndaye
Union Pour la Solidarité et
l'Entraide (USE)
BP 5070
Dakar
Sénégal

University of Laval

Mr Maila Diambomba
Professor
University of Laval
3188 Lavallée
Sainte-Foy
Québec G1X 1J3
Canada

VSO

Ms Lynne Benson
Country Director
VSO
Gambia

World Association of Girl Guides and Girl Scouts (WAGGGS)

Ms Eldrid Midttun
World Association of Girl Guides
and Girl Scouts (WAGGGS)
Slalamv 58
1350 Lommedalen
Norway

World Association of Newspapers (WAN)

Mr Timothy Balding
Director General
World Association of Newspapers
25 rue d'Astorg
75008 Paris
France

Ms Aralynn Abare McMane
Director of Educational
Programmes
World Association of Newspapers
25 rue d'Astorg
75008 Paris
France

World Education

Mr David W. Kahler
Vice-President
World Education
44, Farnsworth Street
Boston, MA 01518
U.S.A.

World Organisation for Early Childhood Education/Organisation Mondiale pour l'Education Préscolaire (OMEP)

Ms Audrey Curtis
World President
World Organisation for Early
Childhood Education/
Organisation Mondiale pour
l'Education Préscolaire (OMEP)
Chiltern College
18 Peppard Road
Caversham
Reading Berks RG48 JZ
United Kingdom

World Organisation of the Scout Movement (WOSM)/Bureau Mondial du Scoutisme

M. Lamine Diawara
Directeur de centre opérationnel
de l'office rétional africain
World Organisation of the Scout
Movement (WOSM)/Bureau
Mondial du Scoutisme
BP 2495
Dakar
Sénégal

World Vision

Mr Chris Herink
International Program Officer
World Vision
220 "I" Street, N.E.
Washington, DC 20002
United States

WOTCLEF-Nigeria

Amina Titi Atiku—Abubakar
WOTCLEF–Nigeria
Aso Rock
Presidential Villa
Abuja
Nigeria

Secretariat of the Meeting

A. EFA Forum Secretariat

UNESCO, ED/EFA
7 place de Fontenoy
75352 Paris 07 SP
France

Mr Svein Osttveit
Executive Secretary,
World Education forum
General Administration

Ms Ulrika Peppler-Barry
Deputy Executive Secretary
Programme Administration

Ms Anne Muller
Assistant Programme Specialist/Media Officer
Media

Mr Olve Hollas
Associate Expert
Exhibitions

EFA Forum Team

Mr Warren Mellor
Senior Programme Specialist
Drafting Group, Framework for Action

Mr Wolfgang Vollmann
Programme Specialist
E–9

Mr Hilaire Mputu
Programme Specialist
Data Information

Ms Karine Brun
Consultant
NGOs

Ms Eliam Nguni
Progamme Specialist
Surveys

Ms Teresa Murtagh
Assistant Programme Specialist
Grassroots Session, Media

Ms Chantal Pacteau
Education Specialist
EFA Reports

Secretarial Assistance

Ms Ramata Diakité

Ms Mercada Hassine

Ms Mary Konin

Ms Jacqueline Lefebvre

Ms Mairéad Maguire

Ms Maral Sanosyan

Ms Cecil Villa-Sayag

Consultants

Mr Peter Herold
Assistant Conference Administrator

Mr Michael Lakin
Strategy Session Organizer

Mr A. Da Costa
Press Room Coordinator

Technical Personnel

Mr Bertrand Ambry
Multimedia Graphist

Ms Jill Britland
Documentation

Ms Jocelyne Fernandes-Barreto
Registration: Conference Center

Mr Edouard N'Diogoye
Documentation

Mr Claude Sauvageot
Statistics

B. Local Organising Committee UNESCO—DAKAR

Secretarial Assistance

Ms Penda Bâ

Mr D. Boubacar

Ms Marietou C. Diagne

Ms Aminata Miranda

Ms Fatou Ndiaye

Ms M. Wade

Registration Desk

Ms Khadid Diop

Ms Natalia Massé

List of Participants

Ms A. Alcantara

Ms Faye Fatime

Mr Boucar Sy

Documents Control

Mr Saloum Diop

Mr Mademba Paye

Mr Aliou Sagna

Mr Demba Sagne

Mr Youssou Seck

Exhibition

Ms Agnes Beynis

Ms Magna Zormelo

Payment Desks

Mr Justin Adjanahoun

Mr Frantz de Laleu

Liaison with Host Country

Mr J. de Bosch Kemper

Mr M. Cabral

Strategy and Plenary Sessions

Mr Bernard Audinos

Mr Souleymane Baldé

Ms Ketrien Beeckman

Mr Ausutin Mariro

Mr Juma Shabani

Translation/Interpretation

Ms Zeynabou Gucye

C. Regional Technical Advisory Group

Mr Victor Billeh
RTAG-Arab States and North Africa
Director
UNESCO Regional Office for the Arab States
Beirut, Lebanon

Ms Aline Bory-Adams
RTAG-West Africa
Regional Education Adviser
UNICEF West Africa and Central Africa
Abidjan, Côte d'Ivoire

Mr Robert Fuderich
RTAG—Europe
Regional Education Adviser
UNICEF Europe and Tokyo Offices
Geneva, Switzerland

Ms Elaine Furniss
RTAG—East Asia
Senior Education Adviser
UNICEF

Mr Shamse Hasan
RTAG—South Asia
Regional Education Adviser
UNICEF South Asia
Kathmandu, Nepal

Ms Claudia Harvey
RTAG—Caribbean
Director UNESCO Kingston
Jamaica

Mr Garren Lumpkin
RTAG—Latin America
Regional Education Adviser
UNICEF Latin America and Caribbean
Bogota, Colombia

Ms Ana Luiza Machado
RTAG—Latin America
Director, UNISCO Regional Office for
Latin America and Caribbean
Santiago, Chile

Mr Moegiadi
RTAG—South and West Asia
Director UNESCO New Delhi
India

Mr Pai Obanya
RTAG—Central and Western Africa
Director
UNESCO Regional Office for Africa
Dakar, Senegal

Mr Victor Ordoñez
RTAG—East Asia
Director
UNESCO Regional Office for Asia and the Pacific
Bangkok, Thailand

Mr Kadayapreth Ramachandran
RTAG—East Africa
Senior Education Programme Officer
Eastern And Southern Africa
UNICEF Ethiopia

Mr Jorge Sequeira
RTAG—Central Asia
Regional Education Adviser
UNESCO Almaty
Kazakhstan

Ms Edna Tait
RTAG—Pacific
Director
UNESCO Apia
Apia, Samoa

Mr Ko-Chin Tung
RTAG—Southern and Eastern Africa
Chair, EFA Sub-Saharan Africa RTAGs
UNESCO Harare
Zimbabwe

D. Drafting Group

Mr Abhimanyu Singh
(Chairman of the Drafting Group)
Joint Secretary
Ministry of Human Resource Development
Government of India

Ms Delia Barcelona
Senior Technical Officer
Technical and Policy Division
UNFPA

Dr Nadia Gamal Eldin
Regional Center for Educational Research and Development
Cairo, Egypt

Mr Tesfamicael Gerahtu
Director General, General Education
Ministry of Education
Asmara, Eritrea

Ms Vena Jules
(Co-writer of the Caribbean Synthesis Report on EFA)
The University of West Indies
Trinidad, West Indies

Mr Warren Mellor
Senior Programme Specialist
ED/EFA
UNESCO

Ms Patricia Miaro
Education Specialist
Africa and Middle East Branch
Canadian International Development Agency (CIDA)
Québec City, Canada

Mr Steve Packer
Deputy Head Education Department
(Policy and Programme Development)
Department for International Development (DFID)
London, United Kingdom

M. Claude Pair
Recteur d'Académie
Membre de la Commission française pour l'UNESCO
Paris, France

Mr Kailash Satyarthi
Global March against Child Labour
New Delhi, India

Mr Ronald Siebes
Sector Expert Basic Education, DCO
Ministry of Foreign Affairs
The Hague, The Netherlands

Ms Camilla Croso Silva
Asociación Brasileria de ONGs (ABONG)
Açao Educativa
Brazil

Mr Naresh Singh
Principal Poverty Advisor
UNDP

Mr Sheldon Shaeffer
Chief, Education Section
Programme Division
UNICEF

M. Gorgui Sow
Responsable Pédagogique
Aide et Action Sénégal
Dakar, Sénégal

Mr Kevin Watkins
Senior Policy Adviser
OXFAM GB
Oxford, United Kingdom

E. Futures Group

Mr John Langmore
(Chairman of Futures Group)
Director, Division for Social Policy and Development, Department of Economic and Social Affairs
United Nations

Mr David Archer
International Education Unit
ActionAid UK
London, United Kingdom

Mr Dieter Berstecher
Director, Global Action Plan on Education for All
UNESCO

Mr Ghanem Bibi
General Co-ordinator
Arab Resource Collective
Beirut, Lebanon

Mme Claudine Bourrel
Chargée de mission
Mission pour la coopération multilatérale
Ministére des affaires étrangéres
Paris, France

Ms Anjimile Mtila Doka
Senior Advisor
Social Analysis and Policy (Education)
UNDP

Dr German Bula Escobar
Minister of Education
Ministry of Education
Bogota, Colombia

Mr Sergio Haddad
Asociación Brasileria de ONGs (ABONG)
Açao Educativa
São Paulo SP, Brazil

Mr Jack Jones
Health Education Sepcialist
Department of Health Promotion
WHO

Mr Elie Jouen
Deputy General Secretary
Education International (EI)
Brussels, Belgium

Mr Alexander Kondakov
Deputy-Minister of Education
Moscow, The Russian Federation

Ms Agneta Lind
Head of Education Division, SIDA
Stockholm, Sweden

Professor Agnela Little
Institute of Education
University of London

Mr Tom Maiyashi
Civil Society Action Committee on EFA (CSAEFA)
Kaduna, Nigeria

Mr Errol Miller
(Resource Person—Futures Group)
Professor, Faculty of Education
University of West Indies
Kingston, Jamaica

Ms Maris O'Rourke
Director, Education, Human Development Network
The World Bank

Ms Mary Pigozzi
Senior Education Advisor
UNICEF

Ms Shaheen Attiqur Rehman
Minister for Literacy
Government of Punjab
Lahore, Pakistan

Mr Pape Momar Sow
Ministry of Education
Senegal

Mr Falai Taafaki
Ministry of Education
Marshall Islands

Mr Ali Ugur Tuncer
Chief, Coordination Branch
Technical and Policy Division
UNFPA

Ms Emily Bargas-Baron
Deputy Assistant Administrator
Director, Center for Human
Capacity Development
USAID

F. Conference Services

Ms Zohra McDoolley-Aimone
Conference Administration

Mr Alain Perry
Conference Clerk

Mr Stephen Hewitt
English Translator

Ms Paula Anne Kacher
English Translator

Ms Chafika Ben-Mehidi
French Translator

Mr J-Pierre Leray
French Translator

Ms D. Thornborough
Engligh Typist

Ms. V Westbrook
English Typist

Ms B. Couturier
French Typist

Ms M. Madoui
Franch Typist

Mr Saied Latifi
Documents Control

G. Interpretation

Mr Mourad Boulares,
Chief Interpreter

Ms A. Abdel Alim

Mr A. Bespalov

Ms C. Bret

Ms L. Carpenter

Ms Emily Fan Chiu Kee

Ms Salmah Farchakh

Ms Li Feng

Ms J. Harding

Ms C. Lattanzio Honthaas

Mr. B. Hubble

Ms G. Leibrich

Ms A. Moran

Ms Lui Ninghui

Ms N. Sideris

Ms L. Ouedraogo

Ms Kathleen Taylor

Ms A. Thaler

Ms V. Viscovi

Interpreters from Abidjan

Ms Faye Avomoka

Ms Isabelle Polneau Anthony

Mr A.K. Bruce

Mr Savane Habbib

Mr Imboua Niava

Ms K. Vieyra

Appendices

Appendix—1

THE DAKAR FRAMEWORK FOR ACTION

Education for All: Meeting Our Collective Commitments

Adopted by the World Education Forum Dakar, Senegal, 26-28 April 2000

1. Meeting in Dakar, Senegal, in April 2000, we, the participants in the World Education Forum, commit ourselves to the achievement of education for all (EFA) goals and targets for every citizen and for every society.
2. The Dakar Framework is a collective commitment to action. Governments have an obligation to ensure that EFA goals and targets are reached and sustained. This is a responsibility that will be met most effectively through broad-based partnerships within countries, supported by co-operation with regional and international agencies and institutions.
3. We re-affirm the vision of the World Declaration on Education for All (Jomtien 1990), supported by the Universal Declaration of Human Rights and the Convention on the Rights of the Child, that all children, young people and adults have the human right to benefit from an education that will meet their basic learning needs in the best and fullest sense of the term, an education that includes learning to know, to do, to live together and to be. It is an education geared to tapping each individual's talents and potential, and developing learners' personalities, so that they can improve their lives and transform their societies.

4. We welcome the commitments made by the international community to basic education throughout the 1990s, notably at the World Summit for Children (1990), the Conference on Environment and Development (1992), the World Conference on Human Rights (1993), the World Conference on Special Needs Education: Access and Quality (1994), the International Conference on Population and Development (1994), the World Summit for Social Development (1995), the Fourth World Conference on Women (1995), the Mid-Term Meeting of the International Consultative Forum on Education for All (1996), the Fifth International Conference on Adult Education (1997), and the International Conference on Child Labour (1997). The challenge now is to deliver on these commitments.
5. The EFA 2000 Assessment demonstrates that there has been significant progress in many countries. But it is unacceptable in the year 2000 that more than 113 million children have no access to primary education, 880 million adults are illiterate, gender discrimination continues to permeate education systems, and the quality of learning and the acquisition of human values and skills fall far short of the aspirations and needs of individuals and societies. Youth and adults are denied access to the skills and knowledge necessary for gainful employment and full participation in their societies. Without accelerated progress towards education for all, national and internationally agreed targets for poverty reduction will be missed, and inequalities between countries and within societies will widen.
6. Education is a fundamental human right. It is the key to sustainable development and peace and stability within and among countries, and thus an indispensable means for effective participation in the societies and economies of the twenty-first century, which are affected by rapid globalization. Achieving EFA goals should be postponed no longer. The basic learning needs of all can and must be met as a matter of urgency.
7. We hereby collectively commit ourselves to the attainment of the following goals:

(i) Expanding and improving comprehensive early childhood care and education, especially for the most vulnerable and disadvantaged children;

(ii) Ensuring that by 2015 all children, particularly girls, children in difficult circumstances and those belonging to ethnic minorities, have access to and complete, free and compulsory primary education of good quality;

(iii) Ensuring that the learning needs of all young people and adults are met through equitable access to appropriate learning are life-skills programmes;

(iv) Achieving a 50 per cent improvement in levels of adult literacy by 2015, especially for women, and equitable access to basic and continuing education for all adults;

(v) Eliminating gender disparities in primary and secondary education by 2005, and achieving gender equality in education by 2015, with a focus on ensuring girls' full and equal access to and achievement in basic education of good quality;

(vi) Improving all aspects of the quality of education and ensuring excellence of all so that recognized and measurable learning outcomes are achieved by all, especially in literacy, numeracy and essential life skills.

8. To achieve these goals, we the governments, organisations, agencies, groups and associations represented at the World Education Forum pledge ourselves to:

(i) Mobilize strong national and international political commitment for education for all, develop national action plans and enhance significantly investment in basic education;

(ii) Promote EFA policies within a sustainable and well-integrated sector framework clearly linked to poverty elimination and development strategies;

(iii) Ensure the engagement and participation of civil society in the formulation, implementation and monitoring of strategies for educational development;

(iv) Develop responsive, participatory and accountable systems of educational governance and management;

(v) Meet the needs of education systems affected by conflict, natural calamities and instability and conduct educational programmes in ways that promote mutual understanding, peace and tolerance, and that help to prevent violence and conflict;

(vi) Implement integrated strategies for gender equality in education which recognize the need for changes in attitudes, values and practices;

(vii) Implement as a matter of urgency education programmes and actions to combat the HIV/AIDS pandemic;

(viii) Create, safe, healthy, inclusive and equitably resourced educational environment conducive to excellence in learning, with clearly defined levels of achievement for all;

(ix) Enhance the status, morale and professionalism of teachers;

(x) Harness new information and communication technologies to help achieve EFA goals;

(xi) Systematically monitor progress towards EFA goals and strategies at the national, regional and international levels; and

(xii) Build on existing mechanisms to accelerate progress towards education for all.

9. Drawing on the evidence accumulated during the national and regional EFA assessments, and building on existing national sector strategies, all States will be requested to develop or strengthen existing national plans of action by 2002 at the latest. These plans should be integrated into a wider poverty reduction and development framework, and should be developed through more transparent and

democratic processes, involving stakeholders, especially peoples' representatives, community leaders, parents learners, non-governmental organisations (NGOs) and civil society. The plans will address problems associated with the chronic under-financing of basic education by establishing budget priorities that reflect a commitment to achieving EFA goals and targets at the earliest possible date, and no later than 2015. They will also set out clear strategies for overcoming the special problems facing those currently excluded from educational opportunities, with a clear commitment to girls' education and gender equity. The plans will give substance and form to the goals and strategies set out in this Frame-work, and to the commitments made during a succession of international conferences in the 1990s. Regional activities to support national strategies will be based on strengthened regional and subregional organisations, networks and initiatives.

10. Political will and stronger national leadership are needed for the effective and successful implementation of national plans in each of the countries concerned. However, political will be must be underpinned by resources. The international community acknowledges that many countries currently lack the resources to achieve education for all within an acceptable time-frame. New financial resources, preferably in the form of grants and concessional assistance, must therefore be mobilized by bilateral and multilateral funding agencies, including the World Bank and regional development banks, and the private sector. We affirm that no countries seriously committed to education for all will be thwarted in their achievement of this goal by a lack of resources.

11. The international community will deliver on this collective commitment by launching with immediate effects a global initiative aimed at developing the strategies and mobilizing the resources needed to provide effective support to national efforts. Options to be considered under this initiative will include:

    (i) Increasing external finance for education, in particular basic education;

(ii) Ensuring greater predictability in the flow of external assistance;

(iii) Facilitating more effective donor co-ordination;

(iv) Strengthening sector-wide approaches;

(v) providing earlier, more extensive and broader debt relief and/or debt cancellation for poverty reduction, with a strong commitment to basic education; and

(vi) Undertaking more effective and regular monitoring of progress towards EFA goals and targets, including periodic assessments.

12. There is already evidence from many countries of what can be achieved through strong national strategies supported by effective development co-operation. Progress under these strategies could—and must—be accelerated through increased international support. At the same time, countries with less developed strategies—including countries in transition, countries affected by conflict, and post-crisis countries—must be given to support they need to achieve more rapid progress towards education for all.

13. We will strengthen accountable international and regional mechanism to give clear expression to these commitments and to ensure that the Dakar Framework for Action is on the agenda of every international and regional organisation, every national legislature and every local decision-making forum.

14. The EFA 2000 Assessment highlights that the challenge of education for all is greatest in sub-Saharan Africa, in South Asia, and in the least developed countries. Accordingly, while no country in need should be denied international assistance, priority should be given to these regions and countries. Countries in conflict or undergoing reconstruction should also be given special attention in building up their education systems to meet the needs of all learners.

15. Implementation of the preceding goals and strategies will require national, regional and international mechanism to be galvanized immediately. To be most effective these mechanisms will be participatory and, wherever possible,

build on what already exists. They will include representatives of all stakeholders and partners and they will operate in transparent and accountable ways. They will respond comprehensively to the word and spirit of the Jomtien Declaration and this Dakar Framework for Action. The functions of these mechanisms will include, to varying degrees, advocacy, resource mobilization, monitoring and EFA knowledge generation and sharing.

16. The heart of EFA activity lies at the country level. National EFA Forums will be strengthened or established to support the achievement of EFA. All relevant ministries and national civil society organisations will be systematically represented in these Forums. They should be transparent and democratic and should constitute a framework for implementation at subnational levels. Countries will prepare comprehensive National EFA Plans by 2002 at the latest. For those countries with significant challenges, such as complex crises or natural disasters, special technical support will be provided by the international community. Each National EFA Plan will:

    (i) Be developed by government leadership in direct and systematic consultation with national civil society;

    (ii) Attract co-ordinated support of all development partners;

    (iii) Specify reforms addressing the six EFA goals;

    (iv) Establish a sustainable financial framework;

    (v) Be time-bound and action-oriented;

    (vi) Include mid-term performance indicators; and

    (vii) Achieve a synergy of all human development efforts, through its inclusion within the national development planning framework and process.

17. Where these processes and a credible plan are in place, partner members of the international community undertake to work in a consistent, co-ordinated and coherent manner. Each partner will contribute according to its comparative advantage in support of the National EFA Plans to ensure that resource gaps are filled.

18. Regional activities to support national efforts will be based on existing regional and subregional organisations, networks and initiatives, augmented where necessary. Regions and subregions will decide on a lead EFA network that will become the Regional or Subregional Forum with an explicit EFA mandate. Systematic involvement of, and co-ordination with, all relevant civil society and other regional and subregional organisations are essential. These Regional and Subregional EFA Forums will be linked organically with, and be accountable to, National EFA Forums. Their functions will be: co-ordination with all relevant networks; setting and monitoring regional/subregional targets; advocacy; policy dialogue; the promotion of partnerships and technical co-operation; the sharing of best practices and lessons learned; monitoring and reporting for accountability; and promoting resource mobilization. Regional and international support will be available to strengthen Regional and Subregional Forums and relevant EFA capacities, especially within Africa and South Asia.

19. UNESCO will continue its mandated role in co-ordinating EFA partners and maintaining their collective momentum. In line with this, UNESCO's Director-General will convene annually a high-level, small and flexible group. It will serve as a lever for political commitment and technical and financial resource mobilization. Informed by a monitoring report from the UNESCO International Institute for Education Planning (IIEP), the UNESCO International Bureau of Education (IBE), the UNESCO Institute for Education (UIE) and, in particular, the UNESCO Institute for Statistics, and inputs from Regional and Subregional EFA Forums, it will also be an opportunity to hold the global community to account for commitments made in Dakar. It will be composed of highest-level leaders from governments and civil society of developing and developed countries, and from development agencies.

20. UNESCO will serve as the Secretariat. It will refocus its education programme in order place to the outcomes and priorities of Dakar at the heart of its work. This will involve working groups on each of the six goals adopted at Dakar.

This Secretariat will work closely with other organisations and may include staff seconded from them.

21. Achieving Education for All will require additional financial support by countries and increased development assistance and debt relief for education by bilateral and multilateral donors, estimated to cost in the order of $8 billion a year. It is therefore essential that new, concrete financial commitments by made by national governments and also by bilateral and multilateral donors including the World Bank and the regional development banks, by civil society and by foundations.

28 April 2000

Dakar, Senegal

Appendix—2

EXPANDED COMMENTARY ON THE DAKAR FRAMEWORK FOR ACTION

Education for All: Meeting our Collective Commitments

This commentary provides details on each goal and strategy of the Framework for Action on the basis of the many suggestions provided before and during the World Education Forum, most notably from its twenty-four strategy sessions.

Prepared by The World Education Forum Drafting Committee, Paris, 23 May 2000

I. Introduction

1. The Dakar Framework for Action is a re-affirmation of the vision set out in the World Declaration on Education for All in Jomtien a decade ago. It expresses the international community's collective commitment to pursue a broad-based strategy for ensuring that the basic learning needs of every child, youth and adult are met within a generation and sustained thereafter.

2. The World Education Forum in Dakar provided the opportunity to assess the achievements, lessons and failures of the past decade. The EFA 2000 Assessment represents an unparalleled effort to take stock of the state of basic education in the world. It includes national assessments of the progress achieved since Jomtien in 183 countries, the problems encountered and recommendations for future action. Synthesis reports summarize the main findings of these assessments by region. In addition, fourteen special thematic studies were undertaken, surveys were conducted on the quality of learning achievement in over thirty countries, and a comprehensive collection and synthesis of case-studies on the involvement of NGOs in education was prepared.

3. The Assessment is a rich store of information and analysis. Five regional EFA conferences (sub-Saharan Africa, Johannesburg; Asia and the Pacific, Bangkok; Arab States and North Africa, Cairo; the Americas and the Caribbean,

Santo Domingo; and Europe and North America, Warsaw) and a conference of the nine high-population (E-9) countries (Recife) discussed and translated the outcomes of the Assessments into regional frameworks for action which are an integral part of this document and underpin the Dakar Framework for Action.

4. The vision of Jomtien remains pertinent and powerful. It provides a broad and comprehensive view of education and its critical role in empowering individuals and transforming societies. Its key points and principles include universal access to learning; a focus on equity; emphasis on learning outcomes; broadening the means and the scope of basic education; enhancing the environment for learning; and strengthening partnerships. Tragically, reality has fallen far short of this vision: millions of people are still denied their right to education and the opportunities it brings to live safer, healthier, more productive and more fulfilling lives. Such a failure has multiple causes: weak political will, insufficient financial resources and the inefficient use of those available, the burden of debt, inadequate attention to the learning needs of the poor and the excluded, a lack of attention to the quality of learning and an absence of commitment to overcoming gender disparities. There can be no doubt that the barriers to achieving Education for All are formidable. Yet they can and must be overcome.

5. The Assessment shows that progress has been achieved, providing that Education for All is a realistic and achievable goal. But it needs to be frankly acknowledged that progress has been uneven and far too slow. At the start of a new millennium, the EFA 2000 Assessment shows the following:

   (i) Of the more than 800 million children under 6 years of age, fewer than a third benefit from any form of early childhood education.

   (ii) Some 113 million children, 60 per cent of whom are girls, have no access to primary schooling.

   (iii) At least 880 million adults are illiterate, of whom the majority are women.

6. These figures represent an affront to human dignity and a denial of the right to education. They stand as major barriers to eliminating poverty and attaining sustainable development, and are clearly unacceptable.

7. The Dakar Framework sets six major EFA goals and proposes twelve major strategies. It puts forward twelve major strategies informed by the experience of the past decade and the changing global context. These include the international development targets for education to which national governments and the international community are already committed.

8. Starting from early childhood and extending throughout life, the learners of the twenty-first century will require access to high quality educational opportunities that are responsive to their needs, equitable and gender-sensitive. These opportunities must neither exclude nor discriminate. Since the pace, style, language and circumstances of learning will never be uniform for all, there should be room for diverse formal or less formal approaches, as long as they ensure sound learning and confer equivalent status.

9. The right to education imposes an obligation upon states to ensure that all citizens have opportunities to meet their basic learning needs. Primary education should be free, compulsory and of good quality. The education systems of tomorrow, however diversified they may be, will need to be transparent and accountable in how they are governed, managed and financed. The indispensable role of the state in education must be supplemented and supported by bold and comprehensive educational partnerships at all levels of society. Education for All implies the involvement and commitment of all to education.

II. Achievements and Challenges

Achievements and Lessons

10. The EFA 2000 Assessment conducted at national, regional and global levels shows that progress has been made over the past decade towards the vision reflected in the Jomtien Declaration.

11. Worldwide, primary school enrolments increased by some 82 million pupils since 1990, with 44 million more girls in school in 1998 than in 1990—figures which more than any other symbolize the serious efforts of many countries to advance in the face of often severe economic constraints and continued rapid population growth. At the end of the 1990s, developing countries as a whole had achieved net enrolment rates in excess of 80 per cent. Repetition and dropout rates had declined. There has been some improvement, albeit limited, in gender equality in primary enrolment in many regions, with the critical exception of sub-Saharan Africa. Early childhood care and education have expanded modestly, mainly in urban areas. Virtually all countries in the world have ratified the United Nations Convention on the Rights of the Child and have thereby accepted an obligation to ensure the right of every child to a basic education. There has been a gradual growth in non-formal education and skills training. While levels of illiteracy remain unacceptably high, a measure of progress has been achieved. The overall adult literacy rate has risen to 85 per cent for men and to 74 per cent for women. Increased levels of education have enabled men and women to make more informed choices about family size. This is having an impact on demographic growth rates, a factor of great importance for both education and development.

12. These quantitative achievements tell nothing of the plight of the millions who are still excluded from education or of alienated youth and their painful struggle to find a place and retain their values in changing societies. Information is also sparse on the nature and quality of teaching and learning and of educational outcomes at all levels in education systems.

13. There is a powerful correlation between low enrolment, poor retention and unsatisfactory learning outcomes and the incidence of poverty. Experience in post-Jomtien decade, however, has demonstrated that significant progress can be made towards the goals of Education for All where there is a strong political commitment, backed by new partnerships with civil society and more strategic support from funding

agencies. It is also clear that ensuring that girls and boys benefit equally from education requires nothing less than the integration of gender equality concerns into the design and implementation of sector policies and strategies. The importance of gathering and carefully analysing reliable gender-disaggregated data at national and subnational levels is evident.

14. The many factors that impinge on the demand for education are now better understood, as are the multiple causes that exclude children, young people and adults from learning opportunities. The range of actions requires to increase the participation and retention of girls in school has received widespread attention. Knowledge about the effectiveness of teachers and other educators, the central role of appropriate learning materials, the need for a context-specific mix of 'old' and 'new' technologies, the importance of local languages for initial literacy and the major influence of the community in the life of schools and other education programmes has increased. The value of early childhood care and education for later school success and the need for strong linkages between the different subsectors of education and among basic education, health, nutrition, safe water and the natural environment have received greater attention and are better understood.

Challenges and Opportunities

15. The tangible but modest gains overall of the past decade still call for caution. Many countries continue to face the challenges of defining the meaning, purpose and content of basic education in the context of a fast-moving world and of assessing learning outcomes and achievement. Many of the qualitative and informal aspects of education have still not been clearly assessed. The huge diversity of contexts makes performance and achievements difficult to measure and compare. Moreover, growing educational disparities within and between countries are a matter for serious concern.

16. Many governments and agencies have focused their efforts on the easy to reach and they have neglected those excluded

from a basic education, whether for social, economic or geographic reasons. What is clear is that quality must not suffer as access expands and that improvements in quality should not benefit the economically well-off at the expense of the poor, as has happened, for example, in the expansion of early childhood care and education.

17. The education of girls remains a major challenge; despite the international attention that it has received, 60 per cent of all children without access to primary education are girls.

18. South Asia and sub-Saharan Africa, where progress has been most difficult to achieve, clearly present a much deeper challenge than world averages imply and will require particular attention if the goals of Education for All are to be reached in each and every country. In the Americas and the Caribbean, deep differences between regions and social groups based on income inequality continue to hamper progress towards Education for All and must receive due attention.

19. A key challenge is to ensure that the broad vision of Education for All as an inclusive concept is reflected in national government and funding agency policies. Education for All must encompass not only primary education, but also early childhood education, literacy and life-skills programmes. Using both formal and non-formal approaches, it must take account of the needs of the poor and the most disadvantaged, including working children, remote rural dwellers and nomads, and ethnic and linguistic minorities, children, young people and adults affected by conflict, HIV/AIDS, hunger and poor health; and those with special learning needs. It is encouraging to see that many governments, funding agencies and civil society organisations are increasingly rallying to this more inclusive and comprehensive view of education.

20. Ensuring the Education for All is provided with adequate, equitable and sustainable resources is the foremost challenge. Many governments do not give education sufficient priority in their national budgets. Too many do not use resources for education effectively and efficiently, and often subsidize

better-off groups at the expense of the poor. At the same time, stabilization programmes often fail to protect education budgets. As a direct consequence, user charges continue to be a major deterrent to poor children attending school and to young people and adults in need of non-formal learning. In some countries, passing the cost burden on to poor parents has had a devastating impact on enrolment and retention. Education must neither exclude nor discriminate. Every government has the responsibility to provide free, quality basic education, so that no child will be denied access because of an inability to pay.

21. Governments need to explore more actively alternative and innovative ways of increasing the resources available to support Education for All and to develop clearly defined strategies for achieving EFA goals, for which they take real and sustained ownership. Debt relief to the poorest countries remains inadequate, with too little being provided to too few countries too late. Debt reduction programmes should offer governments an opportunity to give priority to education within overall poverty reduction frameworks.

22. While the proportion of international assistance allocated to basic education increased in the 1990s, there was an overall decline in total development assistance. The first trend should be supported and the second reversed. There is considerable scope for the international community to demonstrate, in a co-operative and accountable way, that it can be effective in supporting well-defined national sector strategies and in helping to release the significant additional resources that many funding agencies are willing to provide.

23. New ways of working that are emerging within the wider development context also represent opportunities for achieving EFA goals. Greater co-operation between national and international agencies at the country level, through structures and mechanisms such as Comprehensive Development Framework, Poverty Reduction Strategy Plans and United Nations Development Assistance Frameworks, offers the potential for resource-related partnerships for basic education.

24. Genuinely particularly development is more likely to occur where there is a stronger and more vocal recognition of education as a fundamental human right and where representative democracy has taken root. The growing importance of participatory poverty assessments and household surveys also highlights a positive trend in the development of education programmes and systems that are genuinely responsive to well-defined needs and priorities.

25. While inadequate institutional capacity and weak political processes still prevent many governments from responding to the priorities of their citizens, the spread of democratic principles around the world, the growing contribution of civil society to democratic processes, the fight against corruption and the process of decentralization that is ongoing in many countries all have the potential to contribute greatly in building a solid foundation for the achievement of effective, equitable and sustainable Education for All.

26. Globalization is both an opportunity and a challenge. It is a process which must be shaped and managed so as to ensure equity and sustainability. Globalization is generating new wealth and resulting in the greater interconnectedness and interdependence of economies and societies. Driven by the revolution in information technologies and the increased mobility of capital, it has the potential to help reduce poverty and inequality throughout the world, and to harness the new technologies for basic education. Yet globalization carries with it the danger of creating a market place in knowledge that excludes the poor and the disadvantaged. Countries and households denied access to opportunities for basic education in an increasingly knowledge-based global economy face the prospect of deepening marginalization within an increasingly prosperous international economy.

27. The threat posed by HIV/AIDS to the achievement of EFA goals and to development more broadly, especially in sub-Saharan Africa, presents an enormous challenge. The terrifying impact of HIV/AIDS on educational demand, supply and quality requires explicit and immediate attention in national policy-making and planning. Programmes to

control and reduce the spread of the virus must make maximum use of education's potential to transmit messages on prevention and to change attitudes and behaviours.

28. The significant growth of tensions, conflict and war, both within nations and between nations and peoples, is a cause of great concern. Education has a key role to play in preventing conflict in the future and building lasting peace and stability.

III. Goals

Basic learning needs ... comprise both essential learning tools .. and the basic learning content ... required by human beings to be able to survive, to develop their full capacities, to live and work in dignity, to participate fully in development, to improve the quality of their lives, to make informed decisions, and to continue learning.

(World Declaration on Education for All,
Article 1, Paragraph 1)

29. The goals and strategies set out below establish a Framework for Action that is designed to enable all individuals to realize their right to learn and to fulfil their responsibility to contribute to the development of their society. They are global in nature, drawn from the outcomes of the regional EFA conferences and the international development targets to which countries are already committed. Individual countries, through a process of consultation among all stakeholders in education and with the assistance of the wider international community and EFA follow-up mechanisms, should set their own goals, intermediate targets and time-lines within existing or new national education plans.

1. Expanding and improving comprehensive early childhood care and education, especially for the most vulnerable and disadvantaged children

30. All young children must be nurtured in safe and caring environments that allow them to become healthy, alert and secure and be able to learn. The past decade has provided more evidence that good quality early childhood care and

education, both in families and in more structured programmes, have a positive impact on the survival, growth, development and learning potential of children. Such programmes should be comprehensive, focusing on all of the child's needs and encompassing health, nutrition and hygiene as well as cognitive and psycho-social development. They should be provided in the child's mother tongue and help to identify and enrich the care and education of children with special needs. Partnerships between governments, NGOs, communities and families can help ensure the provision of good care and education for children, especially for those most disadvantaged, through activities centered on the child, focused on the family, based within the community and supported by national, multi-sectoral policies and adequate resources.

31. Governments, through relevant ministries, have the primary responsibility of formulating early childhood care and education policies within the context of national EFA plans, mobilizing political and popular support, and promoting flexible, adaptable programmes for young children that are appropriate to their age and not mere downward extensions of formal school systems. The education of parents and other caregivers in better child care, building on traditional practices, and the systematic use of early childhood indicators, are important elements in achieving this goal.

2. **ENSURING THAT BY 2015 ALL CHILDREN, PARTICULARLY GIRLS, CHILDREN IN DIFFICULT CIRCUMSTANCES AND THOSE BELONGING TO ETHNIC MINORITIES, HAVE ACCESS TO AND COMPLETE FREE AND COMPULSORY PRIMARY EDUCATION OF GOOD QUALITY**

32. All children must have the opportunity to fulfil their right to quality education in schools or alternative programmes at whatever level of education is considered 'basic'. All states must fulfil their obligation to offer free and compulsory primary education in accordance with the United Nations Convention on the rights of the Child and other international commitments. The international agreement on the 2015 target date for achieving Universal Primary Education (UPE) in all countries will require commitment and political will

from all levels of government. For the millions of children living in poverty, who suffer multiple disadvantages, there must be an unequivocal commitment that education be free of tuition and other fees, and that everything possible be done to reduce or eliminate costs such as those for learning materials, uniforms, school meals and transport. Wider social policies, interventions and incentives should be used to mitigate indirect opportunity costs of attending school. No one should be denied the opportunity to complete a good quality primary education because it is unaffordable. Child labour must not stand in the way of education. The inclusion of children with special needs, from disadvantaged ethnic minorities and migrant populations, from remote and isolated communities and from urban slums, and others excluded from education, must be an integral part of strategies to achieve UPE by 2015.

33. While commitment to attaining universal enrolment is essential, improving and sustaining the quality of basic education is equally important in ensuring effective learning outcomes. In order to attract and retain children from marginalized and excluded groups, education systems should respond flexibly, providing relevant content in an accessible and appealing format. Education systems must be inclusive, actively seeking out children who are not enrolled, and responding flexibly to the circumstances and needs of all learners. The EFA 2000 Assessment suggests a wide range of ways in which schools can respond to the needs of their pupils, including affirmative action programmes for girls that seek to remove the obstacles to their enrolment, bilingual education for the children of ethnic minorities, and a range of imaginative and diverse approaches to address and actively engage children who are not enrolled in school.

3. Ensuring that the learning needs of all young people and adults are met through equitable access to appropriate learning and life skills programmes

34. All young people and adults must be given the opportunity to gain the knowledge and develop the values, attitudes and skills that will enable them to develop their capacities to

work, to participate fully in their society, to take control of their own lives and to continue learning. No country can be expected to develop into a modern and open economy without a certain proportion of its work force having completed secondary education. In most countries this requires an expansion of the secondary system.

35. Young people, especially adolescent girls, face risks and threats that limit learning opportunities and challenge education systems. These include exploitative labour, the lack of employment, conflict and violence, drug abuse, school-age pregnancy and HIV/AIDS. Youth-friendly programmes must be made available to provide the information, skills counselling and services needed to protect them from these risks.

36. All young people should be given the opportunity for ongoing education. For those who drop out of school or complete school without acquiring the literacy, numeracy and life skills they need, there must be a range of options for continuing their learning. Such opportunities should be both meaningful and relevant to their environment and needs, help them become active agents in shaping their future and develop useful work-related skills.

4. Achieving a 50 per cent improvement in levels of adult literacy by 2015, especially for women, and equitable access to basic and continuing education and all adults

37. All adults have a right to basic education, beginning with literacy, which allows them to engage actively in, and to transform, the world in which they live. There are still some 880 million people who cannot read or write in the world; two-thirds are women. The fragile levels of literacy acquired by many new literates compound the problem. Yet the education of adults remains isolated, often at the periphery of national education systems and budgets.

38. Adult and continuing education must be greatly expanded and diversified, and integrated into the mainstream of national education and poverty reduction strategies. The vital role literacy plays in lifelong learning, sustainable livelihoods, good health, active citizenship and the improved

quality of life for individuals, communities and societies must be more widely recognized. Literacy and continuing education are essential for women's empowerment and gender equality. Closer linkages among formal, non-formal and informal approaches to learning must be fostered to respond to the diverse needs and circumstances of adults.

39. Sufficient resources, well-targeted literacy, programmes, better trained teachers and the innovative use of technologies are essential in promoting these activities. The scaling up of practical, participatory learning methodologies developed by non-government organisations, which link literacy with empowerment and local development, is especially important. The success of adult education efforts in the next decade will be essentially demonstrated by substantial reduction in disparities between male/female and urban/rural literacy rates.

5. ELIMINATING GENDER DISPARITIES IN PRIMARY AND SECONDARY EDUCATION BY 2005, AND ACHIEVING GENDER EQUALITY IN EDUCATION BY 2015, WITH A FOCUS ON ENSURING GIRLS' FULL AND EQUAL ACCESS TO AND ACHIEVEMENT IN BASIC EDUCATION OF GOOD QUALITY

40. Gender-based discrimination remains one of the most intractable constraints to realizing the right to education. Without overcoming this obstacle, Education for All cannot be achieved. Girls are a majority among out-of-school children and youth, although in an increasing number of countries boys are at a disadvantage. Even though the education of girls and women has a powerful trans-generational effect and is a key determinant of social development and women's empowerment, limited progress has been made in increasing girls' participation in basic education.

41. International agreement has already been reached to eliminate disparities in primary and secondary education by 2005. This requires that gender issues be mainstreamed throughout the education system, supported by adequate resources and strong political commitment. Merely ensuring access to education for girls is not enough; unsafe school environments and biases in teacher behaviour and training,

teaching and learning processes, and curricula and textbooks often lead to lower completion and achievement rates for girls. By creating safe and gender-sensitive learning environments, it should be possible to remove a major hurdle to girls' participation in education. Increasing levels of women's literacy is another crucial factor in promoting girls' education. Comprehensive efforts therefore need to be made at all levels and in all areas to eliminate gender discrimination and to promote mutual respect between girls and boys, women and men. To make this possible, changes in attitudes, values and behaviour are required.

6. IMPROVING EVERY ASPECT OF THE QUALITY OF EDUCATION, AND ENSURING THEIR EXCELLENCE SO THAT RECOGNIZED AND MEASURABLE LEARNING OUTCOMES ARE ACHIEVED BY ALL, ESPECIALLY IN LITERACY, NUMERACY AND ESSENTIAL LIFE SKILLS

42. Quality is at the heart of education, and what takes place in classrooms and other learning environments is fundamentally important to the future well-being of children, young people and adults. A quality education is one that satisfies basic learning needs, and enriches the lives of learners and their overall experience of living.

43. Evidence over the past decade has shown efforts to expand enrolment must be accompanied by attempts to enhance educational quality if children are to be attracted to school, stay there and achieve meaningful learning outcomes. Scarce resources have frequently been used for expanding systems with insufficient attention to quality improvement in areas such as teacher training and materials development. Recent assessments of learning achievement in some countries have shown that a sizeable percentage of children is acquiring only a fraction of the knowledge and skills they are expected to master. What students are meant to learn has often not been clearly defined, well-taught or accurately assessed.

44. Governments and all other EFA partners must work together to ensure basic education of quality for all, regardless of gender, wealth location, language or ethnic origin. Successful education programmes require: *(i)* healthy, well-nourished and motivated students; *(ii)* well-trained teachers and active

learning techniques; *(iii)* adequate facilities and learning materials; *(iv)* a relevant curriculum that can be taug'ıt and learned in a local language and builds upon the knowledge and experience of the teachers and learners; *(v)* an environment that not only encourages learning but is welcoming, gender-sensitive, healthy and safe; *(vi)* a clear definition and accurate assessment of learning outcomes, including knowledge, skills, attitudes and values; *(vii)* participatory governance and management; and *(viii)* respect for and engagement with local communities and cultures.

IV. Strategies

45. Education for All is a basic human right at the heart of development. It must be a national and international priority, and it requires a strong and sustained political commitment, enhanced financial allocations and the participation of all EFA partners in the processes of policy design, strategic planning and the implementation of programmes. Achieving the six goals outlined above necessitates a broad-based approach which extends well beyond the confines of formal education systems. Building on the lessons of the last decade, the implementation of the following strategies will be critical in achieving Education for All.

1. Mobilize strong national and international political commitment for education for all, develop national action plans and enhance significantly investment in basic education

46. The Jomtien Framework for Action stated that progress in meeting the basic learning needs of all will depend ultimately on the actions taken within individual countries. This means first that governments must make firm political commitments and allocate sufficient resources to all components of basic education—an absolutely essential step to meeting the state's obligation to all of its citizens. In many countries this will require increasing the share of national income and budgets allocated to education and, within that, to basic education balanced by reduced allocations to sectors of lower development priority. Resources have to be used with much greater efficiency and integrity, and governments

should set goals for more equitable spending across education sub-sectors. Corruption is a major drain on the effective use of resources for education and should be drastically curbed. Structures are needed to enable civil society to be part of transparent and accountable budgeting and financing systems. Achieving Education for All will also require more creative and sustained mobilization of resources from other parts of society, including different levels of government, the private sector and non-governmental organisations.

47. Even with improved mobilization and allocation of domestic resources, and enhanced efficiency in their use, meeting all the education goals will require additional funding from international development agencies. Funding agencies should allocate a larger share of their resources to support primary and other forms of basic education. The regions and countries where challenges are greatest, which include much of sub-Saharan Africa and South Asia, least developed countries and countries emerging from conflicts, deserve particular attention.

48. No countries seriously committed to Education for All will be thwarted in their achievement of this goal by lack of resources. Funding agencies are willing to allocate significant resources towards Education for All. The keys to releasing these resources are evidence of, or potential for, sustained political commitment; effective and transparent mechanisms for consultation with civil society organisations in developing, implementing and monitoring EFA plans; and a well-defined, consultative processes for sector planning and management.

49. This commitment requires that funding agencies coordinate their efforts to provide flexible development assistance within the framework of sectorwide reforms and support sector priorities within sound and coherent government-owned poverty reduction programmes. High priority should be given to providing earlier, deeper and broader debt relief and/or debt cancellation for poverty reduction, with a strong commitment to basic education. Debt relief should not be a substitute for aid.

50. Funding agencies will need to make longer-term and more predictable commitments, and to be more accountable and transparent. They must provide timely and accurate information on their disbursements, and ensure that there is regular, reporting at regional and international levels.

2. Promote EFA policies within a sustainable and well-integrated sector framework clearly linked to poverty elimination and development strategies

51. Education, starting with the care and education of young children and continuing through lifelong learning, is central to individual empowerment, the elimination of poverty at household and community level, and broader social and economic development. At the same time, the reduction of poverty facilitates progress toward basic education goals. There are evident synergies between strategies for promoting education and those for reducing poverty that must be exploited both in programme planning and implementation.

52. A multi-sectoral approach to poverty elimination requires that education strategies complement those of the productive sectors as well as of health, population, social welfare, labour, the environment and finance, and be closely linked with civil society. Specific actions in this regard include: *(i)* integrating basic education strategies into broader national and international poverty alleviation measures such as United Nations Development Assistance Frameworks (UNDAFs), Comprehensive Development Frameworks and Poverty Reduction Strategy Papers; and *(ii)* developing 'inclusive' education systems which explicitly identify, target and respond flexibly to the needs and circumstances of the poorest and the most marginalized.

3. Ensure the engagement and participation of civil society in the formulation, implementation and monitoring of strategies for education development

53. Learners, teachers, parents, communities, non-governmental organisations and other bodies representing civil society must be granted new and expanded political and social

scope, at all levels of society, in order to engage governments in dialogue, decision-making and innovation around the goals of basis education. Civil society has much experience and a crucial role to play in identifying barriers to EFA goals, and developing policies and strategies to remove them.

54. Such participation, especially at the local level through partnerships between schools and communities, should not only be limited to endorsing decisions of, or financing programmes designed by, the state. Rather, at all levels of decision-making, governments must put in place regular mechanisms for dialogue that will enable citizens and civil society organisations to contribute to the planning, implementation, monitoring and evaluation of basic education. This is essential in order to foster the development of accountable, comprehensive and flexible educational management frameworks. In order to facilitate this process, capacity will often have to be developed in the civil society organisations.

4. Develop responsive, participatory and accountable systems of educational governance and management

55. The experience of the past decade has underscored the need for better governance of education systems in terms of efficiency, accountability, transparency and flexibility so that they can respond more effectively to the diverse and continuously changing needs of learners. Reform of educational management is urgently needed—to move from highly centralized, standardized and command-driven forms of management to more decentralized and participatory decision-making, implementation and monitoring at lower levels of accountability. These processes must be buttressed by a management information system that benefits from both new technologies and community participation to produce timely, relevant and accurate information.

56. Country EFA reports and regional action frameworks stemming from the EFA 2000 Assessment recommend the following: *(i)* establish better regulatory frameworks and

administrative mechanisms for managing not only formal and non-formal primary education, but also early childhood, youth and adult education programmes; *(ii)* more sharply delineate responsibilities among different levels of government; *(iii)* ensure that decentralization does not lead to inequitable distribution of resources; *(iv)* make more efficient use of existing human and financial resources; *(v)* improve capacities for managing diversity, disparity and change; *(vi)* integrate programmes within education and strengthen their convergence with those of other sectors, especially health, labour and social welfare; and *(vii)* provide training for school leaders and other education personnel.

5. MEET THE NEEDS OF EDUCATION SYSTEMS AFFECTED BY CONFLICT, NATURAL CALAMITIES AND INSTABILITY, AND CONDUCT EDUCATIONAL PROGRAMMES IN WAYS THAT PROMOTE MUTUAL UNDERSTANDING, PEACE AND TOLERANCE, AND THAT HELP TO PREVENT VIOLENCE AND CONFLICT

57. Conflicts, instability and natural disasters take their toll on education and are a major barrier towards attaining Education for All. The capacity of governments and civil society should be enhanced to rapidly assess educational needs in contexts of crisis and post-conflict situations for children and adults, to restore learning opportunities in secure and friendly environments, and to reconstruct destroyed or damaged education systems.

58. Schools should be respected and protected as sanctuaries and zones of peace. Education programmes should be designed to promote the full development of the human personality and strengthen respect for human rights and fundamental freedoms as proclaimed in the Universal Declaration of Human Rights (Article 26). Such programmes should promote understanding, tolerance and friendship among all nations, and all ethnic and religious groups; and they should be sensitive to cultural and linguistic identities and respectful of diversity and reinforce a culture of peace. Education should promote not only skills such as the prevention and peaceful resolution of conflict, but also social and ethnical values.

6. Implement integrated strategies for gender equality in education that recognize the need for change in attitudes, values and practices

59. Achieving Education for All demands that high-level commitment and priority be given to gender equality. Schools, other learning environments and education systems usually mirror the larger society. Efforts in support of gender equality must include specific actions to address discrimination resulting from social attitudes and practices, economic status and culture.

60. Throughout the education system, there must be a commitment to the development of attitudes and behaviours that incorporate gender awareness and analysis. Education systems must also act explicitly to remove gender bias. This includes ensuring that policies and their implementation are supportive of girls' and boys' learning. Teaching and supervisory bodies must be fair and transparent, and rules and regulations, including promotion and disciplinary action, must have equal impact on girls and boys, women and men. Attention must be given to boys' needs in cases where they are disadvantaged.

61. In the learning environment, the content, processes and context of education must be free of gender bias, and encourage and support equality and respect. This includes teachers' behaviours and attitudes, curriculum and textbooks, and student interactions. Efforts must be made to ensure personal security: girls are often especially vulnerable to abuse and harassment on the journey to and from school and at school.

7. Implement education programmes and actions to combat the HIV/AIDS pandemic as a matter of urgency

62. The HIV/AIDS pandemic is undermining progress towards Education for All in many parts of the world by seriously affecting educational demand, supply and quality. This situation requires the urgent attention of governments, civil society and the international community. Education systems must go through significant changes if they are to survive

the impact of HIV/AIDS and counter its spread, especially in response to the impact on teacher supply and student demand. To achieve EFA goals will necessitate putting HIV/AIDS as the highest priority in the most affected countries, with strong, sustained political commitment, mainstreaming HIV/AIDS perspectives in all aspects of policy; redesigning teacher training and curricula; and significantly enhancing resources to these efforts.

63. The decade has shown that the pandemic has had, and will increasingly have, a devastating effect on education systems, teachers and learners, with a particularly adverse impact on girls. Stigma and poverty brought about by HIV/AIDS are creating new social castes of children excluded from education and adults with reduced livelihood opportunities. A rights-based response to HIV/AIDS mitigation and ongoing monitoring impact of the pandemic on EFA goals are essential. This response should include appropriate legislation and administrative actions to ensure the right of HIV/AIDS affected people to receive education and to combat discrimination within the education sector.

64. Education institutions and structures should create a safe and supportive environment for children and young people in a world with HIV/AIDS, and strengthen their protection from sexual abuse and other forms of exploitation. Flexible non-formal approaches should be adopted to reach children and adults infected and affected by HIV/AIDS, with particular attention to AIDS orphans. Curricula based on life-skills approaches should include all aspect of HIV/AIDS care and prevention. Parents and communities should also benefit from HIV/AIDS-related programmes. Teachers must be adequately trained, both in-service and pre-service, in providing HIV/AIDS education, and teachers affected by the pandemic should be supported at all levels.

8. Create safe, healthy, inclusive and equitably resourced educational environments conductive to excellence in learning, with clearly defined levels of achievement for all

65. The quality of learning is and must be at the heart of EFA. All stakeholders—teachers and students, parents and

community members, health workers and local government officials—should work together to develop environments conducive to learning. To offer education of good quality, educational institutions and programmes should be adequately and equitably resourced, with the core requirements of safe, environmentally friendly and easily accessible facilities; well motivated and professionally competent teachers; and books, other learning materials and technologies that are context specific, cost effective and available to all learners.

66. Learning environments should also be healthy, safe and protective. This should include: (i) adequate water and sanitation facilities, (ii) access to or linkages with health and nutrition services, (iii) policies and codes of conducts that enhance the physical, psycho-social and emotional heaith of teachers and learners, and (iv) education content and practices leading to knowledge, attitudes, values, and life skills needed for self-esteem, good health, and personal safety.

67. There is an urgent need to adopt effective strategies to identify and include the socially, culturally and economically excluded. This requires participatory analysis of exclusion at household, community and school levels, and the development of diverse, flexible, and innovative approaches to learning and an environment that fosters mutual respect and trust.

68. Assessment of learning should include an evaluation of environments, processes and outcomes. Learning outcomes must be well-defined in both cognitive and non-cognitive domains, and be continually assessed as an integral part of the teaching and learning process.

9. ENHANCE THE STATUS, MORALE AND PROFESSIONALISM OF TEACHERS

69. Teachers are essential players in promoting quality education, whether in schools or in more flexible community-based programmes; they are advocates for, and catalysts of, change. No education reform is likely to succeed without the active participation and ownership of teachers.

Teachers at all levels of the education system should be respected and adequately remunerated; have access to training and ongoing professional development and support, including through open and distance learning; and be able to participate, locally and nationally, in decisions affecting their professional lives and teaching environments. Teachers must also accept their professional responsibilities and be accountable to both learners and communities.

70. Clearly defined and more imaginative strategies to identify, attract, train and retain good teachers must be put into place. These strategies should address the new role of teachers in preparing students for an emerging knowledge-based and technology-driven economy. Teachers must be able to understand diversity in learning styles and in the physical and intellectual development of students, and to create stimulating, participatory learning environments.

10. HARNESS NEW INFORMATION AND COMMUNICATION TECHNOLOGIES TO HELP ACHIEVE EFA GOALS

71. Information and Communication Technologies (ICTs) must be harnessed to support EFA goals at an affordable cost. These technologies have great potential for knowledge dissemination, effective learning and the development of more efficient education services. This potential will not be realized unless the new technologies serve rather than drive the implementation of education strategies. To be effective, especially in developing countries, ICTs should be combined with more traditional technologies such as books and radios, and be more extensively applied to the training of teachers.

72. The swiftness of ICT developments, their increasing spread and availability, the nature of their content and their declining prices are having major implications for learning. They may tend to increase disparities, weaken social bonds and threaten cultural cohesion. Governments will therefore need to establish clearer policies in regard to science and technology, and undertake critical assessments of ICT experiences and options. These should include their resources implications in relation to the provision of basic

education, emphasizing choices that bridge the 'digital divide', increase access and quality, and reduce inequality.

73. There is a need to tap the potential of ICTs to enhance data collection and analysis, and to strengthen management systems, from central ministries through sub-national levels to the school; to improve access to education by remote and disadvantaged communities; to support initial and continuing professional development of teachers; and to provide opportunities to communicate across classrooms and cultures.

74. News media should also be engaged to create and strengthen partnerships with education systems, through the promotion of local newspapers, informed coverage of education issues and continuing education programmes via public service broadcasting.

11. Systematically monitor progress towards EFA goals and strategies at the national, regional and international levels

75. Achieving EFA goals requires setting priorities, defining policies, establishing targets and progress indicators, allocating resources, monitoring performance, and assessing qualitative and quantitative outcomes. Robust and reliable education statistics, disaggregated and based on accurate census data, are essential if progress is to be properly measured, experience shared and lessons learned. Information on the success of particular strategies, on national and international budget allocations for basic education and on civil society participation in Education for All must also be sought. These are all key elements in assessing the accountability of EFA partners. Ongoing monitoring and evaluation of EFA, with the full participation of civil society, should be encouraged.

76. When governments are truly committed to educational outcomes, they recognize the fundamental importance of statistics and the need for credible and independent institutions to produce them. The EFA 2000 Assessment identified the existence of important data gaps. Capacity should be increased to fill these gaps, and to produce

accurate and timely data, qualitative and quantitative, for analysis and feed-back to policy-makers and practitioners. Attention to collecting disaggregated data at lower levels of the system, both to identify areas of greatest inequity and to provide data for local-level planning, management and evaluation, is essential.

77. Progress towards meeting EFA goals and targets needs to be assessed regularly and systematically to allow for meaningful comparative analyses. The availability of better data or national and international levels will allow governments, civil society and other agencies to gain a clearer understanding of progress toward the goals, to identify regions, countries, and sub-national levels where there is particular success or difficulty, and then to take appropriate action.

12. Build on Existing Mechanisms to Accelerate Progress Towards Education for All

78. In order to realize the six goals presented in this Framework for Action, broad-based and participatory mechanisms at international, regional and national levels are essential. The functions of these mechanisms will include, to varying degrees, advocacy, resource mobilization, monitoring, and knowledge generation and sharing.

79. The heart of EFA activity lies at the country level. National EFA forums will be strengthened or established and countries will prepare national EFA plans by 2002 at the latest. For those countries with significant challenges such as crises on natural disasters, special technical support will be provided by the international community. Members of the international community commit themselves to working in a consistent, co-ordinated and coherent manner in supporting national EFA plans.

80. Regional and sub-regional activities to support national efforts will be based on existing organisations, networks and initiatives, augmented where necessary. These will work in tandem with national EFA forums.

81. UNESCO will continue its mandated role in co-ordinating EFA partners and maintaining their collaborative momentum. In line with this, UNESCO will convene annually a high-level, small and flexible group to serve as a lever for political commitment and technical and financial resource mobilization. It will be composed of leaders from governments and civil society and development agencies. UNESCO will refocus its education programme in order to place the outcomes and priorities of Dakar at the heart of its work.

82. Achieving Education for All will require that new, concrete financial commitments be made by national governments and by bilateral and multilateral donors including the World Bank and the regional development banks, civil society and foundations.

Appendix—3

EDUCATION FOR ALL, A FRAMEWORK FOR ACTION IN SUB-SAHARAN AFRICA: EDUCATION FOR AFRICAN RENAISSANCE IN THE TWENTY-FIRST CENTURY

Adopted by the Regional Conference on Education for All for Sub-Saharan Africa, Johannesburg, South Africa, 6–10 December 1999.

1. Preamble

If the next century is going to be characterized as a truly African century, for social and economic progress of the African people, the century of durable peace and sustained development in Africa, then the success of this project is dependent on the success of our education systems. For nowhere in the world has sustained development been attained without a well-functioning system of education, without universal and sound primary education, without an effective higher education and research sector, without equality of educational opportunity.

President Thabo Mbeki, Opening Speech, Conference on Education for African Renaissance in the Twenty-first Century, Johannesburg, South Africa, 6 December 1999.

At the close of the twentieth century, we, the Ministers of Education, representatives of civil society and international development agencies, assembled in Johannesburg to reflect on the progress made towards achieving the EFA goals adopted in Jomtien in 1990. We seize this opportunity to launch a renewal of education that will enable Africa to meet the challenges of the twenty-first century. We hereby adopt a framework of action under the theme of *Education for African Renaissance in the Globalized Economy, Communication and Culture.*

We recognize the tremendous efforts made by sub-Saharan African countries to achieve these goals, despite many obstacles and exceptionally harsh conditions. This meeting of major stakeholders from across the continent has enabled us for the first time to analyse the situation from many perspectives. During this decade, the greatest achievements have accompanied comprehensive reform and post-war reconstruction. The greatest losses have been in those countries engaged in war and civil conflict that have engulfed nearly one-third of the countries in the region.

Built often on a weak physical and institutional base, education systems in many African countries are vulnerable to natural and human-made disasters that have hindered progress and, in some cases, even rolled back the achievements already won. Many countries have experienced austere economic adjustment programmes, an increased debt burden, a skewed global economic system, poor governance, inadequate and sometimes poorly used resources, as well as drought and floods. These factors, combined with impact of HIV/AIDS and armed conflict, have continued to have devastating effects on education in Africa.

Remarkable efforts have been made to ensure that every child gets access to quality basic education, but we note that only about ten countries have achieved universal primary education. Although enrolment has increased considerably in many countries, it has not been adequate to accommodate rapid population growth and rural-to-urban migration, thereby giving an impression of being static relative to population size. Early childhood care and education programmes are limited to the few in the urban areas. Based on countries' own estimates, between 1990 and 1998 the net enrolment of boys increased by 9 per cent to 56 per cent, and of girls by 7 per cent to 48 per cent[1] in sub-Saharan Africa. However, these figures mask considerable regional variations. In countries of the Indian Ocean, both girls and boys attained over 70 per cent net enrolment. The most outstanding progress in terms of percentage increase of boys' enrolment was in East Africa (excluding Somalia), where the net enrolment of boys increased by 27 per cent (to 60 per cent) and of girls by 18 per cent (to 50 per cent), and for girls in Southern Africa, where the comparable figures for girls were 23 per cent (to 76 per cent) and for boys, 16 per cent (to 58 per cent).[2] Progress in the peaceful areas of West and Central Africa was counter-balanced by disastrous reversals in the warring countries. Currently available data indicate that about 40 per cent of girls and 50 per cent of boys are enrolled in West Africa, and 50 per cent of girls and 60 per cent of boys in Central Africa.

The real figures may be much lower, however, as several of these countries were unable to collect data in recent years.

Girls represent 56 per cent of the estimated 41 million school-age children who are out of school. Gender parity is highest in Southern Africa, where many countries have attained near universal primary education and high adult literacy. Cases of extreme gender disparity, where girls' enrolment may be only half that of boys, are mostly found along the southern rim of the Sahara, a region characterized by low adult literacy and weak economies. Having entered school, however, girls have a 69 per cent chance of reaching Grade 5, compared with 70 per cent for boys. Here also, regional variations exist: in general, where enrolment and literacy and high, gender equality prevails; where enrolment and adult literacy are low, the survival rate of girls is generally lower than that of boys.

The number of students dropping out of school has increased alarmingly in recent years, mainly due to increased costs or armed conflicts. Participation is particularly low amongst children in remote and rural areas, those with disabilities, refugees and internally displaced people, working children, ethnic minorities, and those affected by HIV/AIDS, conflict and other emergencies that have spawned an increasing number of orphans. The poor from rural areas continue to stream into our cities, where schools are already overcrowded.

Access to education is limited, its quality poor and the curricula often irrelevant to the needs of the learners and of social, cultural and economic development. Emerging new industries need entrepreneurs, managers and skilled labour in order to be competitive; our outdated education systems continue to produce graduates without the requisite knowledge and skills.

The majority of our population still has no access to electricity, clean water and medicine. To solve these shortages, we need the 'know-how' in such basic industrial processes as product development, manufacturing, marketing and distribution. Educational institutions, research centres and industries, working together, could develop indigenous solutions to these problems. The trust needed for this partnership between education and industry, however, is at an all-time low.

Having partaken in the most comprehensive assessment ever conducted in Africa, we recognize the important tasks ahead for education leadership and management. We need to build our capacity for innovation, sensitivity to disparities and flexible responsiveness to changing needs. Education planning and management capacity, however, remains largely underdeveloped. Yet, many African ministry staff have been trained abroad particularly in these areas. We need to effectively implement planned changes as well as respond to crisis and manage adjustment. For this, we need to establish a mechanism for professional partnership and a democratic process for consensus-building with regard to the goals and strategies at various levels, from policy formulation to implementation.

To meet these challenges, it is all the more important to learn from the many examples of good practice and successful policies that have proven to be effective in the African context:

- accelerated access, with particular reference to policies of equity and female enrolment, including affirmative action;
- community involvement in school decision-making and administration;
- employment of teachers in their own community of origin;
- curriculum reform toward locally relevant subjects;
- affordable teaching materials and textbooks;
- use of mother tongue as the language of instruction;
- the use of schools as community learning centres;
- evaluation based on an action-research-action paradigm;
- management/statistical information systems in planning, evaluation, etc.

The resounding success of the EFA 2000 Assessment exercise, in which virtually all the countries of sub-Saharan Africa participated, also demonstrates the potential for partnership between Africa-based organisations, institutions and experts. We shall apply a critical analysis of past successes and failures to the formulation of our future strategies.

We are more convinced than ever that education is the *sine qua non* for empowering the people of Africa to participate in and benefit more effectively from the opportunities available in the globalized economy of the twenty-first century. Our optimism reflects the recent political progress and increased investment in education in parts of Africa and the opportunities offered by new information and communication technologies. With its nation-wide infrastructure and staff specialized in teaching and the design of teaching-learning materials, the education sector shall also address the urgent social issues as HIV/AIDS and violence that are threatening our progress and prospects.

Reflecting on the ten years since the Jomtien Declaration and the four years since the Amman Mid-Term Review, we realize, however, that a fundamental paradigm shift and an ever greater investment in education are essential for achieving our vision of the African Renaissance.

The above being the case, we, Ministers of Education, representatives of civil society and international development agencies:

Reaffirm that education is a basic right and a basic need for all African children, youth and adults, including those with disabilities, as recognized in the international instruments, including the Universal Declaration of Human Rights, the African Charter on Human and Peoples' Rights, the Convention on the Rights of the Child and the recommendations of the Salamanca Conference;

Recognize that investment in quality education is a prerequisite for the empowerment of Africans to fully participate in and benefit from a globalized economy and modern communications technology;

Acknowledge that the provision of basic education must be transformed for inclusiveness, relevance and gender responsiveness and that efforts to improve the participation of girls and women in education, including affirmative action, must be intensified;

Commit ourselves to removing all barriers (social, cultural, economic, political and legal) that hinder African children, youth and adults from having access to quality education and the attainment of the goals of the Jomtien Declaration on Education for All;

Recognize that the HIV/AIDS pandemic, increased poverty, war and civil strife are major hindrances to the achievement of EFA goals, and thus must be taken as priority areas of focus in the region;

Recognize the necessity of education systems to provide all African people with the opportunity to acquire the skills and knowledge essential for access and use of information and communication technology;

Recognize that African indigenous knowledge systems, languages and values should be the foundation for the development of African education systems; and

Recognize the necessity for curriculum transformation to give children, youth and adults the type of quality education that promotes appreciation of diversity, richness and dynamism of our cultures, with a goal to liberate us from psychological, economic and technological dependency.

Having sharpened our vision by this insight, we shall design our policies and programmes, and mobilization partnerships and resources for the realization of African Renaissance in the twenty-first century.

2. The New Vision of African Renaissance

We envision the resurgence of a vibrant Africa, rich in its cultural diversity, history, language and arts, standing united to end its marginalization in world progress and development. A democratic Africa, triumphant over colonialism, apartheid and oppression. A peaceful Africa, having beaten its swords into ploughshares, and respecting the human rights of all, irrespective of colour, gender, ethnicity, religion or abilities. An enlightened Africa, victorious in its struggle for the liberation of the mind. A prosperous Africa, where the knowledge and the skills of its people are its foremost resource. We envision Africa finally integrated in its political, economic and social systems, in pursuit of peace, justice, prosperity and a better life for all.

Our vision seeks, not a nostalgic return to pre-colonialism, but an advance of our cultural heritage. The values that unite us and the knowledge of our own environment, combined with modern management, social and physical sciences and technology, shall be applied to solving the chronic problems of poverty, disease, famine, conflict, misrule and corruption.

Education shall prepare people to take control of their own destiny, liberating them from dependency and endowing them with initiative, creativity, critical thinking, enterprise democratic values, pride and appreciation of diversity. The new Africa will respect the human rights of each individual and demand good governance and accountability. A new social cohesion will resist the forces of violence and division. Access to education will no longer be affected by gender, colour, tribe, ethnic origin, social status, physical and mental ability, religious persuasion or political belief.

It shall be the collective responsibility of government, civil society and development partners at all levels to create dynamic learning organisations, with a clear mission for social, economic and cultural development. The education and training sector shall become an integrated system managing knowledge and human resources development.

Toward the realization of this vision, we are working co-operatively in the area of education. We are cementing African unity and engaging in a continental offensive for African social, economic and cultural development—in short, for African Renaissance.

3. Priority Areas of Focus

Education systems shall provide lifelong learning opportunities to all, focusing on the learner and the learning process. Safe and inspiring learning environments will enable families and individuals to develop their critical thinking and creativity and realize their full potential. The major areas of focus are access and equity, quality and relevance, capacity building and partnerships.

3.1 Improving Access and Equity

- review and develop educational and other policies and legislation within the framework of the African renaissance;
- mobilize resources for restructuring and reallocation of government finances with a view to strengthening basic education;
- develop closer co-operation between central and local government, schools, communities and families to facilitate school ownership, sustainability and accessibility;
- pay special attention to street and working children, nomadic communities, children in remote environments and areas of conflict, minority groups, HIV/AIDS orphans, child prisoners and disabled children;
- expand the provision of early childhood education to all children of the appropriate age;
- develop alternative, non-formal strategies to reach disadvantaged children, youth and adults, and others such as refugees and internally displaced people who are excluded from normal educational opportunities;
- ensure the equal participation of girls and women in all education programmes, including science and technology;
- reduce gender, regional, rural/urban and socio-economic disparities in educational participation.

3.2 Improving the Quality and Relevance of Education

Only a small proportion of children are reaching the minimum required competencies and our education systems are not performing to the standards we expect of them. To address this situation, we shall:

- review and redesign curricula and teaching methods accordingly to make them relevant to the cultural environment and to the educational, psychological and socio-economic needs of the children;

- pay special attention to the life skills needed for coping with such problems as the HIV/AIDS pandemic, children with special needs, people in areas of chronic conflicts and the abuse of drugs;
- improve teacher education and training to enhance competence in participatory, inclusive and gender-sensitive approaches and the use of new technologies;
- validate and apply home-based, traditional approaches to child care in parental guidance and teacher training, reinforcing the principle that learning starts at birth;
- promote the use of the mother tongue in the early childhood education, early years of primary education and adult education; link personal development to the learners' cultural heritage and strengthen their self-confidence;
- improve the development, production and distribution of learning materials that are affordable and more suitable to local conditions;
- undertake research and develop the use of local alternatives to imported manufacturing inputs for the design and production of cost-effective textbooks and learning materials;
- define minimum and basic competencies for the different levels of education;
- develop reliable education management/statistical information systems in order to improve analysis and decision making;
- develop gender–and rights–responsive educational research;
- link formal and non-formal education for mainstreaming the marginalized groups into a lifelong learning system;
- integrate education into the family, community and the workplace;

- introduce democratic values and practices into the conduct of teaching and learning.

3.3 Institutional and Professional Capacity-Building

Institutional and professional capacity for greater efficiency, effectiveness and gender friendliness shall be strengthened at regional, national and local levels. For this purpose, we shall:

- give priority to the social, cultural and economic development of Africa in the design of policies, strategies and programmes;
- assure basic rights to food, shelter, security and health to enable African children to participate fully in education;
- create a supportive policy environment to ensure the inclusion of all in education programmes;
- mobilize existing and new financial and human resources for ensuring the provision of basic education for all;
- develop gender-responsive programmes and child-friendly learning environments for ensuring the full participation of the girl child in education;
- develop institutional capacity and human resources in the areas of statistical and management information systems and research for informed policy formulation, implementation and evaluation;
- involve teachers' unions and teachers in the development of the teaching profession;
- develop institutional and human capacity and curriculum to prevent and manage the HIV/AIDS pandemic and its impact on education.

3.4 Improving Partnership

We recognize that governments have the principal responsibility for ensuring adequate financing of basic education. Included in this responsibility is the leadership that government shall play in facilitating partnership at all levels with civil society, agencies, the private sector, NGOs, religious groups, communities, parents and teachers' associations, teachers' trade unions, families. We seek partnership with stakeholders, not simply in cost sharing, but for the whole education process, including decision-making, management and teaching. Toward this new form of partnership, we shall:

- develop a policy framework for enhancing collaboration between ministries, NGOs, civil society and others;
- jointly plan, monitor and facilitate aid co-ordination toward country leadership, ownership and implementation;
- share knowledge, information, technical know-how and other resources;
- take measures to build mutual confidence, respect and accountability;
- involve the media and other stakeholders in public discourse on education, social and development issues and in reaching out-of-school youth and adults;
- apply aid strategies for eliminating the dependency on aid in the long term, putting more emphasis on local capacity-building and reliance on indigenous solutions;
- create a mechanism of management and co-ordination of partnership, by legislation and consultative and awareness-raising meetings;
- Involve the stakeholders in building the minimum critical infrastructures for decentralization of implementation and management at various levels;
- for countries in conflict, channel assistance to education through operational United Nations Agencies and NGOs;
- collaborate in developing adequate data-collection and information systems to help in assessing the status and trends within the respective education sub-sectors.

4. Strategy

Based on this new form of partnership, we shall forge goal-oriented alliances of stakeholders and focus on building capacity and transforming systems to meet the learning needs of the people and the developmental goals of the community, country and region.

4.1 Strategic Objectives

Our strategic objectives are the five themes of the conference:

1. Transforming education for national and regional development goals with specific reference to social, cultural and economic and technological development.
2. Transforming curriculum content and improving relevance, quality and teaching methodologies with the needs of learners in focus.
3. Transforming the role of the state and education system structures and functions for facilitating active participation of stakeholders in the lifelong learning processes.
4. Building capacity in educational leadership, management, research and information systems.
5. Strengthening partnerships with NGOs, civil society and development partners at community, national, regional and international levels.

We shall convene stakeholders and form consultative councils to address these objectives and to develop strategies for achieving them.

4.2 Basic Strategies

In order to achieve the goals articulated in the Johannesburg Declaration, we shall review our education systems with reference to the five strategic objectives and to the following EFA target dimensions:

- expansion of quality early childhood education and development;
- increasing universal access to, and completion of, primary (basic) education;
- improvement in learning achievement;

- promoting gender equity and enhancement of the education of girls and women;
- reducing adult illiteracy;
- expanding basic education and skills training for out-of-school children;
- developing HIV/AIDS education programmes and response mechanisms;
- improving management and governance.

In formulating country-specific strategies, we shall be guided by the following general strategies that we have adopted:

4.2.1 A Review and Harmonization of Existing Policies and Legislation

Special attention shall be devoted to the rights of disadvantaged groups, including girls and women, ethnic minorities, the disabled, those affected by the HIV/AIDS pandemic and those in specially difficult circumstances in other ways.

Formal, non-formal and informal learning opportunities shall be linked in order to create a 'culture of lifelong learning' that promotes social integration.

4.2.2 An Increase in the Financing and Rationalization of Investment in Education

The principal responsibility for financing education remains with the governments, for which we shall endeavour to devote additional funds, as well as mobilizing endogenous and private-sector resources. By improving the quality of education and the efficiency of education systems, we shall also enhance cost effectiveness.

4.2.3 Development of National, Sub-Regional and Regional Institutional Capacities

We shall enhance our capacity to achieve the EFA goals by effecting institutional reforms and appropriate training programmes, focusing on leadership, strategic resource planning, information management and policy research. By sharing existing regional institutions, expertise, methodologies, and information, we shall ensure feasibility, sustainability and cost-effectiveness.

4.2.4 A Review of Curricula and Validation of African Indigenous Knowledge Systems, Values and Skills

The development of appropriate curricula shall incorporate value systems founded on indigenous languages and knowledge systems, as well as new knowledge, information and technology. New ways shall be found to link the formal, non-formal and informal learning opportunities in order to create a 'culture of lifelong learning' for all, with the aim to promote social integration.

4.2.5 The Improvement of Capacities for Educational Change

Effectiveness in implementing planned changes as well as responding to crisis and managing adjustment require both political consensus and professional competence. In order to enhance capacity for innovation, sensitivity to disparities and flexible responsiveness to changing needs, we shall include the intended implementers and beneficiaries in policy-review and management committees at the respective levels of implementation. To avoid entrenchment of status quo and to broaden the perspectives, the most disadvantaged groups shall be represented, if not directly, then by civil society organisations advocating their cause.

Equally, if not more, important is the capacity to implement the necessary changes. Hence, we shall develop the capacities of the implementing individuals and organisations. The urgent starting point is the level of the teaching-learning process, for example, in the school and the classroom, for this is where most of the intended changes had failed to take place. With this focus, we shall improve professional development of teaching staff, develop school management systems, create a more gender-sensitive and conducive environment for their work, etc.

4.2.6 Improvement of the Teaching and Learning Environment

Urgent attention shall be devoted to the development of materials, methodologies and social learning environments that are feasible and sustainable in the local environment and relevant to the African learner, particularly in respect of girl child and the disabled. We shall develop a learning environment that is safe and intellectually stimulating, and a pedagogy based on learner-centered approach and democratic values and practices in the teaching-learning interaction.

4.2.7 The Adoption of Appropriate and Cost-effective Technologies

New, appropriate and cost-effective technologies shall be adopted, to complement the integration of indigenous educational methodologies. Dependence on imported materials and technology, requiring an ever-increasing supply of scarce hard currency, is not viable and shall be reduced as rapidly as possible. To start with, R & D investment shall be intensified for the development of locally available alternatives to imported paper, books, etc., while import duties on paper and other materials required for domestic book publishing are eliminated. The use of the oral tradition, more effective in appropriate contexts, shall be explored and systematized for teacher training and other education and training applications.

4.2.8 The Promotion and Support of Africa-based Educational Research

Education policies must be anchored to African reality. We shall, therefore, strengthen research on the priority areas in Africa. Research shall be conducted in the language and the environment of the target groups. It shall identify, analyse and solve problems that provoke, for example, exclusion on whatever basis (gender, physical or other handicaps, language, status, race, etc.) relating to culture, educational policies and structures, curriculum and teaching practices. As lack of relevant data continues to be a major problem, those responsible for education research and statistics shall jointly elaborate strategies for research and statistics based on the recommendations of the Johannesburg Conference and submit their report to the national EFA consultative council.

4.2.9 The Development of Genuine and Sustainable Partnerships

Partnerships between all stakeholders shall be built on the principles of trust, accountability and transparency. Governments, however, shall take full responsibility for providing primary education and leadership in facilitating participation of the stakeholders in education as partners. Common goals, consensus on strategies, co-ordination and working relationships shall be established through the national EFA consultative councils and the technical working groups.

5. Target Setting

Based on this framework, each country team shall set goals, strategies and action plans in accordance with the national assessment, using the following guidelines.

5.1 Expansion of Quality, Early Childhood Education and Development

Ensure that Early Childhood Development (ECD) programmes are expanded two-fold by the year 2006, and that they offer safe, secure and stimulating environments. Countries should work towards providing access to ECD programmes to all children from ages 3 to 6 by the year 2015.

5.2 Increasing Universal Access and Completion of Primary (Basic) Education

Ensure that all school-age children have access to quality primary education by the year 2015. At least 80 per cent of those who enrol should complete primary education and at least 90 per cent of these should proceed to secondary level.

5.3 Improvement in Learning Achievement

Ensure that by the year 2015, all teachers have received initial training, and that in-service training programmes are operational. Training should emphasize child-centered approaches and rights and gender-based teaching. Mechanisms should be put into place for carrying out national assessments of learning achievement. All children should master the minimum competencies in language, mathematics and science.

5.4 Enhancement of Education of Girls and Women

Increase the admission, completion and transition rates of girls to equal those of boys. Remove legislative hindrances to the participation of girls and women in education. Create safe learning environments for girls and women, inside and outside school, and institutionalize affirmative action to enhance their access to education, especially in Maths and Sciences. Conduct gender awareness campaigns and training for parents, teachers and education managers.

5.5 Reduction of Adult Illiteracy

Reduce illiteracy rates by at least 50 per cent, by consolidating adult literacy and continuing education as part of lifelong learning. Develop high-quality curricula, teaching methodologies and instructional materials.

5.6 Expansion of Basic Education and Skill Training for out-of-school Learners

Conduct studies within the next two years into the situation of out-of-school children and assess their learning needs in relation to gender, age and community context. Based on the findings of these studies, design and introduce innovative and sustainable non-formal education programmes. Ensure co-operation between education providers and ministries of education in harmonizing programmes and bridging the gap between formal and non-formal education.

5.7 Putting HIV/AIDS Education Programmes and Response Mechanisms into Place

AIDS is no longer simply a public health problem. In many African countries, it constitutes a rapidly growing obstacle to development. Teacher training and recruitment must be accelerated to balance personnel losses. Systems must be developed for keeping the increasing number of orphans in school, and solutions found for their long-term care and development.

Life skills and HIV/AIDS education shall be strengthened or introduced in all education programmes. Working partnerships shall be forged with the media, religious organisations, civil society and communities, to build consensus on implementing HIV/AIDS curriculum and develop effective and viable strategies to fight the HIV/AIDS pandemic.

In collaboration with other ministries and stakeholders, the education sector shall take a leading role in AIDS campaigns, and urge men, including those in the teaching profession, to respect women's dignity and the right to protect themselves.

5.8 Improving Management Governance

The development of quality education must be supported by effective management at all levels. Current practices shall be evaluated and transformed to reflect the new vision of education. Make effective use of new communication and information technologies. Decentralize education management and governance, by building the necessary capacity at the level of implementation, for facilitating the participation of other education providers, parents, communities and learners, so as to guarantee responsiveness to changing needs. Produce a strategic plan on management and governance of the new structure and functions at various levels in accordance with the new principles of partnership.

5.9 Increasing Budgetary Allocation to Education

The implementation of the Framework for Action will depend on the mobilization of additional resources and the rationalization of budgetary allocations to education. Governments should ensure that at least 7 per cent of GDP is allocated to education within five years and 9 per cent within ten years. International agencies should aim to double their financial support, especially for capacity building and management development.

5.10 Institutionalizing the Assessment and Monitoring Functions of the EFA Team

Existing co-ordination teams and consultative structures shall be strengthened in order to monitor progress in implementing the goals of the new vision. Regional Technical Advisory Groups will be transformed into a Regional EFA

Consultative Council, consisting of regional-level partners in education, which will integrate the thematic commissions and technical working groups as sub-structures. These are composed of specialists in the areas of research, statistics, administration, finance, inspection, etc. from various departments, institutions and agencies.

As a target and a benchmark, the first task is to produce, by the end of year 2000, a consensus-based work plan for regular assessment and monitoring of the implementation of the EFA Framework of Action.

6. Agenda of the Alliance for African Renaissance

Having adopted a common vision, we propose an Alliance for African Renaissance, for we are convinced that united we constitute a powerful force capable of achieving the paradigm shift and the investment in education that are required for the envisioned transformation. To this end, we shall jointly plan and co-ordinate our strategies, activities our competence and resources.

We are keenly aware that, for the Alliance to be effective, members must adhere to the principles of membership and assume collective responsibility. As partners in this alliance, we shall strive to meet the responsibilities in our respective domains.

6.1 African Governments shall

- end armed conflicts, ensure security, nurture a culture of peace and re-direct military budget, demobilized soldiers, arms equipment and other assets to constructive use, such as occupational training, adult literacy programmes, school repair and construction, public transport, water management and irrigation, etc.
- promote enlightened, participatory, transparent and accountable governance, and prosecute corruption in all its forms, at every level of government and civil society;
- concentrate resources on teaching-learning processes and delivery systems that enhance efficiency, cost-effectiveness and resource-and cost-sharing;

- invest more resources on basic education by an amount necessary for making a significant impact on quantity and quality;
- ensure that savings from debt reduction are invested in education and the social sector for the betterment of heretofore marginalized and excluded children, youth and adults;
- take the leading role in mobilizing resources, setting standards and facilitating participation of stakeholders in education, including communities, civil society, the private sector and development partners;
- ensure that policies and the legislation are inclusive and supportive of quality education for all;
- create an enabling environment, including affirmative action, for full participation of women in educational leadership;
- develop institutional capacity for strategic resource planning, monitoring and implementation of the Framework for Action; and
- remove legal, administrative and tax constraints hindering the publishing industry and promote indigenous publishers by eliminating custom duties on paper and other required materials.

6.2 Regional and Sub-regional Institutions shall

- establish a Regional EFA Consultative Council, supported by thematic commissions and technical working groups, assimilating the monitoring and evaluation functions of the Regional Technical Advisory Groups;
- give education top priority for the next decade in terms of policy, programmes and activities;
- provide effective leadership in the implementation of regional educational programmes as well as strengthening sub-regional and regional co-operation;
- promote synergies and facilitate the emergence of sub-regional and regional learning institutions, with

integrated educational programmes, information and resource sharing in such areas as development textbooks in indigenous languages, science and technology;

- facilitate regional co-operation of institutions and networks of experts in joint programmes to build capacity in education leadership, management, strategic resource planning, policy research, and statistical information systems;
- promote good governance and prosecute corruption within our own institutions as well as in the wider society;
- take measures to prevent and reduce arms trade and illegal trade in strategic minerals, gold and diamonds which the warring parties are using to finance wars.

6.3 Civil Society, Including NGOs, the Private Sector and Religious Bodies, shall

- re-focus on community empowerment to alleviate poverty and strengthen community participation in education;
- participate in and contribute to education in various ways, such as defining and monitoring relevance and quality, and providing volunteer services;
- advocate the inclusion of the marginalized groups, especially those who are poor and powerless, such as orphans, the disabled and incarcerated, refugees and internally displaced people;
- promote good governance and condemn corruption;
- promote genuine partnerships with other stakeholders in a mutually acceptable manner for the benefit of African children and adult learners through improved management capacities to meet new challenges and responsibilities;
- support government and community efforts in promoting sustainable development through fostering quality education for all;

- increase involvement in campaigns for public awareness, such as HIV/AIDS, as well as for public pressure, such as the reduction of armed conflict.

6.4 African and International Media shall

- popularize and publicize the new vision of African education by developing quality basic education that is holistic, humanizing and transformative, and embedded in African values and indigenous knowledge systems;
- participate in discussions, research, monitoring and mobilization of resources for the development of quality basic education for all;
- develop strategies to inform and educate Africans on issues affecting the development of the continent in general and education in particular, including HIV/AIDS education girls' education, ethnic and social conflicts, and the validation of the African value system and indigenous knowledge;
- provide a forum for public discourse and exchange of views for all stakeholders in education—students, parents, communities, civil society as well as government;
- provide alternative delivery systems for education materials and methods.

6.5 International and Bilateral Agencies shall

- work in partnership with African governments and civil society to enhance the achievement of EFA, through the development of policies and strategies aimed at abolishing, rather than simply reducing, national debt;
- ensure that savings from debt reduction are invested in education and the social sector, and that the highly indebted poor countries (HIPC) initiative is used for the betterment of African children, youth, and adult illiterates, especially targeting the hitherto marginalized or excluded;
- work with African governments and other partners to assess the side effects of SAPs, and other development programmes, on education;

- promote better co-ordination between agencies to improve the coherence of programmes and to avoid duplication, cross-purposes and inefficiency in resource allocation and utilization;
- support the building of Africa's capacity to find its own solutions and political responses, by according priority to locally and regionally based experts, institutions, organisations and education-related initiatives;
- intensify investment in R & D capacity in Africa for developing affordable alternatives to imported paper and books; the pharmaceutical industry for producing affordable medicine to treat HIV/AIDS and tropical diseases; renewable energy for providing electricity; access to Internet for communication and information; and water control, management and purification;
- support and participate in the national and regional EFA consultative councils and support regional partnerships such as the ADEA and the education programmes of such African regional organizations as OAU, ECOWAS, SADC, etc.;
- increase financial and technical support to education in Africa so that it is at least double the current level by 2015; and
- promote the reduction of arms trading and of the illegal trade in strategic minerals as a means of financing wars by the warring parties.

7. Follow-up Timetable

Each country shall draw its own plan of action for achieving EFA goals. The country teams shall review the problems, priorities and mandates of partners and establish a timetable of activities. The following schedule suggests a methodology for starting the process of implementation of this Framework of Action:

7.1 National dissemination and review of the Johannesburg and Dakar Declarations and Frameworks of Action as a Starting point of consensus building and strategic planning.

7.2 National government and other partners disseminate and review their National EFA 2000 Assessment Report after the Dakar meeting and in partnership set specific country goals, targets and strategies.

7.3 National governments and partners complete and update their plans of action to meet defined EFA goals and develop modalities of implementation and monitoring of the activities indentified .

7.4 United Nations and other international agencies review their policies and plans of action to harmonize them with the Johannesburg and Dakar Declarations and Frameworks of Action. Make commitment to supporting country initiatives in EFA and put into place implementation programme.

7.5 Put country co-ordination and implementing teams into place. Refine short and long term implementation plans and set specific benchmarks and indicators for monitoring and evaluation. Start implementation (first three months after Dakar).

8. Conclusion

Guided and supported by our joint commitment, courage, hope and creativity, education in the new African millennium will never be the same again. Education shall be the strategic medium for attaining African Renaissance in the globalized economy, culture and communication in the twenty-first century.

REFERENCES

1. Using United Nations' population estimates, net enrolment of boys increased by 10 per cent to 67 per cent and girls by 8 per cent to 58 per cent in 1998. The difference is due to the assumed population growth rates used in the inter-census projections. The United Nations' estimates are generally lower than the countries' own estimations, in the case of the net enrolment, by nearly 10 per cent for boys and girls respectively.

2. The lower enrolment of boys in this region is due to differences in opportunity costs in countries where mining industries recruit largely uneducated male labour.

Appendix—4

EDUCATION FOR ALL IN THE AMERICAS: REGIONAL FRAMEWORK OF ACTION

Adopted by the Regional Meeting on Education for All in the Americas, Santo Domingo, Dominican Republic, 10—12 February 2000

Preface

Ten years after the World Conference on Education for All (Jomtien, Thailand, 1990) the countries of Latin America, the Caribbean and North America assessed progress made within the region in terms of achieving the objectives and goals outlined in Jomtien. Meeting in Santo Domingo, 10-12 February 2000, the countries agreed to the present *Regional Framework of Action* in which they renewed their commitments to Education for All for the next fifteen years.

The countries of the region base their proposals and actions upon the recognition of the universal right of everyone to high-quality basic education from birth.

This *Regional Framework of Action* ratifies and lends continuity to the efforts by countries during the past decade to achieve ever-higher levels of education for their peoples as attested in numerous international, regional and sub-regional meetings.[1] In these meetings as well as in the actions that countries have carried out, we see them put into practice the conviction that education is the key to sustainable human development. For education stimulates the broadening of opportunities for quality education and promotes in citizens an awareness of their rights and responsibilities.

The *Regional Framework of Action* seeks to fulfil still-pending commitments of the past decade: to eliminate the inequalities that persist in education and to see to it that everyone has access to basic education that prepares them to be active participants in development.

This diversity of situations among countries and the heterogeneity of conditions within them make it difficult to formulate homogeneous strategies aimed at reaching objectives and fulfilling commitments agreed upon by all. This means that countries must convert regional commitments into national goals, according to their own capabilities. Nevertheless, within this diversity there is a common denominator of poverty, inequality and exclusion that affects a large proportion of families in the region, who lack educational opportunities to aid their development and that of their communities. From this arises the countries' shared commitment to give priority to these individuals through differentiated strategies and focuses.

In this *Regional Framework of Action*, countries within the region commit themselves to establish national level mechanisms for public policy co-operation that express the shared responsibilities of government, the private sector and society in general to define and attain specific goals. They also commit themselves to periodic, open review of their actions. Increasingly, the new millennium demands that education, which is a right of all, be the object of State policies that are stable, long-range, arrived at through consensus and backed by the commitment of all members of society. For this reason, processes must be developed that are buttressed by information and by communication, establishing partnerships with all media involved in producing them.

The *Regional Framework of Action* also calls upon organisations of international co-operation to contribute to overcoming intra-regional disparities by giving priority to the efforts of countries that face the greatest challenges in reaching their goals.

I. Achievements and Pending Subjects

The *Regional Framework of Action* seeks to consolidate the major achievements of Education for All attained within the region during the decade of the 1990s. On the regional level these include:

- Substantial increases in early childhood care and education, particularly for the 4-6 year old age-group.
- Significant increases in the availability of schooling and access of nearly all children to primary education.

- An increase in the number of years of compulsory education.
- A relative decrease in illiteracy, without having achieved the goal of diminishing the 1990 rate by one-half.
- Priority given to quality as an objective of education policies.
- Growing concern for the theme of equity and attention to diversity in education policies.
- A progressive inclusion of education for life themes in both formal and non-formal courses.
- Participation of diverse actors such as non-government organisations, parents and others in school life.
- Consensus regarding education as a national and regional priority.

This *Framework* recognizes that, in spite of these achievements, a number of subjects that merit the attention of countries in the region are still pending. Among these are:

- Inadequate attention to comprehensive early childhood development, especially for children under four years of age.
- High rates of repetition and drop-out in primary school, resulting in a high number of over-age children within grades and of others outside school.
- Low priority for literacy training and education of young people and of adults in national policies and strategies.
- Low levels of student learning.
- Little attention to teacher training and professional enhancement.
- Persistent inequalities in the distribution, efficiency and quality of education services.
- Inadequate interface among different actors involved in Education for All.

- Lack of efficient mechanisms for the formulation of state education policies in co-operation with those outside of government.
- Small increases in resources allocated to education and inefficient use of those that are available.
- Insufficient availability and use of information and communication technologies.

II. Challenges Recognized in the Regional Framework of Action

Subjects still pending present challenges that the countries of the region have decided to confront in the coming years. They will do so using the common denominator of the search for equity and equality of opportunity, for quality education and for the sharing of responsibilities by all of society.

The challenges are the following:

- To increase social investment in early childhood care, increasing access to early childhood development programmes and improving coverage of early education programmes.
- To guarantee access and retention of all boys' and girls' basic education programmes, substantially reducing grade repetition, school drop-out and over-age students in grades.
- To assure access to quality education to the entire population with special attention to vulnerable social groups.
- To give greater priority to literacy training and education of young people and of adults as part of national education systems, improving existing programmes and to create alternatives for all young people and adults, especially those at risk.
- To continue to improve the quality of basic education, giving priority to the school and the classroom as

learning environment, recognizing the social value of the teacher and improving assessment systems.

- To formulate inclusive education policies and to design diversified curricula and education delivery systems in order to serve the population excluded for reasons of gender, language, culture, or individual differences.
- To assure that schools encourage health, the exercise of citizenship, and basic life skills training.
- To increase and reallocate resources using criteria of equity and efficiency, as well as to mobilize other resources with alternative delivery systems.
- To offer high levels of professional enhancement to teachers and career development policies that improve the quality of their lives and the conditions of their work.
- To create necessary framework, so that education becomes a task for all, and that guarantee popular participation in the formulation of state policies and transparency in policy administration.
- To co-ordinate education policies that encourage multi-sector actions aimed at overcoming poverty and directed to populations at risk.
- To adopt and strengthen the use of information and communication technologies in the management of education systems and in teaching and learning processes.
- To promote school-based management, granting individual school autonomy with broad citizen participation.
- To strengthen management capacity at local, regional and national levels.

Considering past achievements, pending subjects and challenges, the countries, through this *Regional Framework of Action*, make the following commitments:

III. Commitments of the Regional Framework of Action

1. Early Childhood Care and Education

Considering that:

- A sustained increase of resources for comprehensive early childhood care and development is essential in order to guarantee the rights of citizenship from birth, to assure better learning outcomes in the future, and to reduce educational and social inequalities;
- For this period of life, it is extremely important that pjint actions be undertaken by institutions that offer services in health, nutrition, education and family well-being. It is important that these services be directed toward families and the community, and that they offer literacy training and adult education as well;
- Communication strategies and key, both for education programmes directed at families and in order to establish and strengthen the links among governmental authorities, policy-makers and communities.

The countries pledge to:

- Increase investment in and access to comprehensive early childhood development programmes for children less than 4 years of age. The focus should be centered on the family and give special attention to those who are most at risk;
- Maintain past achievements and increase early childhood education for children 4 years and older, particularly for less advantaged children. Strategies should be centred on the family, the community, or specialized centres;
- Improve the quality of comprehensive early childhood development programme by:
  - — strengthening comprehensive, continuous and high quality training and support programmes for

families and for others who contribute to health, nutrition, and growth during early childhood;

— strengthening monitoring and assessment of early childhood services and programmes, as well as to establish national standards that are flexible, agreed upon, and sensitive to diversity;

— establishing co-operative mechanisms between institutions that offer services and programmes related to the survival and the development of children under 6 years of age;

— better use of communication technologies and media in order to reach families who live in remote areas that are of difficult access for institutionalized programmes.

2. Basic Education

Considering that:

- By *'basic education'* we refer to satisfying learning-for-life needs. These include knowledge, skills, values and attitudes that permit people to
  - — develop their abilities
  - — live and work with dignity
  - — fully participate in the development and improvement of their quality of life
  - — make decisions with access to adequate information, and
  - — continue to learn throughout life.
- Basic learning occurs from birth, and is attained by children, adolescents and adults through strategies that meet the different needs of each age group.
- The empowerment of learners, the promotion of their participation and shared responsibility with families, communities and schools are basic conditions for sustaining past achievements/accomplishments and for facing new challenges.

The Countries Pledge to:

- Maintain and increase access to basic education already achieved, assuring that it will not diminish during emergency situations caused by natural disasters or due to serious deterioration of economic and social conditions;
- Identify groups still excluded from access to basic education for reasons of gender, geographical location, culture or individual differences, and to design and implement flexible and appropriate programmes involving diverse sectors that respond to their specific conditions and needs;
- Give priority to policies and strategies aimed at decreasing repetition and drop-out, assuring permanence, progress and success of boys and girls and of adolescents in basic education systems and programmes until they complete the basic levels required in each country.

3. Satisfying Basic Learning Needs of Young People and of Adults

Considering that:

- Over the years the region has developed its own programmes and rich experiences in the area of popular education and the education of young people and of adults;
- The demands and agreements of international conferences offer new prospects for regional action in the area of education of young people and of adults;
- Providing educational opportunities for young people and adults demands that actions be co-ordinated between social actors and those who work in the fields of health, labour and the environment.

The Countries Pledge to:

- Incorporate the education of young people and of adults into national education systems and give priority to these age-groups in education reforms carried out as part of the key responsibility of governments in the basic education of their peoples.

- Improve and diversify education programmes by:
  - giving priority to groups that are excluded and at risk,
  - guaranteeing and consolidating literacy training,
  - giving priority to the acquisition of basic life skills and encouraging full use of the rights of citizenship,
  - linking parenting education with early childhood care and education,
  - utilizing formal and non-formal quality systems,
  - associating the education of young people and of adults with productive activities and labour, and
  - recognizing previous experience as valid learning for academic credits.
- Define the roles and responsibilities of governments and of society as a whole in this field, as well as stimulate greater participation of society in the formulation of public policies and in the definition of strategies linked to programmes and actions.

4. Learning Achievements and Quality of Education

Considering that:

- The quality of results is a key factor in contributing to retaining children in school and in guaranteeing the social and economic payoffs of basic education;
- Determining learning achievement requires establishing quality standards and permanent process of monitoring and assessment;
- Systems for measuring quality should take into consideration the diversity of individual and group conditions in order to avoid the exclusion from school of children living in high-risk situations.

The Countries Pledge to:

- Continue to move forward with processes of curricular reform and to strengthen curricula by including within its life skills, values and attitudes that encourage families to keep their children in school and that provide people with the necessary instruments to overcome poverty and to improve the quality of life of families and communities;
- Reserve a special place within quality improvement strategies for the school and for the classroom as learning environments characterized by:
  - — the recognition of diversity and heterogeneity of students and of flexibility that responds adequately to their special learning needs;
  - — the encouragement of teamwork on the part of school directors and teachers;
  - — normative frameworks that put into practice the rights of children and adolescents to participate, together with their teachers, parents and the community; and
  - — skill development for autonomous school management and responsibility for processes and results;
- Recognize the social and professional value of teachers as essential actors within quality education by establishing agreed-upon policies for certification, improvement of working conditions, remuneration and incentives for continuing improvement of professional skills;
- Provide books and other didactic and technological resources in order to improve student learning;
- Organize appropriate systems of monitoring and assessment that take into consideration individual and cultural differences, that are based on agreed-upon national and regional standards and that make possible participation in international studies;

- Stimulate on-going action of the media in order to support student learning.

5. Inclusive Education

Considering that:

- Basic education for all requires assuring access, permanence, quality learning, and full participation and integration of all children and adolescents, particularly for members of indigenous groups, those with disabilities, those who are homeless, those who are workers, those living with HIV/AIDS and others;
- Protection against discrimination based on culture, language, social group, gender or individual differences is an inalienable human right that must be respected and fostered by education systems.

The Countries Pledge to:

- Formulate inclusive education policies that define goals and priorities in accordance with different categories of excluded populations in each country, including establishing legal and institutional frameworks that will effectively make inclusion the responsibility of the entire society;
- Design diversified education delivery systems, flexible school curricula and new education environments within the community. These should value diversity, viewing it as a force for social development. They should preserve innovative experiences in formal and non-formal education in order to meet the needs of all boys and girls, adolescents, young people and adults;
- Promote and strengthen intercultural and bilingual education in multi-ethnic, multilingual societies;
- Implement a sustained process of communication, information and education within families that emphasizes the importance and the benefits for countries of educating those who are currently excluded.

6. Education for Life

Considering that:

- Education should provide skills for living and for developing
  - — a culture of the respect for law;
  - — the exercise of citizenship and democratic life;
  - — peace and non-discrimination;
  - — the development of civic and ethical values;
  - — sexuality;
  - — the prevention of drug and alcohol abuse; and
  - — the preservation and care of the environment.
- The inclusion of this learning into either multidisciplinary or subject curricula presents a challenge to new curricula construction, for joint work with communities and for the role of the teacher as a life skills model.

The Countries Pledge to:

- Guarantee that the school be a learner-friendly environment, both physically and socially, one that favours healthy life-styles, the practices of life skills, and early exercise of citizenship and of democratic values, and that it provides opportunities for participation in decision regarding school life and learning;
- Establish flexible curricular norms that allow schools to integrate contents and meaningful experiences into the curriculum that are relevant to the community and that permit the school to interact with the community;
- Train teachers, parents, young people and adults so that they may promote and support this kind of learning in everyday life;
- Include specific indicators on this kind of learning in order to monitor and assess in within the school and to measure its impact on the lives of students;

- Stimulate and carry our activities in education for life developed by the media, by social organisations, NGOs, the private sector, political parties and others.

7. Increase of National Investment in Education and Effective Mobilization of Resources on All Levels

Considering that:

- The priority of education as a key instrument for development should be expressed by the commitment to gradually increase investment in the sector to at least 6 per cent of GDP in order to achieve universal coverage of basic education and to overcome current deficits;
- Systems of information and of assessment are key components in decision-making in education. Data must therefore be sought both on the education system and on its social, economic and cultural contexts. These guide the allocation of resources for the education of children, adolescents, young people and adults.

The Countries Pledge to:

- Develop focus strategies for the allocation of educational expenditures in order to diminish inequalities and to assist at-risk populations;
- Increase the allocation of resources for education based on the efficiency and efficacy of their use, and based upon criteria of equity and affirmative action;
- Establish mechanisms for establishing budgets and allocating resources that include broad social participation, that lend transparency and credibility to the management of resources and that guarantee accountability, for all of which adequate and timely information is of key importance;
- Use decentralization as an opportunity to optimize the use of existing resources and to promote the mobilization of new resources, particularly those coming from the private sector;

- Actively seek alternative mechanisms for financing education, such as public/private sharing and foreign debt/education swaps.

8. Professional Enhancement for Teachers

Considering that:

- Teachers occupy an irreplaceable position in transforming education, in changing teaching practices within the classroom, in the use of teaching and technological resources, in facilitating relevant and quality learning, and in the development of student values;
- The value that society attributes to teachers is associated with the improvement of their performance and their working and living conditions;
- The progressive incorporation of information and communication technologies into society requires that these subjects be included in initial and in-service teacher training;
- Rural schools and those serving at-risk populations require teachers with higher quality academic training and human relations skills.

The Countries Pledges to:

- Offer teachers high quality academic training that is linked to research and the ability to produce innovations, and that prepares them for carrying out their duties in diverse social, economic, cultural and technological contexts;
- Establish teacher career policies that
  - — permit them to improve their living and working conditions,
  - — stimulate the profession and provide incentives for talented young people to enter it,
  - — create incentives for teachers to pursue high levels of pedagogical and academic training,

— develop skills to accompany and facilitate lifelong learning,

— increase commitments with the community,

- Implement systems for assessing teacher performance and for measuring the quality and levels of achievement in the profession, following basic standards agreed upon by teachers' unions and other organisations;
- Establish normative frameworks and education policy in order to incorporate teachers into the management of changes in the education system and to encourage teamwork within the school.

9. New Opportunities for Participation of the Community and the Society

Considering that:

- There is a growing need on the part of many in society to exercise the right to participate in education decisions that affect them, as well as to assume the responsibilities that accompany such decisions;
- Public policies that require long-term stability and continuity are made through processes in which the state and society jointly participate;
- The great potential represented by various social sectors such as workers associations, unions, business groups, political parties, indigenous people, young people, women NGOs, community organisations, artistic and cultural groups, etc., is not sufficiently utilized.

The Countries Pledge to:

- Create normative, institutional and financial frameworks that:

  — create new opportunities for participation,

  — legitimize existing forums and

  — guarantee the participation of society in the elaboration, monitoring and assessment of education policies, and in the development of national plans and programmes in these areas;

- Create and strengthen channels for communication and consultation, facilitating the interface among different actors in education, whether governmental, private , or non-governmental.

10. Linking of Basic Education to Strategies for Overcoming Poverty and Inequality

Considering that:

- During the decade of the 1990s, countries within the region developed policies and programmes to promote basic education, seeking to make an impact on overcoming poverty and inequality through various measures;
- One must keep in mind past attempts to increase education opportunities that were linked to providing food, clothing, basic health services; to budgetary strategies of redistribution and targeting; to support measures for families through study grants and education activity carried out by leaders, institutions and/or community groups;
- Education, in order to have a more effective impact on overcoming poverty and inequality, must be part of more broad-based social policies and developed within a multi-sector strategic framework.

The Countries Pledge to:

- Bring together various activities designed to:
  - strengthen education within the ambit of social policies;
  - convert assistance policies into policies to promote the skills of people;
  - combine, at all levels, education policies and programmes with policies and programmes for generating employment, improving health and developing communities,

— include contents and values with education that promote solidarity and improvement of the quality of life.

- Guarantee equity in the distribution of both public and private resources for education and for social development, and assure greater efficiency in their utilization to benefit at-risk populations;
- Promote programmes for the support and accompaniment of children, adolescents, young people, and adults of poor families and those affected by social and economic inequalities in order to guarantee their basic education and full participation in the design, management, follow-up and assessment of such training;
- Improve living conditions for teachers themselves as a necessary condition for their professional growth.

11. Utilization of Technologies in Education

Considering that:

- The current technological revolution in information and communication has produced new ways for people and organisations to relate to one another. Education cannot remain outside of these changes. Increasingly, teachers assume the role of facilitator and mediator so that students may critically utilize these new technologies;
- These technologies should be included as a key factor in the improvement of processes and opportunities of teaching and learning;
- Information and communication technologies fulfil a crucial role in the administration, planning, management and follow-up of education policies and processes;
- These technologies, which are tools, should not be merely one more factor for exclusion and discrimination; on the contrary, they should be accessible to all students and teachers.

The Countries pledge to:

- Support use in the classroom of information and communication technologies;
- Promote permanent and equitable access to communication and information technologies to teachers and to communities as well as provide ongoing opportunities for training through information centres, better practices networks and other mechanisms for the dissemination and interchange of experiences;
- Adopt, and strengthen where currently in use, information and communication technologies in order to improve policy decision-making and planning of education systems and school administration. This will facilitate the processes of decentralization and autonomy of school management, and the training of administrators and teachers in the introduction and use of information and communication technologies;
- At the same time, re-emphasize the importance of books as key instruments for access to culture as a fundamental means of using the new technologies.

12. Management of Education

Considering that:

- The improvement of quality and equity of education is closely related to improvement in management at all levels of the education system;
- With increasing decentralization and greater participation of the school community, the role of school principals acquires broader and more complex dimensions;
- Information and assessment systems are vital for education policy decision-making.

The Countries Pledge to:

- Define administrative structures that consider the individual school as the basic unit, with managerial autonomy progressively generating mechanisms for citizen participation and establishing levels of responsibility for each actor in the management process, in the control of results and in accountability;

- Promote national and regional mechanisms that offer school principals and teachers professional training in school and curricular management, in the use of technology, and in values, attitudes and practices that foster transparency in education management;
- Develop systems for the collection of information, data analysis, research and innovations as tools in improve policy decision-making;
- Establish parameters that identify the responsibilities of personnel that work in the education system, as well as support mechanisms and policies for personnel administration;
- Improve systems for measuring results, assessment and accountability, adjusted to comparable indicators and standards, supported by assessment mechanisms that are outside the education system itself.

IV. A Call for International Co-operation

The countries of the region, upon assuming the above commitments:

- Call upon the international community and co-operation agencies to increase and perfect support mechanisms to countries in order to contribute to the fulfilment of goals established in this framework of Action and to assume a shared responsibility for their fulfilment, particularly in the support of countries facing the most critical problems;
- Agree to foster country-to-country co-operation for the exchange of lessons learned and of useful experiences for improving education;
- Appeal to international financing agencies to align their funding policies with the directions of national education policies and to increase the amount of

resources dedicated to education, especially in less-favoured countries;

- Call upon governments and societies to make every effort to co-operate in the development of policies, strategies and action plans that will give a new thrust to policies that guarantee to all people the right of access to basic, quality education and to reap its benefits.

REFERENCE

1. Since the 1980s at a number of forums, the countries have agreed upon goals and guidelines for regional action: the Major Project in the Field of Education for Latin America and the Caribbean; the Convention on the Rights of the Child; the Action Plan of the World Summit for Children; the World Conference on Special Needs Education (Salamanca, Spain); the Fifth International Conference on Adult Education; the Summits of the Americas; the Ibero-American Summits, and the meetings of Ministers of Education and of Ministers responsible for social areas and for early childhood.

Appendix—5

EDUCATION FOR ALL IN THE ARAB STATES: RENEWING THE COMMITMENT

The Arab Framework for Action to Ensure Basic Learning Needs in the Arab States in the Years 2000-2010

Adopted by the Regional Conference on Education for All for the Arab States Cairo, Egypt, 24–27 January 2000

Preamble

Based on the assessment of the efforts and achievements made in the Arab States as regards basic education. Education for All, since the Jomtien Conference (1990) until the end of the decade (the year 2000), in preparation for the International Forum on EFA (Dakar, April 2000).

According to:

— the Convention on the Rights of the Child, the World Declaration on Education for All, the Arab Document on Children, the Arab Plan for Childhood Care, Protection and Development, and other Arab and international documents on education; and

— the strategies adopted by the Arab Ministers of Education during their meetings;

Aware of world challenges and changes and their consequences on the development of the Arab Region, and in order to benefit from their positive achievements while avoiding their negative consequences;

Conscious of the importance of education as a key for human development which constitutes a generator of global sustainable development;

In order to achieve education for all, both quantitatively and qualitatively, an education of high quality that is aimed at enabling all to achieve excellence and to develop, strengthen and promote their capacities to the fullest extent;

Reaffirming the role of education in providing equal educational opportunities for boys and girls, both urban and rural, and in keeping with the spirit of the century represented by the scientific, computer and technological revolutions that reaffirm the concept of self-learning which constitutes the basis for lifelong learning, in order to allow individuals to have access to data and to criticize, select, classify, treat and use this data in the different areas of social, economic and cultural life;

Considering the fact that education is a social issue, and that all Arab and international forces, institutions and organisations as well as government and non-governmental associations, unions and organisations, should join efforts to meet the Education for All needs and goals;

Inspired by the cultural and spiritual values of the Arab nation which reaffirm that education is an essential dimension of our cultural identity today and in the future;

We, the participants in the Arab Regional Conference on Education for All—EFA 2000 Assessment, held in Cairo from 24 to 27 January 2000, recommend that Arab States adopt the document entitled *Education for All in the Arab States: Renewing the Commitment* as the Arab Framework for Action to Ensure Basic Learning Needs in the Arab States in the Years 2000-2010.

Introduction

1. The Arab Framework for Action to Ensure Basic Learning Needs in the Arab States in the Years 2000-2010 is based upon the following:

   (i) The World Declaration on Education for All and the Framework for Action to Meet Basic Learning Needs, respectively adopted and agreed on by the World Conference on Education for All (Jomtien, Thailand, 1990);

   (ii) The Mid-decade Review of the International Consultative Forum on EFA (Amman, 1996) and the various international and Arab activities related to the Declaration and Framework for Action undertaken in the 1990s as regards the substance of the two aforementioned documents;

   (iii) The documents about childhood and Education for All adopted by the Ministers of Education in the Arab States;

(iv) EFA 2000 Assessment made by the Arab States in preparation for The Arab Regional Conference on Education for All (Cairo, 24-27 January 2000);

(v) The Preliminary Draft Framework for Action elaborated by the International Consultative Forum on EFA and proposed to discussion in preparation of the World Education Forum (Dakar, April 2000); and

(vi) The discussions of the Arab Regional Conference on Education for All—EFA Year 2000 Assessment held in Cairo (24-27 January 2000).

2. The objectives of the Framework are twofold:

(i) To form a reference and guide for all stakeholders concerned with education in the Arab Region and committed to achieving the goals of Education for All, in their strategies, plans and programmes;

(ii) The convey the concerns of the Arab States while discussing the EFA issues at the World Education Forum (Dakar, Senegal, April 2000)

I. Background

Learning is the key to human sustainable development and is the foundation for enlightened existence and the sustenance of all livelihood

3. Learning, this treasure within, is the product of open and diversified access to knowledge and experience. Thus, the concept of learning throughout life emerges as one of the keys to life in the twenty-first century. It goes beyond the traditional distinction between school and lifelong education. It is designed to meet the challenges posed by a rapidly changing world.

4. Four pillars were proposed as the foundation of education by the International Commission on Education for the Twenty-first Century, i.e. *learning to know, learning to do, learning to be* and *learning to live together, learning to live with others*. The capacity to learn is at the heart of human development. It is the foundation for enlightened existence and the sustenance of all livelihoods.

5. Education aims not only at providing equal opportunities for individuals to learn, but also at achieving a *learning society* based on the acquisition, renewal and use of knowledge. This involves increasing the scope and opportunities for access to knowledge for all individuals. Education should enable everyone to gather information and to select, arrange, manage and use it. Learning is the key to sustainable human development.

Enhancing Learning is Improving the Quality of Life

6. The provision of equal opportunities for learning is a mandatory social service that must be provided to all individuals, as one of their basic rights and a condition for improving the quality of life. Health care is another important social service. It encompasses fighting diseases, providing nutrition and pure water, and ensuring an unpolluted environment.

7. Among these mandatory social services other than education is health care, which encompasses the eradication of diseases, the provision of nutrition, safe water and a non-polluted environment. The expansion of education has led to greater health awareness. Education for women leads not only to enhanced child health care but also to the enhancement of the general care of children, including their education. Enhancement of the educational level of the mother is no doubt the most crucial factor underlying participation in education and improving the quality of life.

8. Moreover, the expansion of education leads to a more enhanced environments awareness, a greater knowledge of basic rights and duties, and a generally increased sense of citizenship and enlightened involvement in civic life. It is generally believed today all over the world that education is the most important means to fight poverty.

Meeting Basic Learning Needs is an International Priority

9. The World Declaration on Education for All (Jomtien, 1990) affirmed the necessity to provide basic learning needs by stating that '*Every person—child, youth and adult—shall be able*

to benefit from educational opportunities designed to meet their basic learning needs.'

10. Furthermore, the Jomtien Conference agreed on a framework, derived from the World Declaration on Education for All, to be taken as a guide for action at the national, regional and international levels.

Re-Affirmation of the Jomtien Message at the International Level

11. During the ten years after the Jomtien Conference, the international community, with the participation of the Arab States, has witnessed a series of conferences, all of which re-affirmed the message of the Jomtien Declaration and linked education to development, quality of life, human rights, democracy, social integration and justice. These conferences called for a special emphasis on the education of girls and women, and the struggle against poverty, unemployment and social exclusion (the World Summit for Children, 1990; the United Nations Conference on Environment and Development, 1992; the World Conference on Human Rights, 1993; the International Conference on Population and Development, 1994; the World Conference on Special Needs Education: Access and Quality, 1994; the World Summit for Social Development, 1995; the Fourth World Conference on Women, 1995; the Fifth International Conference on Adult Education, 1997; etc.)

12. The Mid-Decade Meeting on the International Consultative Forum on Education for All (Amman, 1996) was held to assess what has been achieved in the five years that followed the Jomtien Conference. The meeting discussed various new challenges and the continuing challenges that still have to be addressed. The Amman Affirmation recommended 'stressing the forms of learning and critical thinking that enable individuals to understand changing environments, create new knowledge and shape their own destinies.' It further noted that the continuing challenges to the goals of EFA include mainly the education of women and girls, the training, status and motivation of teachers, the role of the

family and the local community in education, and the broad partnership to achieve EFA goals.

Re-Affirmation of the Jomtien Message at the Arab Level

13. At the Arab level, the Cairo Declaration (1994) emphasized the role of education in achieving sustainable development. The Conference expressed its determination 'to frame educational programmes that would bring the region into a position of world prominence in the next century.' The Conference concluded that two major areas stand out as pressing priorities requiring concerted action: the problem of illiteracy and the quality of education.

14. Furthermore, the Arab Declaration on Adult Education (Cairo, 1997) re-affirmed the contents of Jomtien Declaration (1990) and Amman Affirmation (1996), and renewed its commitment towards the Arab Strategy for Education, the Strategy to Eradicate Illiteracy in the Arab States and the recommendations of the Arab conferences on education, particularly the Fifth Conference of Ministers of Education and Those Responsible for Economic Planning in the Arab States (MINEDARAB V) held in Cairo, 1994. The Arab Declaration on Adult Education called for the necessity to consider illiteracy eradication as a top priority for the development of the Arab States. It also confirmed its endeavour to ensure new opportunities and educational programmes for continuous education of adults.

II. Achievements and Problems

15. The efforts exerted at the international, regional and Arab levels have culminated in various policies, laws, measures, programmes and activities at the level of each Arab State. This in turn has lead to an improvement in the quality of life and to providing learning opportunities and improving education quality.

16. Yet, all that has been achieved by the end of the twentieth century remains below the expectations. Poverty is still widespread and, where it exists, educational opportunities decrease and so does the quality of health care. In addition,

there is a spread of other problems, like unemployment, violence, conflicts and the continuous threat to family ties and social integration. Poverty generates poverty, as illiteracy generates illiteracy conducive to social decline. In some countries, the suffering is greater than in others; in rural areas more than in urban ones; in geographically remote areas and among marginalized minorities and nomads more than among others.

17. Although various studies have highlighted the importance of educating females as a positive investment factor, girls and women have not sufficiently benefited from the allocated resources. Where girls do complete a primary education, there is often a large gender gap in the transition rate to secondary school. The gap between males and females becomes wider when literacy is considered. When combined with other factors related to the quality of life (especially in rural areas and shanty towns) such as poverty, disability violence against females, malnutrition, rapid social changes, unemployment and risks of acquiring diseases such as AIDS, it appears that the females are more systematically disadvantaged than their male counterparts, on the basis of discrimination by gender.

Early Childhood Education Still does not Receive the Required Attention

18. Most of the Arab States have a pre-primary system of education for children aged 3-5 years. In some States, this takes on a traditional form, such as the *Kuttabs*, supported by government as in Morocco and Mauritania. The gross enrolment ratio (GER), however, varies between 0.7 per cent and 99 per cent—the educational indicator showing the widest discrepancy between Arab States. But all states reported improvement between 1990 and 1999. In the latter, the ratio is less than 13 per cent in ten states, between 13 and 50 per cent in six states, and more than 70 per cent in only two states (Lebanon 71 per cent and Kuwait 99 per cent). This shows that Arab States, rich and poor countries alike, do not devote the require attention to ECCD. It seems that, for the Arab States, education at this stage is primarily a family matter.

19. On the other hand, the percentage of children who attend the first grade of primary education after pursuing certain per-primary schooling (for one or more) is higher than GER in pre-primary. This indicates, first, that pre-primary schooling is short term in most states, and second, that the tendency towards schooling at the pre-primary level is increasing. In most Arab States, ECCD still generally constitutes an important challenge, since it affects school life at the primary level.

Increase in Primary Education Enrolment

20. The most important achievements in the Arab States in the previous decade relate to enrolment in primary education. Most of the Arab States either maintained or improved their enrolment ratio in the first grade (6-7 years old). The countries which still show low GER at this level (82 per cent and below in late 1990s) are Djibouti, the Sudan, Mauritania and Yemen. Where enrolment ratios are high, the gender gap is smaller (1 to 4 percentage points), and where they are low it increases (10 percentage points). Yet, when looking at the net enrolment ratio (NER) at the first grade the picture is different: nine countries show a NER of 82 per cent and below.

21. In terms of GER in primary education, the Arab States have demonstrated significant progress. Only in three countries is GER equal to 68 per cent and below, versus thirteen countries where it is 90 per cent and above (and where gender parity index is 0.9 and above). Two countries have shown a very high rate of progress between the early and late 1990s: the Sudan and Mauritania.

22. Besides this progress, the discrepancies between rural and urban areas are still high, and female participation in primary education is always less than that of males (the parity index is equal to 1.0 and above in one country). In addition, the problem of enrolment appears more striking when looking at the NER. In spite of a real improvement in the 1990s, there are still six countries which have a NER of less than 80 per cent, and where the gap between boys and girls widens in this regard: the parity index is equal to or less than 0.9 in six countries.

Illiteracy yet Prevails

23. The number of illiterates in the Arab States is estimated today at 68 million (of which 63 per cent and women). Despite the expanded efforts, one fourth of these is found in one country; Egypt (17 million), and 70 per cent in five countries: Egypt, the Sudan, Algeria, Morocco and Yemen. In most of these countries illiteracy is accompanied by population size, high population growth rates, poverty and concentration of population in rural areas.

24. It is clear that the feature of illiteracy in the Arab States is different from that of the expansion of primary education, for illiteracy is the negative product of education that had not been completely expanded in the past. The strongest element in the spread of illiteracy in the Arab States and its strongest explanatory factor is the gender gap. The Gender Parity Index in these countries is 0.69. This indicates that illiteracy in the Arab Region is caused not only by poverty, but also by attitudes against education of girls and by the absence of effective policies to change these attitudes.

25. The presence of 68 million illiterates in the Arab Region and the existence of illiteracy in all Arab States, though in widely varying rates, not only represent a great challenge to these states in terms of development, social justice and the quality of life, but also serves as a serious indictment to the education systems themselves. These marks are reflected in the failure of schools to draw children and to retain them enough to prevent them from returning to illiteracy as well as in the low level of learning achievement.

Quality Education is Still a Privilege for a Few

26. After Jomtien, learning achievement was adopted as a key indicator of the quality of education. Nine Arab States participated (between 1993 and 1999) in the Monitoring Learning Achievement (MLA) project conducted by UNESCO and UNICEF. The results show that competencies acquired by pupils in primary education (4th grade) are far below the standard proposed in Jomtien: only 12 per cent, 10 per cent and 25 per cent showed high skills (80 per cent

of the competencies or more) in Arabic, mathematics and life skills, respectively. In Arabic language, only Tunisia and Morocco achieved and benchmark rate suggested at Jomtien (80 per cent of pupils). None of the participating states achieved the suggested level in mastering mathematics competencies. Only Tunisia and Jordan reached the suggested level of achievement in life-skills testes. In average, the achievement of girls was better than that of boys. Achievement among pupils in urban schools was higher than in rural schools.

27. According to the results of the Monitoring Learning Achievement project, primary education in the Arab States appears to be of poor quality and not providing for the basic learning needs to the pupils. This means that, in the past, these states focused more on providing school places than on enhancing the quality of education. Therefore, improving the quality of education constitutes a main challenge to the Arab States.

28. Among the components of learning acquisition, basic skills for a better life are to be taken into consideration. Many Arab States include, in their educational goals and objectives, elements related to these skills, such as vocational training, health, environment and citizenship education. Mass media are also mentioned as a means for the transmission of values and knowledge in relation to these skills. However, in general, these essential aspects of learning have not received sufficient attention and the information about the acquisition of basic skills related to the quality of life is still very scarce.

Teachers' Qualifications Need Improvement

29. Data from Arab States show that the teachers fulfilling the minimum required national qualifications vary widely between 21 per cent and 100 per cent (late 1990s). In addition, the required entry qualifications vary from completing secondary school to completing four or five years at a higher education institution. They also differ in terms of pedagogical requirements from nil to a full programme approaching international standards. This is a large

discrepancy. The concept of teaching licence is still not common in educational circles and professionalization of teaching remains a rhetorical discourse. However, the pupil/teacher ratio is low in general. It ranges between 11 and 25 in fourteen states, as opposed to 26 and 30 in three states and 31 and above in two. Furthermore, more efforts should be exerted in order to resolve many problems facing the status of teachers, mainly concerning their work conditions and their social position, in order to attract young and qualified people.

Improvements in Internal Efficiency

30. Available data on internal efficiency show slight decline in repetition rates, improvement in the number of pupils staying at school until the 5th grade and better performance of girls as compared to boys. However, the primary level of the education systems in the Arab States still shows weaknesses in internal efficiency; persistence of drop-out and repetition (which increase the higher one goes up the educational ladder), and the long time needed to complete primary education.

Expenditure on Education

31. Achievements and problems of education in the Arab States depend largely, among other factors, on expenditure. Arab States exerted a substantial effort that led to a greater expenditure on education in the last decade. But, in view of what has been mentioned about enrolment ratios and quality of education, the expenditure on primary education seems to be suffering from different problems: inadequacy, in some countries, between financial resources and educational requirements; wastage or lack of rationalization of spending; weakness in capital expenditure (investment); high cost of educating remote and widespread population; and weakness in budgeting techniques. Such problems raise questions about the potential role of non-governmental organisations, diversification of financial sources, mobilization of resources, accountability, and the means to build the national capacity for planning, budgeting and assessment.

Poor Management of Education Systems

32. If the increase of financial resources may be pressing need for poor countries, the major problem in most of Arab States is how to make a good use of available resources, human as well as financial. Surveys on learning achievement showed the absence of developed systems of monitoring. Reports on expenditure show problems in terms of planning and budgeting. Education Management Information Systems (EMIS) are lacking in general. Problems of centralization versus decentralization are still debated. Thus, the issue of efficient educational management constitutes, a serious challenge in the Arab States in order to meet the goals of EFA.

III. Challenges and Opportunities

33. Time is passing and, in the Arab Region, millions of individuals remain deprived of education and millions are getting education of poor quality, while most of the rest are not appropriately prepared for the technological era and the international competition in the new millennium. We are faced with the challenge of achieving what has not been achieved since Jomtien and with the new challenges after 2000.

34. There is general consensus on EFA goals, and that education for all is pivotal in addressing increasing poverty, sustaining socio economic progress, and honouring the human rights of every individual. Lacking are the necessary resources. And despite the political will, and although education stands high on rhetorical agendas of governments, commitments made at Jomtien by Arab States remain highly visible but significantly unmet.

35. It is more starkly evident that failure to quicken the pace of progress towards Jomtien goals will have grave consequences for peace, stability and prosperity. The stage is now set for a stronger, more action-oriented approach of country initiatives for basic education, with important international commitment and support, reset within the circumstances and imperatives of the new millennium.

The Challenges of the Twenty-First Century—Outlook for 2010

36. Globalization imposes a labour market that surpasses the boundaries of countries and a tough competition according to the acquired qualifications. These qualifications are primarily the product of learning.

37. Globalization furthermore dictates the increasing use of technology, which is the most efficient means for production and communication. But the ability to make use of technology and what that entails in terms of skills and knowledge is also a product of learning. So what can the Arab educational authorities and organisations do to prevent marginalization and to positively participate in the globalization process?

38. Technology also includes in people a deep transformation in how to learn, how to use what they have learned, and how to evaluate the importance and relevance of what they have learned. We live in a period where economical progress is essentially based on knowledge. Thus, learning becomes more than ever a decisive factor in prosperity.

39. This also means that the cost of learning will increase. This is as true for households as it is for countries. Poor countries, unable to enter more technology-intensive-based markets, run the risk of excessive marginalization in trade are investment. In developed and developing countries alike, poverty and inequality at the household levels are increasingly associated with educational attainment. And the gap is widening between those who have access to information and the capacity to use technology of communication (e-mail, e-commerce and e-learning) and those who don't or can't.

40. The Arab States furthermore face the problem of the usage of foreign language as the technological medium. Mastering a foreign language is not generalized, nor is the Arabization of technology.

41. The unpredictable changes surrounding our lives give daily new meaning to the imperatives of the Jomtien

commitments. That is because, as skills requirements for adequate, livelihood sustaining employment rise, basic education becomes ever more essential for work, or for school success and transition to secondary and higher levels of education.

42. Demographic growth poses another challenge to the education systems. While the annual average growth rate is estimated for the years 2000-2010 at 1.2 per cent for the world and 1.5 per cent for the developing countries, it is 2.5 per cent for the Arab States. In 2010, the estimated population of the age group 5-18 years old is 110 million. If the enrolment ratio in general education will be around 80 per cent for this age group, Arab States have to ensure educational opportunities to 88 million students, i.e. to provide resources for an additional 29 million students (present figure: 59 million students). This demographic increase places severe pressure on the education systems in terms of expenditure, management, qualified human resources, etc. At the same time, the population growth entails competing demands for resources to ensure other basic needs such as nutrition, housing, health services, etc. Some education systems in the Arab States have suffered from high indebtedness and the consequences of applying structural adjustment and economic reform policies.

43. Furthermore, in the past decade a number of Arab States suffered from persistent troubles and conflicts (Algeria and the Sudan), embargoes (Iraq, Lybian Arab Jamahiriya and the Sudan), occupation and wars (Lebanon, Palestine, Syrian Arab Republic and the Sudan). The education systems in these countries suffered deeply from these troubles which hindered their capacities and delayed the achievement of their objectives according to the Jomtien Declaration. The return to peace and normal life through the elimination of all forms of occupation, embargoes, conflicts and tensions appears to be a *sine quo non* precondition to ensure education for all in troubled areas. In parallel, education has a role to play in contributing to create a peaceful environment in the region.

Building on Available Opportunities and Progress Made

44. Facing these challenges does not initiate from a void. It has to be recognized that there are opportunities available that were not there a decade ago. An unequivocal global consensus has been forged around the critical role of education for sustainable human development. There is an even stronger reaffirmation of the importance of human rights. Since the Copenhagen Summit (1995), there is renewed concern for the rights of the socially excluded, marginalized, and impoverished, and mounting recognition of the benefits for societies of educating females.

45. Donors are answering the calls for countries to strengthen ownership of competencies and the development of national capacities. The educational deterioration that many developing countries experienced in the 1990s has been stemmed. And it is noticeable that civil society has become more likely to assume its responsibilities.

46. New and creative ways are now available also for reaching out to learners with disabilities or learning difficulties, as a means of ensuring that their capacities for learning are given the utmost chance to flourish.

47. Modern information and communication technologies offer in general enormous potential for educational outreach, enhancing access, self-paced learning and meticulous assessment of learning outcomes.

48. At the national level, new synergies are beginning to develop around more comprehensive governance systems and the participation of a wider set of actors, such as NGOs representing civil society in educational planning and implementation.

49. At the global level, original core sponsorship of education for all (by UNESCO, UNICEF, the World Bank and UNDP) has extended through the International Consultative Forum to engage another United Nations agency (UNFPA) and representation from a wide set of public, private and non-governmental constituencies.

The Year 2000: Renewing the Commitment to the Jomtien Declaration

50. Ten years after the Jomtien Declaration, the definition of basic education and the commitments surrounding it still stand as a persistent challenge to the Arab States. This Declaration focused, for the first time, on the basic learning needs of neglected minorities and on learning achievement rather than on mere school enrolment.

51. The ten articles of the Jomtien Declaration shed light, illuminating the road ahead: *(i)* meeting basic learning needs; *(ii)* shaping the vision; *(iii)* universalizing access and promoting equity; *(iv)* focusing on learning acquisition; *(v)* broadening the means and scope of basic education; *(vi)* enhancing the environment for learning; *(vii)* strengthening partnerships; *(viii)* developing a supporting policy context; *(xi)* mobilizing resources; and *(x)* strengthening international solidarity.

52. The Jomtien Declaration remains even more vibrant and relevant today. The commitment should be renewed. And the follow-up efforts already exerted by the states must be continued and enriched by the experiences and the information gained during the past decade. We have a shared responsibility to ensure that failure is prevented.

The Arab Framework for Action: A Guide for all the Partners to Achieve EFA

53. Taking into account the above-mentioned background, the achievement and the problems in the Arab States and the challenges—those imposed by what was unmet in the 1990s and those imposed by the developments of the twenty-first century—the Arab States are called upon to adopt this Framework for Action and to act in conformity with it.

54. The purpose of the Arab Framework for Action is to act as a reference and a guide for all stakeholders concerned with education in the Arab States and committed to achieving education for all, in their plans and programmes, each within its adopted goals, missions, and target groups, with the view of strengthening partnerships at the global, regional and

local levels, in the single aim of meeting basic learning needs of all by 2010.

55. The main *stakeholders* to this Framework are:

(i) the governments of the Arab States which hold responsibility for immediate action towards achieving the goals of education for all, and for leading and co-ordinating actions aimed at achieving these goals;

(ii) all stakeholders from civil society at the national level, i.e. universities and other educational institutions, NGOs, the private sector, etc., which should take a proactive role in contributing significantly to the achievement of the goals of education for all;

(iii) Arab and other regional organisations in the Arab States Region responsible for providing support and for promoting bilateral and multilateral co-operation at the Arab regional level; and

(iv) international agencies and organisations responsible for providing support and promoting bilateral and multilateral co-operation at the international level.

IV. Principles for Action

56. The following five principles are proposed as guidelines for all actions aiming at ensuring the provision of basic learning needs in the Arab States.

57. The principle of *comprehensiveness*, which includes the following:

— viewing education for all through the expanded vision confirmed in Jomtien;

— considering learning as one of the key components of the quality of life, and an essential factor in improving this quality;

— the acknowledgment at all levels and sectors of society that learning in the cornerstone to sustainable human development;

— dealing with learners in a holistic manner, in order to understand their surrounding environment and to meet their needs and develop their personalities in an integrated and harmonious manner.

58. The principle of *equity*, which consists of the following:
    - considering access to educational opportunities as an absolute right to be provided by society to all citizens of all ages without discrimination;
    - considering social and geographical inequality of educational opportunities as a factor leading to the creation of a gap in society that is hard to close;
    - integrating in the educational plans and processes the various excluded groups, such as the impoverished, rural populations, the marginalized, the displaced, refugees, nomads, immigrants, street and working children, and others in difficult circumstances;
    - addressing the needs of special groups and racial, religious, and cultural minorities when generalizing programmes and curricula;
    - considering gender discrimination in basic education as incompatible with social equity and with development needs, and as a breach in human rights;
    - considering the inclusion of learners with special needs, especially those with disabilities and learning difficulties, in educational programmes, as a right and an essential means for their self-actualization and social integration;
    - providing the gifted and talented with special care and an appropriate teaching/learning environment so as to develop their talents and capacities in order to contribute in the development process and to meet the challenges of the future.

59. The principle of a *learner-friendly environment*, which includes the following:
    - providing a healthy and secure environment to learners;
    - providing quality education relevant to learners' needs and to the requirements of the changing society;

— providing an educational environment based on mutual rights and responsibilities, and non-discrimination between genders;

— fostering the attitudes that enhance the values of respect, tolerance, and understanding of others;

— promoting independent thinking and expression among learners;

— providing committed teachers keen to discover the learners' potentials and to work for their development;

— making this environment available and affordable to all.

60. The principle of *commitment*, which includes the following:

— high-level re-commitment at all levels of government and leadership in civil society, regional and international organisations and other partners, to renewed efforts towards meeting the basic learning needs of all, children, youth and adults, in line with national and international goals and targets;

— commitment by all relevant bodies to a renewed campaign for resource mobilization at all levels, global and local, to provide more innovative and equitable formulas to resolve the problem of human and financial resources of countries in the greatest need.

61. The principle of *keeping pace with technological advancements*, which includes the following:

— considering the rapid transformations in technology of communication as a supporting factor for the provision of education, starting from basic education. Among other things, technology helps in classifying learning objectives and determining the expected performance from learners, subdividing subject matters and facilitating their presentation, individualizing learning, assessing learning and analysing learner's performance, and conducting examinations, and using distant education to get access to populations in geographically remote areas;

— considering the use of technology, which includes, in addition to hardware and software, the use of Arabic and of foreign languages, as indispensable to help education meet the challenges of the new century.

V. Objectives and Orientations for Implementation

62. The Jomtien Framework for Action invited all Member States to develop their special goals and objectives in their efforts to meet the basic learning needs of children, youth and adults.

63. The EFA mid-decade review meeting (Amman, 1996) emphasized five major areas of concern: improving learning achievement, mobilizing resources, developing partnerships, building national capacities and meeting the basic learning needs for all in the twenty-first century.

64. With the end of the decade, it is necessary to acknowledge the difficulties facing education systems which have prevented the Jomtien goals from being achieved. Among these difficulties have been shortage of financial and human resources on their misallocation and waste, poor mobilization, the difficulties related to the management of a complex system such as education and the complexity of its relationship with other systems, the mismatch between the size of the pressure to meet the goals and the size of the exerted efforts, etc.

65. The successes achieved should also be recognized and the commitment among the four major groups of partners that hold responsibility for achieving the goal in the future, i.e. governments, civil society, regional agencies and organisations, and international agencies and organisations renewed, and all have to set clear goals and objectives.

Seven Objectives

66. Therefore, building on the Jomtien Declaration and the present needs of the Arab States, the new objectives and targets for achieving the ultimate goal of *education for all in the Arab States* could be re-defined for the coming years

(2000-2010) as follows (these objectives allow for periodical assessment of the progress achieved):

(i) *Expanded and improved early childhood care and development*, which includes, besides providing health care, nutrition and other basic social services to young children, providing them opportunities for learning and development at educational institutions with a view to fully developing their capacities including their physical, cognitive, creative and psycho-social abilities.

(ii) *Extending basic education and its provision to achieve high quality education leading to excellence for all children, with special emphasis on those with special needs.* This requires ensuring compulsory basic education, supporting needy families in enrolling their children in schools, categorically prohibiting child employment, and providing for the inclusion in schools of all children, including those with special needs.

(iii) *Extended opportunities for basic education and training programmes to acquire life and vocational skills for all youth and adults.* This includes enhancing the existing non-formal learning structures, developing new ones and providing diversified forms of technical and vocational training and lifelong learning for both males and females.

(iv) *Universalizing literacy among adolescents, and decreasing illiteracy rates among adults* by setting realistic yet still ambitious targets, which would lead to significant progress.

(v) *Ensuring mastery of basic learning skills and excellence for all through the empowerment of all learners to attain outstanding achievement levels that make full use of their potential, starting with the mastery of basic skills, vocational and life skills, and attaining excellence in creativity and inventiveness.* This will require improving the quality of education in all its aspects, including teachers' qualifications and conditions of employment, curricula, teaching and assessment methods, and the learning environment.

(vi) *Full equality and effective participation in basic education for girls and women, and the elimination of gender biases and disparities in all schools and education systems.*

(vii) *Improving educational governance and management, which* entails improving decision-making processes, accountability systems, building capacities, and extending and strengthening partnerships in planning implementation, monitoring and evaluation.

Each state sets its own targets for each of those objectives in such a manner as to allow the assessment of the progress made, reviewing these targets periodically and modifying them according to new developments.

Five Orientations for Implementation

67. Five orientations for implementation constitute the approaches to be adopted at the national level towards reaching the determined objectives.

Orientation 1: *Promote partnerships,* which includes the following mechanisms:

— organizing the support provided by regional and international organisations, and by bilateral and multilateral co-operation in a concerted manner and orienting it according to national priorities;

— greater participation of civil society in designing, implementing and monitoring basic education programmes, and allowing for the participation of the private sector, NGOs, local communities and religious foundations, in the achievement of EFA goals;

— better co-operation, exchange of information, transparency, accountability and trust amongst all partners in the process of universalizing basic education.

Orientation 2: *Integrate programmes and projects,* through:

— implementing integrated health, social and educational policies. Health problems can prevent children from attending school and from learning. Ensuring that children are healthy and able to learn is especially relevant to efforts to increase enrolment and learning achievement, i.e. it encourages the poorest and most disadvantaged children to attend school and to devote the needed efforts for success;

— incorporating all programmes for the education of children, youth and adults into an integrated national vision and linking the educational plans to the economic and social development plans within the framework of sustainable development efforts and strategies. Also, employment policies based on training, education, and the eradication of illiteracy increase the value of learning in society, with its subsequent rewards;

— ensuring synergies between the different programmes of education, considering that adult education affects the education of children and that expanding secondary education creates incentives to expanding enrolment in primary education;

— using all available media and technological channels in co-ordination with the efforts exerted in education.

Orientation 3: *Promote knowledge-based decision-making and information for all.* This includes:

— assessing curricular objectives, contents, teaching methods, forms of evaluation and activities, and examining the needs, aspirations and achievements of each learner through scientific research, in order to take objective decisions thereon;

— providing society with a clear picture of educational reality, after collection, analysis and dissemination of relevant data, in order to ensure societal accountability.

Orientation 4: *Mobilize all possible resources* through the enhancement of national investments in education, effective use of available human and material resources, and the mobilization of support from all concerned parties (the public sector, the private sector, the local communities, non-governmental organisations, bilateral and multilateral co-operation agencies and regional and international organisations) towards education for all.

***Orientation 5**: Enhance management and monitoring efficiency,* which encompasses the following:

— Setting clear targets to be achieved at the national (and local) level, that reflect what had been agreed upon internationally and nationally, and any other commitments. These objectives should emphasize, along with quantitative aspects, the qualitative aspects, such as the levels of expected achievement in terms of knowledge and skills to be acquired, the quality of educational material and environment. These objectives must identify and categories that should receive priority;

— designing and implementing schemes for the monitoring and assessment of curricula, and for the adjustment of processes;

— developing the management systems, enhancing the qualifications of human resources, and building national capacities;

— institutionalizing assessment and follow up;

— rationalizing expenditure.

Each state is invited to develop a self-monitoring system of its commitment to each orientation proposed in this Framework for Action and of its implementation of these orientations, as well as the difficulties related to them.

VI. Priorities

Two Priorities for All Arab States

68. In view of the achievements of the Arab States collectively in the expansion of basic education (Objective 2), the problem occupying the first priority in the Arab Region as a whole is that of the quality of education. Therefore, and in accordance with the Cairo Declaration as well, *improving the quality of education is to be considered as the first priority in the Arab Framework for Action for meeting the goals of education*

for all at both quantitative and qualitative levels. This means that Arab countries must aim at ensuring mastery of basic learning skills and excellence for all. In spite of all efforts made to universalize basic education, the provision of a high-quality education remains a goal imposed by the sustainable development requirements, a positive attitude towards globalization, and the challenges of the world market competition and free trade. This priority encompasses all educational processes and skills, including the achievement by all learners of nationally defined and objectively measured levels, of learning in literacy, numeracy and life skills, including technology skills, that entail open-mindedness, development of thinking, the desire for knowledge and the desire to seek knowledge from all sources. Within this priority, the emphasis goes to improving the teachers' status, including their qualifications and work conditions. The slogan for the coming years in the Arab States should be: teachers' empowerment, professionalization and training to reach the highest possible levels in scientific, professional and cultural specialization.

69. In view of the limited human and financial resources available, it is of utmost importance in the Arab States to mobilize efforts and capabilities. That will require good governance and good management, both to assist in the achievement, of the quality of education and other goals, and to ensure the implementation of the determined principles adopted in the framework for Action. Therefore, *improving educational governance and management (Objective 7) can be considered as the second priority* in the Arab Region as a whole. This includes the development of education decision-support systems and building national capacities at central, regional and local levels, to ensure the use of knowledge in decision-making at all these levels and in all educational endeavours, from policies to planning and management of operational activities, and from mobilization of resources to monitoring and assessment of results. Within this priority the emphasis would be in the coming years on *capacity-building*.

Eradication of Illiteracy: A Top Priority for National Regional and International Mobilization

70. The Arab States, singly and jointly, are concerned with all objectives of the Arab Framework for Action. But, considering the massive and important problems facing them, whether in catching up with previous commitments or in meeting the demands of the coming century, the greatest problem for the Arab States, is in general, that of *illiteracy*. There are two reasons for this: the first relates to the number of illiterates in these centuries (around 68 million, or 38.5 per cent of the population 15 years of age or older) and with the wide gender gap in literacy (Parity Index = 0.69). The second relates to the multiplier effect of literacy. Illiteracy among adults, especially women, lower children's school enrolment and the educational achievement (quality of education) of those in school, and exacerbates failure and early school drop-out rates (effectiveness of education). Illiteracy is also associated with early marriage, high fertility and high infant mortality rates. Illiteracy reinforces gender discrimination in society, while literacy helps improve the overall quality of life.

71. Therefore, and in accordance with the Cairo Declaration (1994), *the eradication of illiteracy is today (in the year 2000) a high priority in the Arab States for national, regional and international mobilization of resources to achieve EFA goals (Objective 4)*. For, as stated in the Cairo Declaration: 'It is impossible to imagine the development and resurgence of the Arab world without putting an end to the problem of illiteracy in all the Arab countries.' Within this priority, the emphasis goes first to the *education of girls and women*.

Two Other Priorities for Arab Co-operation and National Development

72. In view of the relative neglect of early childhood education in the Arab States and the potential of such education for the enhancement of learning achievement and improving internal efficiency in primary school, *early childhood care and development* deserves much more attention in the coming ten

years, particularly in regional co-operation activities and among those states where illiteracy does not constitute a heavy burden. Efforts should be devoted both to the expansion and diversification of ECCD delivery services, and to the innovation and improvement of educational curricula, bearing in mind that early childhood care and development is not confined to pre-schooling but includes care given by the whole family from birth onwards.

73. In parallel to the above-mentioned priorities, efforts should be made to diversify delivery systems of educational services to youth and adults, in order to broaden educational opportunities. The enormous potential of new information and communication technologies should be exploited at the national, sub-regional and regional levels. In terms of educational methods, priority should be given to the *development of a multimedia environment to be used both for formal and non-formal education,* encouraging the investment in cultural industries related to teaching/learning activities.

Each Arab State has its Own National Priorities

74. The aforementioned sets of priorities apply to the Arab States as a whole, but it is difficult to apply to them individually. In fact, some states are close to overcoming the problem of illiteracy and to gender gap related to it. These include Jordan, the United Arab Emirates, Bahrain, Palestine, Qatar, Kuwait and Lebanon, followed by the Libyan Arab Jamahiriya, Saudi Arabia and the Syrian Arab Republic. For other countries, illiteracy remains the number one challenge, and these include Egypt, the Sudan, Morocco, Mauritania and Yemen, followed by Tunisia, Algeria, Djibouti, Iraq and Oman. This discrepancy in positions changes the scale of priorities from one group to another. The same should be said about early childhood education, where Kuwait and Lebanon are approaching full enrolment.

75. In all cases, each country is called upon to define its priorities and their sequence of importance according to the problems facing it and to review these priorities in a periodical manner according to what has been achieved. This is a necessary step to define the plan of action in each

country and, in that light, to define the extent of Arab regional and international co-operation.

VII. Arab Regional and International Co-operation

Increasing the Efficiency of Arab Co-operation

76. The Arab Region is composed of twenty-one states, most of which share a common language and a common culture. Furthermore, and more important, they are bonded by a sense of belonging to one nation, in that what besets one state affects the others, and by a sense of combined strength of will for the general progress of the Arab nation. A condition for that progress is the achievement of the goals of education for all, both quantitatively and qualitatively.

77. Arab States are also brought together by Arab regional organisations concerned with the issues of co-ordination and co-operation among the different states. In the year 2000, the Arab States will renew their commitments for co-operation and their faith in its returns for all. The disparity in development levels is an additional incentive for the establishment of that co-operation. Achieving the education for all goals will be the product of their individual and collective efforts.

78. This co-operation will take place mainly through two channels:

    — Bilateral and multi-lateral relations, where the exchange of information and experiences take place, where assistance is provided, agreements are concluded, and the flow of human resources and investments is encouraged;

    — Networks, and regional and sub-regional organisations (ALECSO, ISESCO, ABEGS, AGFUND) which develop joint programmes and projects in co-operation with international organisations, and provide technical information and expertise.

79. In view of the experience of the past decade where the achievements of the Arab States, collectively and individually, did not meet the requirements, the Arab States are invited to do the following:

(i) Assess the previous co-operation experiences through the two above-mentioned channels, to enhance co-operation in the coming years and extend the benefits derived from co-operation on everyone, including the establishment of specialized regional centres, joint programmes and projects, as well as common lists of learning competencies expected from learners.

(ii) Renew the mobilization of bilateral and multilateral co-operation. This requires that each country lists its priorities for co-operation, in terms of partners, as well as in terms of types of co-operation, capabilities to assist and the areas where assistance is needed. More developed countries are called upon to provide assistance for less developed countries.

(iii) Strengthen Arab organisations, specialized regional centres, and Arab networks and programmes. This will involve enhancing the capacities of these agencies and helping them direct their activities towards more assistance for needier countries.

(iv) Consider efforts to address shortcomings in the achievement of the set objectives of basic education in any state of the Region as a joint Arab responsibility.

Increasing the Benefit of Arab-International Co-operation

80. In their approach to co-operation with international institutions and organisations, especially those located in the Arab region, the Arab States should refer to the Jomtien Declaration concerning international co-operation:

(i) '*Meeting basic learning needs constitutes a common and universal human responsibility. It requires international solidarity and equitable and fair economic relations in order to redress existing economic disparities*. All nations have valuable knowledge and experiences to share in designing effective educational policies and programmes.

(*ii*) 'Substantial and long-term increases in resources for basic education will be needed. The world community, including governmental agencies and institutions, has an urgent responsibility to alleviate the constraints that prevent some countries from achieving the goals of education for all.'

81. Arab States should also refer to the Jomtien Framework for Action on action priorities at the international level. These include:

(*i*) 'Enhancing national capacities' for designing and managing programmes and services for basic education;

(*ii*) 'Providing sustained long-term support for national and regional actions', which includes providing 'increased international funding....to help the less developed countries implement their own autonomous plans for action in line with the expanded vision of basic Education for All';

(*iii*) 'Providing technical assistance on policy issues.'

82. Therefore, taking into consideration the experience of the past decade, Arab States call upon the international community to do the following:

— *Renew the international commitment to provide financial assistance to the less developed Arab States* that are unable, with their own resources and with those provided by Arab co-operation, to fulfil the requirements for achieving the education for all goals within the coming ten years;

— *Renew the commitment of international agencies and organisations,* especially those sponsoring the Arab Regional Conference on Education for All (Cairo), and those participating in the World Education Forum (Dakar), *to provide sustained and long-term assistance for national and Arab regional activities,* especially those linked to developing national capacities and to designing and implementing priority strategies, plans, programmes and projects for education.

83. *For their part, Arab States will renew their commitment for positive interaction with international agencies and organisations,* under the banner of the Jomtien Declaration, especially in the area of knowledge development and data-base construction. They will undertake periodical assessment studies on education in these states, in line with the goals and orientations adopted in this Arab Framework for Action.

VIII. Designing National Autonomous Plans for Action

84. The EFA 2000 Assessment allowed each Arab State to recognize its decade's achievements and what it was unable to achieve. It helped each state to understand what prevented it from achieving the EFA goals. These countries are invited to perform such an assessment in a periodic manner.

85. The Arab Framework provides a guide for each country to work towards achieving its own targets based upon the principles, objectives, strategies, priorities and forms of Arab and international co-operation set out in this document.

86. Each Arab State is now called upon to determine a time frame for future action, identifying specific targets to be achieved by the year 2010. These targets should be phased so that at the end of each phase a new assessment could be made of what has and what has not been achieved.

87. In this respect, each Arab State is invited to define, according to its own circumstances and possibilities, the upper and lower limits that it shall strive to attain with regard to each individual EFA objective contained in this Framework for Action. It is also called upon to enshrine its commitments in official and public texts.

88. Defining objectives and targets to achieve requires more than political will and intentions. It also requires educational and scientific research reflecting the actual educational situation and examining possible action alternatives, including governance and management methods, centralization versus decentralization, public versus private sector, role of civil society, sources of local, national, regional and international

funding, forms and direction for co-operation, etc. At this stage, national stakeholders should initiate and maintain the necessary communication with other states and organisations, and survey the local human and financial resources so that planning for maximal mobilization of resources and capacities can be undertaken in a realistic manner. Based on all this, the minimum and maximum thresholds for achievement can be defined for each of the seven objectives mentioned in this Framework for Action.

89. Therefore the Arab States are called upon to meet again in 2002 in a regional Arab Ministerial Conference, the subject of which would be education for all in the Arab States—targets for 2010. At this meeting, the Arab States, and the Arab and international organisations, could deliberate on the orientation of the national plans within the context of Arab and international support and co-operation.

90. The regional organisations and the international community are called upon to assist all Arab States to develop their autonomous plans for achieving the goals of education for all, in preparation of the Ministerial Conference proposed for 2002.

APPENDIX—6

ASIA AND PACIFIC REGIONAL FRAMEWORK FOR ACTION: EDUCATION FOR ALL GUIDING PRINCIPLES, SPECIFIC GOALS AND TARGETS FOR 2015

Adopted by the Asia-Pacific Conference on EFA 2000 Assessment in Bangkok, Thailand, 17-20 January 2000

Introduction

During the Asia-Pacific Conference on EFA 2000 Assessment, 17 to 20 January, 2000, the Regional Drafting Committee produced the Draft Outline of the Asia and Pacific Regional Framework for Action: Education for All. The Draft Outline document drew on the following information:[1]

- the Draft Dakar Framework for Action, Preliminary Discussion Document (5 November 1999);
- the Asia-Pacific Region Draft Synthesis Report;
- the four Sub-Regional Draft Synthesis Reports; and
- points raised during the Plenary sessions on 17 and 20 January and the Sub-Regional Meetings on 18 and 19 January, 2000.

On the final day of the Conference, all delegates received a copy of the Draft Outline of the Asia and Pacific Regional Framework for Action: Education for All and were asked to make further suggestions and comments. In subsequent weeks, the Regional Technical Advisory Group's Secretariat received forty-three submissions from Education Ministries, United Nations Agencies and non-governmental organisations throughout the region. All of the submissions were considered when constructing this document; many suggestions have been simply incorporated into the Draft Outline, while other comments have been listed in the Appendix, Asia and Pacific Regional Framework for Action—Additional Concerns.

I. Preamble

Education is a fundamental human right of all people—of value in and of itself, for improving the quality of life, and as an essential part of social and human development. The provision of basic education, whether it be formally on non-formally delivered, is a core responsibility of the state with active and genuine collaboration of parents, communities, and civil society. All people, especially those most disadvantaged and excluded,[2] must be guaranteed access to a basic education of decent quality.

II. The Gains

- Increase in primary school enrolment
- Expansion of early childhood care and education programmes
- Higher priority given to quality
- Increase in functional adult literacy
- Improvement in educational management information systems
- Increase in national budgets for basic education
- Effective use of existing resources
- Increase in 'international' assistance to basic education
- Increase in the number of legislative measures, campaigns, projects and reforms in basic education
- More innovative initiatives in basic education
- More partnership between the private sector and civil society

III. The Challenges[3]

- Growing disparities within countries, particularly a persistent urban/rural gap
- Persistent gender gap against girls, especially in South Asia
- Relative lack of emphasis on alternative, non-formal approaches to basic education and lack of interest in workplace education[4]
- While much emphasis is placed on getting children into school, not enough attention is paid to the retention rate nor to the completion of schooling

- Urban bias of early childhood programmes
- Continuing shortfalls in national education budgets, especially for countries in economic crisis and in transition, and in relation to school-age population growth
- Continuing shortfalls in international resources for basic education
- Weakness in identifying, refining, and expanding best practices in basic education
- Difficulty in re-casting curricula to address the new risks and challenges facing youth in the region
- Inability to implement the required management reforms for the education systems of countries in transition
- Lack of broad participation of communities and local leadership in management and delivery of education
- Lack of reliable data and statistics
- Increasing the visibility of people with disabilities and other disadvantaged groups
- Disruption or cessation of basic education provisions, facilities and support as a result of national or sub-national armed conflict or emergency
- Lack of capacity to assess educational problems and contributing factors
- Limited testing, assessment and evaluation processes for learning often isolated from previous learning experiences
- The (still) large number of illiterates in the region and the challenge of delivering meaningful and relevant literacy programmes to people living in different social, economic and political circumstances
- Inadequate means of assessing learning performance and achievement
- Disparities between big countries and small island states

IV. Regional Objectives and Strategies

A. GOALS

1. Early Childhood Care and Education (ECCE)[5]

At all stages of life, children should be provided with quality, comprehensive, integrated care and education. Child-centered, family-focused, community-based, holistic care and education of pre-school children is essential for securing the well-being and rights of all children, and should be supported by national policies and sufficient funds. This should be the result of synergistic partnership among families, communities, civil society, NGOs and the government.

ECCE programmes, whether they be family or community based, or linked to schools or learning centres, must focus on caring for and educating the whole child, from birth to school entry. These programmes must promote the child's optimum physical, psycho-social, emotional, cognitive and linguistic development in ways that are culturally and socially relevant.

Investments in capacity-building to improve the quality of care and education through the diverse programme options and services for young children and families are critical. Improved data-gathering and analysis of both programme access and quality indicators, regular monitoring of programme implementation and regulatory frameworks linked to both local and national systems are essential.

ECCE programmes should remain flexible and adaptable to the needs of pre-school children and not become mere extensions of formal school systems. In addition, they should be developmentally appropriate and responsive to the needs and interests of children, and should be firmly anchored on the family and community as the child's primary caring and learning environment.

2. Universal Basic Education

All must have the opportunity to receive a basic education of good quality that focuses on the 'whole' person, including health, nutrition and cognitive and psycho-social development.[6] In order for this to happen, education systems must be able to adapt to the individual needs of child, youth and adult learners, by incorporating formal and non-formal approaches and programmes within an integrated and inclusive system of basic education.

A strong and serious commitment must be made to include the excluded. Clearer analyses must be made of reasons for exclusion, including issues such as language of instruction, and there must be more innovative approaches made to address these reasons.

Greater, more explicit focus and commitment must be given to the identification of unreached children who are not in school and to the promotion of innovative and varied approaches by government and NGOs to meet their diverse educational needs.

There is a need to improve demand as well as increase supply through the closer collaboration and genuine involvement of parents, communities and the private sector in education.

There is also a need to mitigate the direct and indirect costs of basic education, especially for the disadvantaged. In order to achieve universal basic education, systems must become more internally and externally efficient, and focus more sharply on training children in school.

3. Basic Learning and Skills Programmes[7]

There have been impressive gains in Children's, youth and adult literacy in the region, especially for girls and women. These, nonetheless, remain fragile and need constant reinforcement and recommitment.

Conflict, violence, social injustice and other risks affect the lives of people in almost every country in the region. Basic education must focus increasingly on developing skills and capacities for life and work in a rapidly changing world. Values and cultural identity and their preservation must continue to find a prominent place in all learning programmes and teaching practices.

So, too, basic literacy and numeracy skills must be developed in the context of relevant life skills—whether these be work-related or address any of the risks increasingly confronting children, youth and adults. Such programmes should adopt participatory, age-appropriate, culturally sensitive and integrated approaches to peace education and conflict resolution, gender relations, sexual and reproductive health, and HIV/AIDS education.

There is also a need to integrate functional education into equivalency programmes to provide opportunities for out-of-school youth and adults to gain access to relevant and meaningful learning programmes leading to educational certification.

4. Learning Achievement[8]

Improvement in the quality of education is critical to economic and social development, and is therefore a national imperative. Approaches to improving the quality of education require adoption of curriculum content and processes that are learner centered, recognize the diversity of learning needs and stages of cognitive, social and emotional development, and develop knowledge, skills, and attitudes required for independent learning and problem-solving. Improving the quality of education also requires access to appropriate learning resources. Assessment strategies at all levels should reflect such changing emphases, especially the focus on learning how to learn, and include appropriately diverse, continuous and responsive assessment strategies. Training of teachers and educational managers is required to support curriculum reforms and should include modalities which strengthen teacher monitoring and support mechanisms which ensure continuity of reform.

5. Education of Women and Girls and the Elimination of Gender Disparities

It is essential to eliminate systemic gender disparities, where they persist, amongst girls and boys throughout the education system—in enrolment, achievement and completion; in teacher training and career development; in curriculum, and learning practices and learning processes. This requires better appreciation of the role of education as an instrument of women's equality and empowerment.

Furthermore, specific measures should be taken to ensure the inclusion of women and girls with disabilities in all educational processes.

Where possible, also, specific programmes, both formal and non-formal in approach, should be developed to target the increased enrolment, retention and completion of education by girls and women.

6. Literacy and Continuing Education[9]

Via the support of literacy campaigns, the goal of universal literacy should be aspired to in the next decade.

7. Life Skills and Values: Education for Peace and Global Understanding[10]

The education system should strive to address issues of peace, order and socio-political cohesion. Whether school-based or delivered non-formally, basic learning tools should increase the capacities of learners to deal with issues of day-to-day survival, to resolve community conflict and to enjoy human, political and civil rights to a greater extent.

B. STRATEGIC OBJECTIVES

1. Investment and Resource Mobilization

Lack of resources is often a matter of political will, both within national governments and among international funding agencies. Both must continue to increase the absolute and relative size of their budgets devoted to basic education (without sacrificing needed resources for higher levels of education) and to push for more rapid debt relief and new funding mechanisms to complement existing resources directed towards education and health, if necessary through the transfer of budget allocation from the defence sector. Money saved through increased efficiency must continue to be reinvested in education systems and not subtracted from the overall allocation for education.

Special attention and support should be given to the most excluded and least-accessible people in each country, and those suffering the consequences of armed conflict, civil dislocation and natural disasters. The needs of these people should be continually reassessed and the necessary actions defined and taken.

In addition, education policy-making must assume a more central position in public policy dialogue and decision-making. There must be greater recognition of the interconnectedness of public policy issues so that the effects of actions taken in one sector on other sectors are clearly understood. This implies a need for more integrated processes and governmental mechanisms for public policy-planning and a balancing of the influence of Treasury and Finance ministries with the advice of Ministries of Education, Health, Social Welfare, Labour and Regional Development.

2. New Opportunities for Civil Society

The need to broaden the way education in conceptualized, implemented and evaluated requires the greater involvement of NGOs, the media, the private sector and other civil society stakeholders—including families and children—at all levels and all stages of education programme development.

To reach EFA goals, we must ensure that genuine decision-making responsibilities are shared among all elements of society. The strong trend toward decentralization has important implications in terms of the provision of adequate support from the centre and the transfer of both responsibility and decision-making authority to all levels in the administrative hierarchy. The latter requires both a more localized EMIS and stronger management training at lower levels of the system.

More effective collaboration and equal partnership between governments and NGOs must be encouraged. A commitment has already been made between NGOs and governments in the region to create new opportunities for genuine engagement and dialogue, bringing to the partnership strength in innovation, participatory processes, critical analysis, social mobilization, and school-community partnerships—but not at the risk of *user pay* scenarios, polarized education systems and the increased exclusion of disadvantaged children.

3. Education and Poverty Elimination

Attempts must be made to ensure stronger linkages between education policies and programmes, poverty alleviation strategies and public policy-making. A strong focus must be placed on more and better education for excluded groups, culturally appropriate and cognitively stimulating early-childhood care, and education for girls and women, as well as education for life skills and employment.

In addition, the EFA process at all levels must be made barrier-free in attitudinal, informational and physical terms so that people with disabilities and socially disadvantaged groups can participate meaningfully in EFA activities.

Decentralized micro-planning and delivery with people's participation may be utilized on a wider scale for provision of basic education to unserved and underserved populations. NGOs working for the underprivileged should receive support and assistance on a sustainable basis.

4. Equitable Harnessing of New Technologies

The information and telecommunication technologies of the twenty-first century offer new ways of managing the educational processes as well as delivering particular programmes. The ability to access and analyse data and information about formal and non-formal education, and about the community context in which education takes place, encourages better decision-making at local levels. At other levels, policy decisions about technology can be taken to enhance equity and reduce disparities between groups within society at large.

Such technologies can also help to deliver learning programmes at adult and professional levels, such as teacher education through distance education. Further study may be required to see where such technologies are cost-effective in serving the learning needs of children, youth and adults more widely.

In many part of the region, learning is increasingly taking place in an informal, media-based context. This wealth of information resources must be accessible by *all*, and the growing disparity between rich and poor, and the urban/rural divide in terms of access to technology must be taken into account when policies about technology are formulated. In addition, these information resources must be accessible in an equitable and structured way to ensure overall improvement in learning achievement. Information resources should in particular be accessible to people with sensory impairments and in a format that permits ready assimilation of content. Further, the deployment of technology in basic education should be done in a culturally sensitive manner.

Governments must promote popular access to relevant media and technology systems, and incorporate media and technology as both a learning tool and as an interface for the expansion of information dissemination critical to better management.

5. Enabling Teachers and Learning Facilitators

Public perceptions of teachers and teaching must be enhanced; incentives to identify, attract and retain good teachers must be provided; for example, policies should be in place to protect teachers' salaries, rights and welfare. In addition, strong and ongoing teacher, supervisor and manager support and professional development services, at the level of the school and classroom, must be introduced. Teachers themselves must be more genuinely involved in decisions that affect their work. Adequate time and investment must be given to re-train the existing teacher work-force and to reform pre- and in-service training.

The role of teachers and learning is changing in the new decade and is crucial in the fulfilment of the goals of Education for All. New contexts—including new challenges—in which teachers and their learners operate must be clearly understood. Above all, teachers must be able to make learning environments more inclusive and welcoming to children—healthier, more effective and more nurturing.

Adequate learning materials, textbooks, teaching aids and supplemental readers are critical to educating all children. They should reflect learning outcomes and the time available for instruction in the classroom. Values and subject content should be gender-fair and reflective of acceptance of diversity and cultural differences. Policy should foster and development and adaptation of learning experiences and materials to ensure social and cultural relevance for learners.

6. Education Management Reform[11]

Increased emphasis on decentralization of education management should be accompanied by the development of enhanced and comprehensive EMISs that provide timely, relevant, accurate and valid information for local decision-making. Locally relevant indicators compatible with national standards and curriculum frameworks, and that cover quantitative and qualitative aspects of learning, must be developed and monitored. The accountability of the school system to learners themselves, to parents and to communities should be emphasized.

Effective decentralization also requires extensive training of school leaders and local managers, both at the institutional level and in district and provincial offices. Decentralization of authority and responsibility that is supported by improved EMISs and management training will lead to greater accountability and transparency in the allocation and utilization of resources. At the central level, enhancement of EMISs will increase the capacity of policy-makers to model the effects of proposed policy reforms as a basis for policy dialogue aimed at identifying optimal linkages between resource inputs and education outputs.

In addition, mechanisms must be put in place to ensure that managers and policy-makers have access to the latest information and research in the field of education.

7. Integration of Development Activities

Partnership between government, non-government and donors/non-government organisations should encompass policy planning, implementation, monitoring and evaluation.

8. Exchange of Information, Experience and Innovations

With the increasing availability of communication technologies in the region, governments and all stakeholders must promote an equitable exchange of information and experiences about educational innovations that have been, and continue to be, successfully developed by countries and communities in the region. This exchange should cover a wide range of educational dimensions: policy reform, planning and management, resource mobilization, curriculum, teacher training, measurement and evaluation, community participation and linkages between education and poverty alleviation. As a means of exchanging information and experiences, subregional resource centres could be set up in each country.

Asia and Pacific Regional Framework for Action: Additional Concerns

1. Comments were received about the language of the Draft Framework for Action. These comments highlighted the need for stronger and more action-oriented language. Feedback received on the Draft Framework for Action pointed out that it failed to offer mechanisms for translating the vision into reality, it did not outline the new commitments from the partner agencies UNICEF, UNDP, UNFPA, UNESCO and the World Bank, and nor did it propose new directions for the future. Some went further, urging that a statement, acknowledging that some of the commitments and promises made at Jomtien were not achieved, be added to the Dakar Framework for Action.
2. Continuing education for lifelong learning was highlighted by a number of participants, notably APPEAL, as being an important goal if a society is to truly become a learning society. After the completion of basic literacy, it was recommended that post-literacy and continuing education be provided in order to sustain and expand literacy skills.
3. Emphasis must be placed on continuing education for the newly literate and on including in this continuing education the means of achieving scientific and technological literacy.

4. Scientific and technological illiteracy was highlighted as a concern in the region, as well as the need for adequate teacher training in science and technology.
5. Non-formal education should be developed in quality, comparable with the formal education sector, leading to the establishment of an equivalency programme. Furthermore, non-formal education should be given institutional shape.
6. Much debate was centered on the meaning and concept of *quality education*. A suggestion was made that the EFA Forum promote measures and indicators of quality that are common to both formal and non-formal modalities of learning, focusing on competencies, aptitudes and functionality of the things learners learn and how they can apply them to their day-to-day existence.
7. Although many argued for basic education to cater to the needs of disabled people, the fact remains that data on the educational experiences of disabled people remain difficult to access. One way of rectifying this situation could be to include the issue of disability as an indicator in all future country assessments.
8. Children's participation in the Education for All process should be encouraged, considering that childhood is the time when most people begin formal basic education.
9. Care must be taken, however, not to place too much emphasis on child learners at the expense of adult learners. Learning is a lifelong process, and the language of the Dakar Framework for Action must be inclusive of all learners, whether young or old. Likewise, care should be exercised with official EFA documents, pronouncements and pictures, so as not to convey the false impression that EFA is only about children.
10. Attention must be given to the learning needs of adolescents.
11. The Dakar Declaration must state in very clear terms whether secondary education will form part of basic education that should be universalized.
12. Aside from the concern for access of those not in school, a concern for quality, relevance and content of basic education

for those already in school was also expressed. It was felt that a fundamental re-examination of the curriculum and content of all forms of basic education was called for to meet the learning needs of a more complex and interconnected society in the future.

13. The structural reform of a country's basic education system could be viewed as an economic and effective way of meeting that the country's EFA objectives. Consideration of structural reform is particularly pertinent in those countries where the projected rate of growth of the school-age population over the next ten years far exceeds any reasonable expectation concerning the rate of growth of public expenditure on basic education. Many countries would, understandably, by reluctant to attempt to meet the implied funding gap over the next decade by taking up further education loans from either the World Bank or the Asian Development Bank because of the additional burden it placed on their capacity to service such foreign debt.

REFERENCES

1. Some delegates suggested that ten years may be a better timeframe for assessment, rather than the fifteen years suggested in the Draft Dakar Framework for Action.

2. For the purpose of this document, excluded groups include the poor, ethnic minority groups, remote populations, the displaced, people affected by civil unrest or emergency, child workers and people with disabilities, whether they be physical, intellectual or emotional.

3. The point was raised that the challenges be ordered according to importance, though of course this is entirely subjective.

4. Some delegates suggested that this sentence be rephrased in a more positive way, expanded on (see Appendix, par. III) and be included as a Strategic Objective, rather than as a challenge.

5. Some participants mentioned that Early Childhood Care and Development was a more appropriate term.

6. A point of contention was whether a *good* education could be quantified and how many years constituted a *good* education. Bangladesh suggested that good quality should include at least eight years of education, whereas the Maldives want ten. Other

countries, for example the Lao People's Democratic Republic, did not agree to this and felt it should be left to the country to decide what constituted a *good* education. It really depended on country-specific goals and the level of development in the country.

7. Other titles—*'Linking Literacy and Skills Programmes'* and *Adult Literacy and Skills Programmes*—were suggested.
8. Other titles—*'Quality of Learning'* or *'Learning Achievement and Quality of Education'*—were proposed.
9. This additional goal was suggested.
10. This additional goal was suggested.
11. It was suggested that Strategic Objective 6 be expanded to cover not only EMIS, but other aspects of education management, for example, reforms in general systems of management and institutional management and delivery systems.

Appendix—7

REGIONAL FRAMEWORK FOR ACTION EUROPE AND NORTH AMERICA

Adopted by the Conference on Education for All in Europe and North America, Warsaw, Poland, 6-8 February 2000

Preamble

At the invitation of UNESCO, UNDP, UNICEF, UNFPA and the World Bank, government representatives of thirty-nine European and North American countries, and representatives of intergovernmental and non-governmental organisations met in Warsaw from 6 to 8 February 2000. The participants read and took note of the preliminary document concerning the action framework to be adopted at the World Education Forum (Dakar). Discussion was based on the report presented by the Consultative Forum on Education for All, a report based on contributions from thirty-one countries, as well as on two syntheses: one on Central and Eastern Europe, and the other produced by the Organisation for Economic Co-operation and Development (OECD) on its member countries.

Ten years ago, the Jomtien Conference asserted the need to implement the right to education that was provided for in the Universal Declaration of Human Rights, and to meet basic educational needs in each country in the world. Over the past decade all European countries have ratified the Convention on the Rights of the Child.

A number of international conferences have since then repeatedly insisted on the importance of basic education in social and economic development. The World Summit for Social Development (Copenhagen, 1995) fixed 2015 as the ultimate date for Universal Primary Education and this is now the time reference for the EFA movement.

Learning and the learner are at the heart of lifelong learning, itself a cyclical, episodic and continuous concept that involves both intended and unanticipated episodes of learning of both informal and formal nature. Basic education is a part of life-long learning. The importance of valuing the learners' experiences in order to create both the curriculum and opportunities for learning is paramount: education from all as well as for all. Participation in learning builds self-confidence, citizenship and autonomy.

Evolution Over the Past Ten Years

Throughout the world, the trend is towards the development of free market economies and globalization; this is accompanied by an awareness of the importance of education and training. For most of our countries, common characteristics include declining demographic trends. This is turn increases the importance of the quality of education, be it for children, youth or adults of all ages, and the need for education throughout life.

The Jomtien assertions have not always been properly taken into account in Europe and North America: basic education was considered to have been implemented, since primary and lower secondary education were practically universal. However, although our region remains the one in which the outcomes of basic education are the closest to the Jomtien *'enlarged vision'*, the past decade has been marked by regressions and difficulties linked in particular to an increase in social inequalities and violence, and in some countries to war.

In the Eastern part of the European continent, the political and economic system is being transformed. However, from a basic education viewpoint, the transition of these countries towards the free market economy has not been positive:

- in financial terms, in most cases there has been a reduction in expenditure on education;
- in terms of quality and non-discrimination for teachers, whose salary levels have led them to seek supplementary resources; for pedagogical equipment, in particular textbooks and computers; and for teaching conditions related to teaching premises and their facilities;
- in terms of equity, the increased contribution requested from families and from local communities is leading to inequality to the detriment of the most underprivileged families and of the poorest areas, in particular rural

areas. In the context of societies where social inequalities are increasing, this is especially true with the education of young children, whether it concerns access to educational institutions or parents' available resources.

These difficulties have not significantly reduced the percentage of children in full-time education, which remains high, despite a slight decline in a number of cases. However, in the long term they are certain to have a negative influence on the results obtained.

In West Europe and North America, an already universal schooling in primary and lower secondary education has provided a basis for development drives on the other levels. Educational expenditure has continued to increase, in line with GDP and often more rapidly. The education of young children has been reinforced in many countries, even though situations remain quite varied.

However, in Central and Eastern European countries, concern has been expressed with respect to quality and non-discrimination. Disturbing signs and emerging: increase in numbers of drop-outs; low motivation of a number of pupils resulting in endemic truancy; weaker performance of the most disadvantaged pupils—10 per cent, 20 per cent, sometimes more—who do not have access to the level required, in particular, for satisfactory work integration; and development of social exclusion phenomena, of disaffiliation, of drug addiction, of violence, at increasingly young ages. Not only has progress failed significantly to reduce inequality in education according to social, geographical and ethnic origin, but the gap is widening between the majority of young people and a fringe made up by children from the most underprivileged backgrounds with increasing difficulties. This gap also exists among adults, in particular those who have no professional qualification or who are functionally illiterate.

European and North American countries have a responsibility towards the regions of the world where education is less widespread. They meet this responsibility by means of co-operation and development provided in bilateral and multilateral forms. In the field of education, this assistance appears now to focus more on basic education. However, despite the commitments for increases declared by Heads of States of Jomtien and Copenhagen, the level of the aid has decreased over the last decade.

Shaping the Vision

The World Declaration on Education for All called for an expanded vision and a renewed commitment, by stating the objective of basic education in its Article I. It can be summarized as allowing women and men to develop their personal potential to achieve intellectual autonomy, integrate into society and take part in society's development.

Integration into a society depends on the nature of the society. Education therefore has a national aspect, and even sometimes a sub-national aspect. According to the Jomtien Declaration, 'The scope of basic learning needs and how they should be met varies with individual countries and cultures, and inevitably, changes with the passage of time.'

For the past ten years, we have been increasingly aware of a stronger and stronger interaction between countries, influenced by technical evolution and the sharing of ideas: this is the phenomenon known as globalization. It is characterized by, among other things, the fundamental importance of knowledge, so as to allow change, and education, so as to make the change acceptable. The evolution mentioned in the Jomtien Declaration should therefore lead to a convergence in levels of education for the countries in the world. However, an education system cannot be severed from its historical, cultural, religious and linguistic roots, which our fellow citizens consider as essential, no doubt in reaction to the threat of loss of identity that globalization can represent.

To ensure sustainable and peaceful development in North American and European countries, renewed emphasis is required on '*learning to live together*' in the Education for All context. This should enable individuals to better understand themselves and others, and to contribute to the world's progress towards a unity respectful of and founded on creative diversity.

In this context, renewed efforts to fight racism, ethnocentrism, anti-Semitism and xenophobia are needed.

Education for democratic citizenship concerns not only the teaching of democratic norms but essentially the development of reflective and creative persons. It is based on the understanding that democracy is not fixed and immutable, but rather that it must be built and rebuilt every day in every society. Over the past ten years, our countries have joined together in the will to form democratic societies; for such societies, the future is to be invented and built; the mission of education is to prepare future citizens so that they can take part in this initiative.

In the past, basic education was defined in terms of an obligation fixed by the state and covering the childhood period, and therefore meant primary school. Today, such a definition has several deficiencies:

- with the development of knowledge and of its influence on the lives of people, basic education takes more time: in our countries, it covers at least lower secondary education and touches other levels;
- basic education cannot be defined solely by an obligatory duration, but must now be defined in terms of outcomes;
- basic education should indeed become an 'education for everybody' regardless of age, social and economic background, gender and residence, founded on the respect for difference. The problems to be solved concern those who do not reach the level required for successful integration into working life and who cannot take part in social development; children who fail often come from very underprivileged families and, conversely, failure in school often leads to social exclusion; and the solution to these problems is therefore closely linked to anti-poverty strategies;
- the definition of basic education is no longer fixed by the state alone: in many cases, the expectations of society and of families, and the economy, along with

the supply of knowledge from outside of the formal education system, have led to the evolution of educational duration and content;

- because as society is rapidly changing, each individual needs lifelong learning: learning how to learn is seen as a fundamental skill for all. The expanding area of adult basic education for out-of-school children, youth and adults is essential to achieving learning throughout life.

The foundation of this process begins at birth. Early childhood education and care must be holistic and integrated to ensure the survival, growth and development of young child. In particular, more attention should be paid to young children under 3 years old, children in difficult and emergent situations and in rural areas for their participation in and access to quality early childhood programmes.

The primary child caretakers are parents, and the family and community environment plays an important role. In this regard, an effort to link early childhood education and care with adult education deserves attention. The learning that parents and grandparents do enhances the learning that children do. In turn, the success or failure of learning at school has an impact on how adults learn later on in their lives. The vision, provision, policy and system of early childhood education and care can vary across countries, but there is a growing consensus that some form of early childhood programme focusing on the child's holistic development is essential to favour the social, psychological, affective and cognitive development of the young child.

THREE LEVELS OF ACTION

In Each Country

1. Definition of Basic Education

The definition of basic education must be in terms of levels to be attained, and knowledge and skills to be acquired along the lines of the Jomtien 'enlarged vision', not in terms of a period of compulsory school education.

Basic education allows personal development, intellectual autonomy, integration into professional life and participation in the development of the society in the context of democracy. In order to achieve these aims, basic education must lead to the acquisition of:

- key skills used as personal development tools and, later on, as a basis for lifelong learning;
- initial vocational guidance;
- the knowledge, values and abilities that are needed for individual development, and for the exercise of participatory and responsible citizenship in a democracy.

2. Operational Goals for 2015

- All young women and men achieve basic education as defined in their country, through their initial education.
- Young people and adults who have not achieved the set level of basic education, or who have lost the corresponding skills, are offered the means to undergo training in order to attain this level; in particular promotion of literacy is an essential task.
- In the framework of their right to education, children of at least 3 are offered access to pre-primary education on request from their parents.

3. Strategies

3.1 National Action Plan

Develop, in constitution with all stakeholders, a national action plan with precise goals and objectives, and agreed milestones for assessing progress. This plan should include and deal with very precise questions on all aspects of curriculum. It will pay particular attention to the right of disadvantaged groups to education.

3.2 Allocation of Resources

The investment level currently dedicated to education, despite decreasing, demographic trends, must be maintained;

and if reductions have been made in the level of education expenditure since 1990, investment should be increased to what it was then. Benchmark resources are needed to increase the efficiency in the use of resources.

Education should be given high priority, and not less than 6 per cent of a country's GNP should be devoted to education, as recommended by the International Commission on Education for the Twenty-first Century, chaired by Jacques Delors.

3.3 Equitable Allocations

Ensure that the allocation of public resources for education across sub-sectors and communities serve to reduce inequities in access and quality rather than to exacerbate them, particularly through the use of positive discrimination measures.

3.4 Effective Partnerships

Set up the institutional and legal formulas to ensure a real sharing of responsibility among the various levels (central, regional and local) of public authorities responsible for education.

Promote effective and formal partnerships between schoolteachers, families, communities, civil society, employers, voluntary bodies, social services and political authorities. This is particularly important for excluded groups: parents must have the possibility to express the difficulties that hinder the educational success of their children and to take part in the definition of solutions so as to achieve this success. Education for democratic citizenship also relies on effective partnership in order to ensure commitment of the whole of society to prevent racism and xenophobia. Partnerships alone allow taking advantage of all the opportunities society provides for learning, especially to ensure that all adults have a right to education. Many adults never participate in learning opportunities after leaving school. Education for all must address this. The development of the International Adult Learners' Week (September 2000) following on from International Literacy Day is one way of encouraging participation in adult learning, increasing international solidarity.

Moreover, partnership contributes to linking education to working life; and to take full advantage of the changing employment environment that community service provides for increasing opportunities for employment (not necessary paid or fully paid employment) and the student's need to be aware of this. Career guidance and consulting services for both young people and adults need strengthening.

3.5 Address Specific Issues

Identify a specific set of problem issues and develop strategies to address them. The experience of the past decade in this region suggests that these might include identifying children excluded from basic education (rural children, disabled children, girls, street children, ethnic minorities and children affected by conflict or HIV/AIDS), and implementing flexible and creative programmes to restore their right to basic education.

Promising directions include:

- more opportunities for teachers' initiative, creativity and decision-making;
- more attention to cultivating a positive attitude to learning;
- a focus on general skills, life skills and competencies;
- rethinking the content and organisation of general education by relating it to contemporary life and student interests;
- improving the quality of education by ensuring that schools are healthy for children, effective with children and protective of children. This implies a broader definition of quality that includes addressing the quality of learners (health, nutrition, etc.), the quality of the curricula including assessment and materials, the quality of the learning process (teachers and technologies to enhance learning) and the quality of the learning environment (child-centered, gender-sensitive, healthy and safe). Furthermore, basic education can play a role in reducing risks of infection by HIV/AIDS and other health hazards;

- intergenerational learning: the learning that parents and grandparents do enhances the learning that children do. In turn, the success or failure of learning at school impacts on how adults learn later on in their lives;
- develop and support awareness of the cultures present in each country, understanding differences, intercultural exchanges and creativity as well as defending democratic and universal values by all forms and practices of formal and non-formal education;
- support lifelong education for citizenship efforts of non-governmental organisations and citizens, associations that participate in the democratic dynamic and cultural development.

3.6 Monitoring

- Set up a monitoring plan that allows levels achieved to be measured against levels required and in particular to determine, in social and geographical terms, the populations that have the most difficulties in attaining the objectives set. Research-based policies should explore how individuals and their communities can learn, and why they do not.
- Establish quality-improvement systems to enable the responsible education personnel to allocate resources according to locally perceived needs and priorities. Enlisting parents, teachers and community representatives in this process can promote ownership and help to enhance a sense of local responsibility.

3.7 Personnel

Basic education and basic training personnel include all the actors related to the educational, social, cultural and health sectors.

The main objective is to instil in the institutions and the personnel that are responsible for education, the will that is needed in order to attain the goal of the educational success of each pupil and to develop the practices that are required for this purpose. It implies, in particular, training and retraining teachers, assessing schools and teachers, co-ordinating their action, and training teachers and social interveners in how to dialogue with excluded families and with the parents of pupils in difficulty.

The Warsaw regional EFA conference refers to the already internationally adopted documents such as the ILO Convention on the Status of Teachers and the 1996 recommendations of the 45th International Conference on Education. Measures to increase the social status of teachers of all school levels should be taken; this has to do not only with salaries but also with academic qualification and access to Post-graduate studies. At the same time it should be emphasized that the nature of the teaching profession is related to decision-making and planning, and to identifying and solving problems, rather than to transmitting knowledge and following rules. The recognition of this fact has consequences for the goals and style of in-service teacher-education programmes. Teacher must have the possibility with their organisations to participate in the process of formulating educational policies.

Moreover, the essential role of universities and other institutions of higher education should also be emphasized both in educational research and in pre-service teacher education.

In the Region

1. Sharing information, good practices and interesting experiences in the management and improvement of basic education systems across the region should be facilitated in order to find common convergent solutions. This regional co-operation should rely on existing intergovernmental (Council of EUROPE, UNESCO, OECD, EU, CIS, NAFTA, OSCE, etc.) and non-governmental structures. These exchanges can be encouraged to take place in a variety of ways, including e-mail, written communication, ad hoc meetings and committees.
2. Given the need for further improvement of education systems, particularly in hard-hit economies of Central and Eastern Europe, enhanced flows of financial assistance are

needed and should be provided. In this context, bilateral, regional and multilateral agencies are invited to re-assess their priorities and to consider significant increases of assistance to education.

With the Whole World

Education must be allowed to play its key role for lasting development in the context of globalization and by respecting the responsibilities of each country. This can be achieved by implementing the following measures:

1. Empower developing countries to identify their needs, and to lead and own their development by working in close partnership towards achieving the goals defined at the Dakar Forum.
2. Encourage international organisations, notably the UNESCO Institute for Statistics, to improve and collect internationally comparable data and develop quality research and thus enable to worldwide community to assess achievement of the goals established in Dakar. This process should be done in concentration and co-operation with national and regional research and statistical institutions international agencies will be asked to assist in national capacity-building for statistical collection and analysis.
3. Rectify the level of assistance that is provided by the countries in our region and reserve an adequate portion for basic education in order to met the expectations of all actors in the field of Education for All.
4. Since there is no common model for Overseas Development Aid, an early rethinking of its levels, ways and means by the North American and European countries should be considered in light of the Dakar Forum.
5. The revised draft Dakar Declaration should be made available to all ministries, institutions and authorities concerned by 30 March at the latest to allow for proper consultation and consensus building.

Appendix—8

RECIFE DECLARATION OF THE E–9 COUNTRIES

Adopted by the E–9 Ministerial Review Meeting Recife, Brazil, 31 January—2 February 2000

Preamble

1. We, the Ministers of Education and representatives of the E-9 countries comprising Bangladesh, Brazil, China, Egypt, India, Indonesia, Mexico, Nigeria and Pakistan, and accounting for more than 50 per cent of the world's population, having assembled in Recife, Brazil from 31 January to 2 February 2000, have reviewed the progress of EFA in our countries. Having taken note of the national reports of the nine countries, we recognize with deep satisfaction that, since the Jomtien Conference, March 1990, and the EFA Summit of Heads of State of the E–9 countries, New Delhi, December 1993, there have been significant breakthroughs in all of the nine countries.

2. Despite the diversities among E–9 countries, there is a consensus regarding the achievements recorded during the past ten years in the field of education as well as the need to draft a new visionary agenda for the new millennium that will reaffirm basic education as a human right.

3. We believe that the objectives of Education for All should be pursued through evaluations of the programmes specific to each country and by targeted actions to address the multiplicity of problems. We also believe that the realities of the twenty-first century demand that we adopt the newest methods and most modern technologies in our pursuit of truly global modernization in the field of education in order to achieve excellence for all. These challenges affect not only the E-9 countries but are also shared by all countries throughout the world.

4. The key challenge is the promotion of social and economic development with equity through quality education for all. Besides formal organisations for basic education, we should seek to engage civil society in a broader context with all its

creativity and commitment. We underline that education is for excellence and excellence is for all.

5. The fact is that some of the E–9 countries are in a state of transition, confronted simultaneously by the challenges of advancing to higher levels of development while also addressing the problems of underdevelopment. These countries work to meet advanced standards of excellence while still dealing with pockets of backwardness in education.

6. We attest to the crucial role of national governments in partnership with provincial governments, local bodies, NGOs and civil society in meeting EFA goals with renewed enthusiasm.

7. New paradigms of international solidarity are urgently needed. These new models require increased technical co-operation among countries and regions as well as broad technical and financial support from international agencies and development partners. Such co-operation in turn requires the careful designing of specific projects that will allow us to draw on the experience garnered throughout the world in solving educational problems over the past decade.

We Acknowledge the Achievements of the Decade which include

- massive reduction in adult illiteracy;
- increase in early childhood education strategies that involve parents and that support vulnerable families;
- substantial increase in pre-school educational services;
- significant advance towards universal elementary education;
- improved gender equity in school access for boys and girls and for school attendance;
- addressing early development of attitudes and values for coexistence and civic education;
- decentralization of educational services;
- development of a national curriculum framework;

- advance in the process of inclusion of children with special needs in mainstream schools;
- use of distance education for the expansion of learning and for teacher training;
- development of programmes for specific target groups with appropriate inbuilt incentives;
- strengthening of national database, evaluation and accreditation systems for education;
- expansion of partnerships with NGOs, civil society and private sector;
- increasing public awareness for EFA through media and advocacy.

We Recognize the Following Challenges

- persistence of large numbers of illiterates in some countries;
- provision of access to basic education in remote and inaccessible areas;
- expansion of provision of early childhood education and development;
- further massive reduction of illiteracy and promotion of technological learning and life skills;
- improved quality and learning achievement in education;
- addressing adequately existing inequalities in education, particularly in regard to girls' and women's education.
- mastery learning and excellence for all.

We Declare the Following as Our Goals

- according highest national priority to EFA and in particular to the eradication of adult illiteracy;
- increasing the number of students that complete basic, middle and higher education;
- total inclusion of children with special needs in the mainstream schools;

- effecting changes in legislation to extend basic education and include education for all in policy statements;
- implementation of new educational modalities that link education to the work force;
- ensuring access and equity for population located in inaccessible areas;
- developing national networks of communication systems for universal school access to internet and all forms of electronic media;
- strengthening moral values in the basic education curriculum, stressing the importance of democratic values such as justice, fairness, tolerance, and respect for diversity and equity for teachers and students;
- enhancement of quality education measured not only by national standards attained in traditional subjects but also by the acquisition of knowledge, life skills and technological abilities;
- improvement of the quality of initial and in-service teacher education;
- development of special programmes that respond directly to the problems of groups that have been traditionally excluded from development;
- increasing the participation of civil society including the local community to promote basic learning and lifelong learning for all;
- increasing modern technology and distance learning in all aspects of EFA;
- establishing an effective programme for post-literacy and continuing education;
- paying greater attention to education of adolescents (HIV/AIDS) to equip them with life skills;
- strengthening databases for education;
- continuing necessary reforms in management of education to improve administration and supervision;

- sharpening focus on gender equity;
- ensuring excellence for all in education.

Resource Mobilization

We wish to strengthen our resolve to further increase resource allocations for EFA, at the level of national government down to the provincial, state and local bodies, and by mustering the support of civil society, NGOs as well as industry and business towards contribution and involvement in EFA.

The success of the EFA programme critically depends on mobilization of adequate resources for education. While all the countries acknowledge this requirement, some of the countries of the group face enormous constraints in mobilizing adequate resources.

The Role of the International Community

Acknowledging the valuable support and assistance offered at the national level by UNDP, UNESCO, UNFPA, UNICEF, the World Bank and bilateral donors in pursuing the goals of EFA, we would like to invite these agencies to renew and review their role and strategies in conformity with national plans and priorities and to evolve a more co-ordinated framework for providing international assistance to quality education for all.

We unequivocally call on the international community to prioritize assistance to:

1. support National Plans for Basic Education of each Member State;
2. facilitate reduction and writing off of debt burden in a manner that provides additional funding for education as well as commits further resources to education;
3. promote advocacy and awareness of the benefits of literacy in alleviating poverty, promoting health and mitigating social tensions in order to assure sustainable development;
4. provide technical assistance to improve educational statistics and information systems and strengthening the evaluation for quality education for all.

Vision for the Future

We acknowledge that quality education for all will be our biggest challenge and also our greatest hope. Universal access to education will allow our peoples to participate more effectively in an interactive world.

The onset of the information and knowledge revolution is changing our lives in an unprecedented manner. Knowledge has become the capital and the currency of the twenty-first century. New technologies, new mechanisms and immensely large and varied sources of information are influencing our private and public lives. While remaining committed to utilizing the advanced and modern technologies, we shall remain equally committed to maintaining the cultural identities of our respective societies and countries.

We realize that we can help the world advance the cause of humanity by striking a balance between acquisition of information and knowledge and enrichment of the essence of our rich heritage. We realize the need for a synergy between technological modernity and traditional values. We look ahead to a future in which our countries are liberated from the burden of illiteracy and are fully empowered to move in fruitful harmony towards peace, prosperity and global stability, security and technological development.

The Way Forward

We, the Ministers and representatives of E–9 countries, reaffirm our joint commitment and pledge to sustain, intensify and accelerate our efforts and policies for achieving the laudable goals of EFA. While appreciating the sincerity and enormity of efforts made by governments and civil society in our countries, we acknowledge the seriousness of the problems that continue to impede our progress towards EFA. We appreciate that new challenges have surfaced over the past decade that need to be addressed in an innovative and creative manner. We see renewed hope in the emerging technologies that provide undreamed-of opportunities for lifelong learning and that have the potential to enable our countries to leap-frog into the new millennium with hope.

We call on the international community to express their solidarity and to continue to lend their support to our endeavours in this regard. We believe that a continuous sharing of knowledge and experiences could make a visible contribution towards a more efficient implementation of national EFA policies and programmes. We wish to strengthen alliances and effective partnerships between countries and the international community to give a fresh impetus to EFA. We approach the new millennium with the hope and optimism generated by our achievements and resolve to address the challenges of EFA with even greater determination and commitment to achieve excellence for all.

Appendix—9

WORLD DECLARATION ON EDUCATION FOR ALL

Meeting Basic Learning Needs

Adopted by the World Conference on Education for All. Meeting Basic Learning Needs, Jomtien, Thailand, 5-9 March 1990

Preamble

More than 40 years ago, the nations of the world, speaking through the Universal Declaration of Human Rights, asserted that 'everyone has a right to education'. Despite notable efforts by countries around the globe to ensure the right to education for all, the following realities persist:

- more than 100 million children, including at least 60 million girls, have no access to primary schooling;
- more than 960 million adults, two-thirds of whom are women, are illiterate, and functional illiteracy is a significant problem in all countries, industrialized and developing;
- more than one-third of the world's adults have no access to the printed knowledge, new skills and technologies that could improve the quality of their lives and help them shape, and adapt to, social and cultural change; and
- more than 100 million children and countless adults fail to complete basic education programmes; millions more satisfy the attendance requirements but do not acquire essential knowledge and skills;

At the same time, the world faces daunting problems; notably mounting debt burdens, the threat of economic stagnation and decline, rapid population growth, widening economic disparities among and within nations, war, occupation, civil strife, violent crime, the preventable deaths of millions of children and widespread environmental degradation. These problems constrain efforts to meet basic learning needs, while the lack of basic education among a significant proportion of the population prevents societies from addressing such problems with strength and purpose.

These problems have led to major setbacks in basic education in the 1980s in many of the least-developed countries. In some other countries, economic growth has been available to finance education, expansion, but even so, many millions remain in poverty and unschooled or illiterate. In certain industrialized countries, too, cutbacks in government expenditure over the 1980s have led to the deterioration of education.

Yet the world is also at the threshold of a new century, with all its promise and possibilities. Today, there is genuine progress toward peaceful detente and greater co-operation among nations. Today, the essential rights and capacities of women are being realized. Today, there are many useful scientific and cultural developments. Today, the sheer quantity of information available in the world—much of it relevant to survival and basic well-being—is exponentially greater than that available only a few years ago, and the rate of its growth is accelerating. This includes information about obtaining more life-enhancing knowledge—or learning how to learn. A synergistic effect occurs when important information is coupled with another modern advance—our new capacity to communicate.

These new forces, when combined with the cumulative experience of reform, innovation, research and the remarkable educational progress of many countries, make the goal of basic education for all—for the first time in history—an attainable goal.

Therefore, we participants in the World Conference on Education for All, assembled in Jomtien, Thailand, from 5 to 9 March, 1990:

Recalling that education is a fundamental right for all people women and men, of all ages, throughout our world;

Understanding that education can help ensure a safer, healthier, more prosperous and environmentally sound world, while simultaneously contributing to social, economic, and cultural progress, tolerance, and international co-operation;

Knowing that education is an indispensable key to, though not a sufficient condition for, personnel and social improvement;

Recognizing that traditional knowledge and indigenous cultural heritage have a value and validity in their own right and a capacity to both define and promote development;

Acknowledging that, overall, the current provision of education is seriously deficient and that it must be made more relevant and qualitatively improved, and made universally available;

Recognizing that sound basic education is fundamental to the strengthening of higher levels of education and of scientific and technological literacy and capacity and thus to self-reliant development; and

Recognizing the necessity to give to present and coming generations an expanded vision of, and a renewed commitment to, basic education to address the scale and complexity of the challenge;

proclaim the following

World Declaration on Education for All: Meeting Basic Learning Needs

---

Education for All: The Purpose

Article 1. Meeting Basic Learning Needs

1. *Every person—child, youth and adult—shall be able to benefit from educational opportunities designed to meet their basic learning needs.* These needs comprise both essential learning tools (such as literacy, oral expression, numeracy, and problem solving) and the basic learning content (such as knowledge skills, values, and attitudes) required by human beings to be able to survive, to develop their full capacities, to live and work in dignity, to participate fully in development, to improve the quality of their lives, to make informed decisions, and to continue learning. The scope of basic learning needs and how they should be met varies with

individual countries and cultures, and inevitably, changes with the passage of time.

2. The satisfaction of these needs empowers individuals in any society and confers upon them a responsibility to respect and build upon their collective cultural, linguistic and spiritual heritage, to promote the education of others, to further the cause of social justice, to achieve environmental protection, to be tolerant towards social, political and religious systems which differ from their own, ensuring that commonly accepted humanistic values and human rights are upheld, and to work for international peace and solidarity in an interdependent world.

3. Another and no less fundamental aim of educational development is the transmission and enrichment of common cultural and moral values. It is in these values that the individual and society find their identity and worth.

4. Basic education is more than an end in itself. It is the foundation for lifelong learning and human development on which countries may build, systematically, further levels and types of education and training.

Education for All: An Expanded Vision and A Renewed Commitment

Article 2. Shaping the Vision

1. *To serve the basic learning needs of all requires more than a recommitment to basic education as it now exists. What is needed is an 'expanded vision' that surpasses present resource levels, institutional structures, curricula, and conventional delivery systems while building on the best in current practices.* New possibilities exist today which result from the convergence of the increase in information and the unprecedented capacity to communicate. We must seize them with creativity and a determination for increased effectiveness.

2. As elaborated in Articles 3–7, the expanded vision encompasses:

   - universalizing access and promoting equity;
   - focusing on learning;

- broadening the means and scope of basic education;
- enhancing the environment for learning;
- strengthening partnerships.

3. The realization of an enormous potential for human progress and empowerment is contingent upon whether people can be enabled to acquire the education and the start needed to tap into the ever-expanding pool of relevant knowledge and the new means for sharing this knowledge.

Article 3. Universalizing Access and Promoting Equity

1. *Basic education should be provided to all children, youth and adults.* To this end, basic education services of quality should be expanded, and consistent measures must be taken to reduce disparities.
2. For basic education to be equitable, all children, youth and adults must be given the opportunity to achieve and maintain an acceptable level of learning.
3. The most urgent priority is to ensure access to, and improve the quality of education for girls and women, and to remove every obstacle that hampers their active participation. All gender stereotyping in education should be eliminated.
4. An active commitment must be made to removing educational disparities. Underserved groups—the poor; street and working children; rural and remote populations; nomads and migrant workers; indigenous peoples; ethnic, racial, and linguistic minorities; refugees; those displaced by war; and people under occupation—should not suffer any discrimination in access to learning opportunities.
5. The learning needs of the disabled demand special attention. Steps need to be taken to provide equal access to education to every category of disabled persons as an integral part of the education system.

Article 4. Focusing on Learning

Whether or not expanded educational opportunities will translate into meaningful development—for an individual or for society—

depends ultimately on whether people actually learn as a result of those opportunities, i.e. whether they incorporate useful knowledge, reasoning ability, skills, and values. The focus of basic education must, therefore, be on actual learning acquisition and outcome, rather than exclusively upon enrolment, continued participation in organised programme and completion of certification requirements. Active and participatory approaches and particularly valuable in assuring learning acquisition and allowing learners to reach their fullest potential. It is, therefore, necessary to define acceptable levels of learning acquisition for educational programmes and to improve and apply systems of assessing learning achievement.

Article 5. Broadening the Means and Scope of Basic Education

The diversity, complexity, and changing nature of basic learning needs of children, youth and adults necessitates broadening and constantly redefining the scope of basic education to include the following components:

- *Learning begins at birth.* This calls for early childhood care are initial education. These can be provided through arrangements involving families, communities, or institutional programmes, as appropriate.
- *The main delivery system for the basic education for children outside the family is primary schooling.* Primary education must be universal, ensure that the basic learning needs of all children are satisfied, and take into account the culture, needs, and opportunities of the community. Supplementary alternative programmes can help meet the basic learning needs of children with limited or no access to formal schooling, provided that they share the same standards of learning applied to schools and are adequately supported.
- *The basic learning needs of youth and adults are diverse and should be met through a variety of delivery systems.* Literacy programmes are indispensable because literacy is a necessary skill in itself and the foundation of other like skills. Literacy in the mother-tongue strengthens cultural identity and heritage. Other needs can be served by:

skills training, apprenticeships, and formal and non-formal education programmes in health, nutrition, population, agricultural techniques, the environment, science, technology, family life including fertility awareness, and other societal issues.

- *All available instruments and channels of information, communications and social action could be used to help convey essential knowledge and inform and educate people on social issues.* In addition to the traditional means, libraries, television, radio and other media can be mobilized to realize their potential towards meeting basic education needs of all.

These components should constitute an integrated system—complementary, mutually reinforcing, and of comparable standards and they should contribute to creating and developing possibilities for lifelong learning.

Article 6. Enhancing the Environment for Learning

Learning does not take place in isolation. Societies, therefore, must ensure that all learners receive the nutrition, health care, and general physical and emotional support they need in order to participate actively in and benefit from their education. Knowledge and skills that will enhance the learning environment of children should be integrated into community learning programmes for adults. The education of children and their parents or other caretakers is mutually supportive and this interaction should be used to create, for all, a learning environment of vibrancy and warmth.

Article 7. Strengthening Partnerships

National, regional and local educational authorities have a unique obligation to provide basic education for all, but they cannot be expected to supply every human, financial or organisational requirement for this task. New and revitalized partnerships at all levels will be necessary: partnerships among all sub-sectors and forms of education, recognizing the special role of teachers and that of administrators and other educational personnel; partnerships between education and other government departments, including planning, finance, labour, communications and other social sectors; partnerships between government and non-governmental organisations, the private sector, local communities, religious groups, and families. The recognition of the vital role of both families and teachers is particularly important. In this context, the terms and conditions of services of teachers and their status, which constitute a determining factor in the implementation of education for all, must be urgently improved in all countries in line with the joint ILO/UNESCO. Recommendation Concerning the Status of Teachers (1966). Genuine partnerships contribute to the planning, implementing, managing and evaluating of basic education programmes. When we speak of 'an expanded vision and a renewed commitment', partnerships are at the heart of it.

Education for All: The Requirements

Article 8. Developing A Supportive Policy Context

1. *Supportive policies in the social, cultural and economic sectors are required in order to realize the full provision and utilization of basic education for individual and societal improvement.* The provision of basic education for all depends on political commitment and political will backed by appropriate fiscal measures and reinforced by educational policy reforms and institutional strengthening. Suitable economic, trade, labour employment and health policies will enhance learners' incentives and contributions to societal development.
2. Societies should also insure a strong intellectual and scientific environment for basic education. This implies improving higher education and developing scientific research. Close contact with contemporary technological and scientific knowledge should be possible at every level of education.

Article 9. Mobilizing Resources

1. *If the basic needs of all are to be met through a much broader scope of action than in the past, it will be essential to mobilize existing and new financial and human resources, public, private and voluntary.* All of society has a contribution to make, recognizing that time, energy and funding directed to basic education and perhaps the most profound investment in people and in the future of a country which can be made.

2. Enlarged public-sector support means drawing on the resources of all the government agencies responsible for human development, through increased absolute and proportional allocations to basic education services with the clear recognition of competing claims on national resources of which education in an important one, but not the only one. Serious attention to improving the efficiency of existing educational resources and programmes will not only produce more, it can also be expected to attract new resources. The urgent task of meeting basic learning needs may require a reallocation between sectors, as for example, a transfer from military to educational expenditure. Above all, special protection for basic education will be required in countries undergoing structural adjustment and facing severe external debt burdens. Today, more than ever, education must be seen as a fundamental dimension of any social, cultural, and economic design.

Article 10. Strengthening International Solidarity

1. *Meeting basic learning needs constitutes a common and universal human responsibility. It requires international solidarity and equitable and fair economic relations in order to redress existing economic disparities.* All nations have valuable knowledge and experiences to share for designing effective educational policies and programmes.
2. Substantial and long-term increases in resources for basic education will be needed. The world community, including inter-governmental agencies and institutions, has an urgent responsibility to alleviate the constraints that prevent some countries from achieving the goal of education for all. It will mean the adoption of measures that augment the national budgets of the poorest countries or serve to relieve heavy debt burdens. Creditors and debtors must seek innovative and equitable formulae to resolve these burdens, since the capacity of many developing countries to respond effectively to education and other basic needs will be greatly helped by finding solutions to the debt problem.

3. Basic learning needs of adults and children must be addressed wherever they exist. Least developed and low-income countries have special needs which require priority in international support for basic education in the 1990s.

4. All nations must also work together to resolve conflicts and strife, to end military occupations, and to settle displaced populations, or to facilitate their return to their countries of origin, and ensure that their basic learning needs are met. Only a stable and peaceful environment can create the conditions in which every human being, child and adult alike, may benefit from the goals of this Declaration.

We, the participants in the World Conference on Education for All, reaffirm the right of all people to education. This is the foundation of our determination, singly and together, to ensure education for all.

We commit ourselves to act co-operatively through our own spheres of responsibility, taking all necessary steps to achieve the goals of education for all. Together we call on governments, concerned organisations and individuals to join in this urgent undertaking.

The basic learning needs of all can and must be met. There can be no more meaningful way to begin the International Literacy Year, to move forward the goals of the United Nations Decade of Disabled Persons (1983-92), the World Decade for Cultural Development (1988-97), the Fourth United Nations Development Decade (1991-2000), of the Convention on the Elimination of Discrimination against Women and the Forward Looking Strategies for the Advancement of Women, and of the Convention on the Rights of the Child. There has never been a more propitious time to commit ourselves to providing basic learning opportunities for all the people of the world.

We adopt, therefore, this *World Declaration on Education for All: Meeting Basic Learning Needs* and agree on the *Framework for Action to Meet Basic Learning Needs*, to achieve this goals set forth in the *Declaration*.

Framework for Action to Meet Basic Learning Needs

Guidelines for implementing the World Declaration on Education for All

Introduction

1. This *Framework for Action to Meet Basic Learning Needs* derives from the *World Declaration on Education for All*, adopted by the World Conference on Education for All, which brought together representatives of governments, international and bilateral development agencies, and non-governmental organisations. Based on the best collective knowledge and the commitment of these partners, the *Framework* is intended as a reference and guide for national governments, international organisations, bilateral aid agencies, non-governmental organisations (NGOs), and all those committed to the goal of Education for All in formulating their own plans of action for implementing the *World Declaration*. It describes three broad levels of concerted action: *(i)* direct action within individual countries, *(ii)* co-operation among groups of countries sharing certain characteristics and concerns, and *(iii)* multilateral and bilateral co-operation in the world community.

2. Individual countries and groups of countries, as well as international, regional and national organisations, may use the *Framework* to develop their own specific plans of action and programmes in line with their particular objectives, mandates and constituencies. This indeed has been the case in the ten-year experience of the UNESCO Major Project on Education for Latin America and the Caribbean. Further examples of such related initiatives are the UNESCO Plan of Action for the Eradication of Illiteracy by the Year 2000, adopted by the UNESCO General Conference at its 25th session (1989); the ISESCO Special Programme (1999-2000); the current review by the World Bank of its policy for primary education; and USAID's programme for Advancing Basic Education and Literacy. Insofar as such plans of action, policies and programmes are consistent with this Framework, efforts throughout the world to meet basic learning needs will converge and facilitate co-operation.

3. While countries have many common concerns in meeting the basic learning needs of their populations, these concerns do, of course, vary in nature and intensity from country to country depending on the actual status of basic education as well as the cultural and socio-economic context. Globally by the year 2000, if enrolment rates remain at current levels, there will be more than 160 million children without access to primary schooling simply because of population growth. In much of sub-Saharan Africa and in many low income countries elsewhere, the provision of universal primary education for rapidly growing numbers of children remains a long-term challenge. Despite progress in promoting adult literacy, most of these same countries still have high illiteracy rates, while the numbers of functionally illiterate adults continue to grow and constitute a major social problem in much of Asia and the Arab States, as well as in Europe and North America. Many people are denied equal access on grounds of race, gender, language, disability, ethnic origin, or political convictions. In addition, high drop-out rates and poor learning achievement are commonly recognized problems throughout the world. These very general characterizations illustrate the need for decisive action on a large scale, with clear goals and targets.

Goals and Targets

4. The *ultimate goal* affirmed by the *World Declaration on Education for All* is to meet the basic learning needs of all children youth, and adults. The long-term effort to attain that goal can be maintained more effectively if *intermediate goals* are established and progress toward these goals is measured. Appropriate authorities at the national and subnational levels may establish such intermediate goals, taking into account the objectives of the *Declaration* as well as overall national development goals and priorities.

5. Intermediate goals can usefully be formulated as specific targets within national and subnational plans for educational development. Such targets usually *(i)* specify expected attainments and outcomes in reference to terminal performance specifications within an appropriate time-frame,

(ii) specify priority categories (e.g. the poor, the disabled), and *(iii)* are formulated in terms such that progress toward them can be observed and measured. These targets represents a *floor* (but not a *ceiling*) for the continued development of education programmes and services.

6. Time-bound targets covey a sense of urgency and serve as a reference against which indices of implementation and accomplishment can be compared. As societal conditions change, plans and targets can be reviewed and updated. Where basic education efforts must be focussed to meet the needs of specific social groups or population categories, linking targets to such priority categories of learners can help to maintain the attention of planners, practitioners and evaluators on meeting the needs of these learners. Observable and measurable targets assist in the objective evaluation of progress.

7. Targets need not be based solely on current trends and resources. Initial targets can reflect a realistic appraisal of the possibilities presented by the *Declaration* to mobilize additional human, organisational, and financial capacities within a co-operative commitment to human development. Countries with low literacy and school enrolment rates, and very limited national resources, will need to make hard choices in establishing national targets within a realistic timeframe.

8. Countries may wish to set their own targets for the 1990s in terms of the following proposed dimensions:

   (i) Expansion of early childhood care and developmental activities, including family and community interventions, *especially* for poor, disadvantaged and disabled children;

   (ii) Universal access to, and completion of, primary education (or whatever higher level of education is considered as *basic*) by the year 2000;

   (iii) Improvement in learning achievement such that an agreed percentage of an appropriate age cohort (e.g. 80% of 14 year-olds) attains or surpasses a defined level of necessary learning achievement;

(iv) Reduction of the adult illiteracy rate (the appropriate age group to be determined in each country) to, say, one-half its 1990 level by the year 2000, with sufficient emphasis on female literacy to significantly reduce the current disparity between male and female illiteracy rates;

(v) Expansion of provisions of basic education and training in other essential skills required by youth and adults, with programme effectiveness assessed in terms of behavioural changes and impacts on health, employment and productivity;

(vi) increased acquisition by individuals and families of the knowledge, skills and values required for better living and sound and sustainable development, made available through all education channels including the mass media, other forms of modern and traditional communication, and social action, with effectiveness assessed in terms of behavioural change.

9. Levels of performance in the above should be established, when possible. These should be consistent with the focus of basic education both on universalization of access and on learning acquisition, as joint and inseparable concerns. In all cases, the performance targets should include equity by gender. However, setting levels of performance and of the proportions of participants who are expected to reach these levels of specific basic education programmes must be an autonomous task of individual countries.

Principles of Action

10. The first step consists in identifying, preferably through an active participatory process involving groups and the community, and traditional learning systems which exist in the society, and the actual demand for basic education services, whether expressed in terms of formal schooling or non-formal education programmes. Addressing the basic learning needs of all means: early childhood care and development opportunities; relevant, quality primary schooling or equivalent out-of-school education for children; and literacy, basic knowledge and life skills training for

youth and adults. It also means capitalizing on the use of traditional and modern information media and technologies to educate to public on matters of social concern and to support basic education activities. These complementary components of basic education need to be designed to ensure equitable access, sustained participation, and effective learning achievement. Meeting basic learning needs also involves action to enhance the family and community environments for learning and to correlate basic education and the larger socio-economic context. The complementarity and synergistic effects of related human resources investments in population, health and nutrition should be recognized.

11. Because basic learning needs are complex and diverse, meeting them requires multisectoral strategies and action which are integral to overall development efforts. Many partners must join with the education authorities, teachers, and other educational personnel in developing basic education if it is to be seen, once again, as the responsibility of the entire society. This implies the active involvement of a wide range of partners—families, teachers, communities, private enterprises (including those involved in information and communication), government and non-governmental organisations, institutions, etc.—in planning, managing and evaluating the many forms of basic education.

12. Current practices and institutional arrangements for delivering basic education, and the existing mechanisms for co-operation in this regard, should be carefully evaluated before new institutions or mechanisms are created. Rehabilitating dilapidated schools and improving the training and working conditions of teachers and literacy workers, building on existing learning schemes, are likely to bring greater and more immediate returns on investment than attempts to start afresh.

13. Great potential lies in possible joint actions with non-governmental organisations on all levels. These autonomous bodies, while advocating independent and critical public views, might play roles in monitoring, research, training and

material production for the sake of non-formal and life-long educational processes.

14. The primary purpose of bilateral and multilateral co-operation should appear in a true spirit of partnership—it should not be to transparent familiar models, but to help develop the endogenous capacities of national authorities and their in-country partners to meet basic learning needs effectively. Actions and resources should be used to strengthen essential features of basic education services, focussing on managerial and analytical capacities, which can stimulate further developments. International co-operation and funding can be particularly valuable in supporting major reforms or sectoral adjustments, and in helping to develop and test innovative approaches to teaching and management, where new approaches need to be tried and/or extraordinary levels of expenditure are involved and where knowledge of relevant experiences elsewhere can often be useful.

15. International co-operation should give priority to the countries currently least able to meet the basic learning needs of their populations. It should also help countries redress their internal disparities in educational opportunity. Because two-thirds of illiterate adults and out-of-school children are female, wherever such inequities exist, a most urgent priority is to improve access to education for girls and women, and to remove every obstacle that hampers their active participation.

1. Priority Action at National Level

16. Progress in meeting the basic learning needs of all will depend ultimately on the actions taken within individual countries. While regional and international co-operation and financial assistance can support and facilitate such actions, government authorities, communities and their several in-country partners are the key agents for improvement, and national governments have the main responsibility for coordinating the effective use of internal and external resources. Given the diversity of countries' situations, capacities and development plans and goals, this *Framework*

can only suggest certain areas that merit priority attention. Each country will determine for itself what specific actions beyond current efforts may be necessary in each of the following areas.

1.1 Assessing Needs and Planning Action

17. To achieve the targets set for himself, each country is encouraged to develop or update comprehensive and long-term plans of action (from local to national levels) to meet the learning needs it has defined as *basic*. Within the context of existing education-sector and general development plans and strategies, a plan of action for basic education for all will necessarily be multisectoral, to guide activities in the sectors involved (e.g. education information, communications/media, labour, agriculture, health). Models of strategic planning, by definition, vary. However, most of them involve constant adjustments among objectives, resources, actions, and constraints. At the national level, objectives are normally couched in broad terms and central government resources are also determined, while actions are taken at the local level. Thus, local plans in the same national setting will naturally differ not only in scope but in content. National and subnational frameworks and local plans should allow for varying conditions and circumstances. These might, therefore, specify:

   - studies for the evaluation of existing systems (analysis of problems, failures and successes);
   - the basic learning needs to be met, including cognitive skills, values, attitudes, as well as subject knowledge;
   - the languages to be used in education;
   - means to promote the demand for, and broadscale participation in, basic education;
   - modalities to mobilize family and local community support;
   - targets and specific objectives;
   - the required capital and recurrent resources, duly costed, as well as possible measures for cost effectiveness;

- indicators and procedures to be used to monitor progress in reaching the targets;
- priorities for using resources and for developing services and programmes over time;
- the priority groups that require special measures;
- the kinds of expertise required to implement the plan;
- institutional and administrative arrangements needed;
- modalities for ensuring information sharing among formal and other basic education programmes; and
- an implementation strategy and timetable.

1.2 Developing a Supportive Policy Environment

18. A multisectoral plan of action implies adjustments to sectoral policies so that sectors interact in a mutually supportive and beneficial manner in line with the country's overall development goals. Action to meet basic learning needs should be an integral part of a country's national and subnational development strategies, which should reflect the priority given to human development. Legislative and other measures may be needed to promote and facilitate co-operation among the various partners involved. Advocacy and public information about basic education and important in creating a supportive policy environment at national, subnational and local levels.

19. Four specific steps that merit attention are: *(i)* initiation of national and subnational level activities to create a broad, public recommitment to the goal of education for all; *(ii)* reduction of inefficiency in the public sector and exploitative practices in the private sector; *(iii)* provision of improved training fro public administrators and of incentives to retain qualified women and men in public service; and *(iv)* provision of measures to encourage wider participation in the design and implementation of basic education programmes.

1.3 Designing Policies to Improve Basic Education

20. The preconditions for educational quality, equity and efficiency, are set in the early childhood years, making attention to early childhood care and development essential to the achievement of basic education goals. Basic education must correspond to actual needs, interests, and problem of the participations in the learning process. The relevance of curricula could be enhanced by linking literacy and numeracy skills and scientific concepts with learners' concerns and earlier experiences, for example, nutrition, health and work. While many needs vary considerably within and among countries, and therefore much of a curriculum should be sensitive to local conditions, there are also many universal needs and shared concerns which should be addressed in education curricula and in educational messages. Issues such as protecting the environment, achieving a balance between population and resources, slowing the spread of AIDS, and preventing drug abuse are everyone's issues.

21. Specific strategies addressed to improve the conditions of schooling may focus on: learners and the learning process, personnel (teachers, administrators, others), curriculum and learning assessment, materials and physical facilities. Such strategies should be conducted in an integrated manner; their design, management, and evaluation should take into account the acquisition of knowledge and problem-solving skills as well as the social, cultural, and ethical dimensions of human development. Depending on the outcomes desired, teachers have to be trained accordingly, whilst benefiting from in-service programmes as well as other incentives of opportunity which put a premium on the achievement of these outcomes; curriculum and assessment must reflect a variety of criteria while materials—and conceivably buildings and facilities as well—must be adapted along the same lines. In some countries, the strategy may include ways to improve conditions for teaching and learning such that absenteeism is reduced and learning time increased. In order

to meet the educational needs of groups not covered by formal schooling, appropriate strategies are needed for non-formal education. These include but go far beyond the aspects described above, but may also give special attention to the need for coordination with other forms of education, to the support of all interested partners, to sustained financial resources and to full community participation. An example for such an approach applied to literacy can be found in UNESCO's Plan of Action for the Eradication of Illiteracy by the Year 2000. Other strategies still may rely on the media to meet the broader education needs of the entire community. Such strategies need to be linked to formal education, non-formal education or a combination of both. The use of the communications media holds a tremendous potential to educate the public and to share important information among those who need to know.

22. Expanding access to basic education of satisfactory quality is an effective way to improve equity. Ensuring that girls and women stay involved in basic education activities until they have attained at least the agreed necessary level of learning, can be encouraged through special measures designed, wherever possible, in consultation with them. Similar approaches are necessary to expand learning opportunities for various disadvantaged groups.

23. Efficiency in basic education does not mean providing education at the lowest cost, but rather the most effective use of all resources (human, organisational, and financial) to produce the desired levels of access and of necessary learning achievement. The foregoing considerations of relevance, quality, and equity are not alternatives to efficiency but represent the specific conditions within which efficiency should be attained. For some programmes, efficiency will require more, not fewer, resources. However, if existing resources can be used by more learners or if the same learning targets can be reached at the lower cost per learner, then the capacity of basic education to meet the targets of access and achievement for presently underserved groups can be increased.

1.4 Improving Managerial, Analytical and Technological, Capacities

24. Many kinds of expertise and skills will be needed to carry out these initiatives. Managerial and supervisory personnel, as well as planners, school architects, teacher educators, curriculum, developers, researchers, analysts, etc., are important for any strategy to improve basic education, but many countries do not provide specialized training to prepare them for their responsibilities; this is especially true in literacy and other out-of-school basic education activities. A broadening of outlook toward basic education will be a crucial prerequisite to the effective co-ordination of efforts among these many participants, and strengthening and developing capacities for planning and management at regional and local levels with a greater sharing of responsibilities will be necessary in many countries. Pre-and in-service training programmes for key personnel should be initiated, or strengthened where they do exist. Such training can be particularly useful in introducing administrative reforms and innovative management and supervisory techniques.

25. The technical services and mechanisms to collect, process and analyze data pertaining to basic education can be improved in all countries. This is an urgent task in many countries that have little reliable information and/or research on the basic learning needs of their people and on existing basic education activities. A country's information and knowledge base is vital in preparing and implementing a plan of action. One major implication of the focus on learning acquisition is that systems have to be developed and improved to assess the performance of individual learners and delivery mechanisms. Process and outcome assessment data should serve as the core of a management information system for basic education.

26. The quality and delivery of basic education can be enhanced through the judicious use of instructional technologies. Where such technologies are not now widely used, their introduction will require the selection and/or development of suitable technologies acquisition of the necessary

equipment and operating systems, and the recruitment or training of teachers and other educational personnel to work with them. The definition of a suitable technology varies by societal characteristics and will change rapidly over time as new technologies (educational radio and television, computers, and various audio-visual instructional devices) become less expensive and more adaptable to a range of environments. The use of modern technology can also improve the management of basic education. Each country may reexamine periodically its present and potential technological capacity in relation to its basic educational needs and resources.

1.5 Mobilizing Information and Communication Channels

27. New possibilities are emerging which already show a powerful impact on meeting basic learning needs, and it is clear that the educational potential of these new possibilities has barely been tapped. These new possibilities exist largely as a result of two converging forces, both recent by-products of the general development process. First, the quantity of information available in the world—much of it relevant to survival and basic well-being—is exponentially greater than that available only a few years ago, and the rate of its growth is accelerating. A synergistic effect occurs when important information is coupled with a second modern advance—the new capacity to communicate among the people of the world. The opportunity exists to harness this forces and use it positively, consciously, and with design, in order to contribute to meeting defined learning needs.

1.6 Building Partnerships and Mobilizing Resources

28. In designing the plan of action and creating a supportive policy environment for promoting basic education, maximum use of opportunities should be considered to expand existing collaborations and to bring together new partners: e.g., family and community organisations, non-governmental and other voluntary associations, teacher's unions, other professional groups, employers, the media, political parties, co-operatives, universities, research

institutions, religious bodies, as well as education authorities and other government departments and services (labour, agriculture, health, information, commerce, industry, defence, etc.). The human and organisational resources these domestic partners represent need to be effectively mobilized to play their parts in implementing the plan of action. Partnerships at the community level and at the intermediate and national levels should be encouraged; they can help harmonize activities, utilize resources more effectively, and mobilize additional financial and human resources where necessary.

29. Governments and their partners can analyze the current allocation and use of financial and other resources for education and training in different sectors to determine if additional support for basic education can be obtained by *(i)* improving efficiency, *(ii)* mobilizing additional sources of funding within and outside the government budget, and *(iii)* allocating funds within existing education and training budgets, taking into account efficiency and equity concerns. Countries where the total fiscal support for education is low need to explore the possibility of reallocating some public funds used for other purposes to basic education.

30. Assessing the resources actually or potentially available for basic education and comparing them to the budget estimates underlying the plan of action, can help identify possible inadequacies of resources that may affect the scheduling of planned activities over time or may require choices to be made. Countries that require external assistance to meet the basic learning needs of their people can be use the resource assessment and plan of action as a basis for discussions with their international partners and for coordinating external funding.

31. The individual learners themselves constitute a vital human resource that needs to be mobilized. The demand for, and participation in, learning opportunities cannot simply be assumed, but must be actively encouraged. Potential learners need to see that the benefits of basic education activities exceed the costs of participants must bear, such as earnings foregone and reduced time available for community and

household activities and for leisure. Women and girls, especially, may be deterred from taking full advantage of basic education opportunities because of reasons specific to individual cultures. Such barriers to participation may be overcome through the use of incentives and by programmes adapted to the local context and seen by the learners, their families and communities to be *productive activities*. Also, learners tend to benefit more from education when they are partners in the instructional process, rather than treated simply as *inputs* or *beneficiaries*. Attention to the issues of demand and participation will help assure that the learners' personal capacities are mobilized for education.

32. Family resources, including time and mutual support, are vital for the success of basic education activities. Families can be offered incentives and assistance to ensure that their resources and invested to enable all family members to benefit as fully and equitably as possible from basic education opportunities.

33. The preeminent role of teachers as well as of other educational personnel in providing quality basic education needs to be recognized and developed to optimize their contribution. This must entail measures to respect teachers' trade union rights and professional freedoms, and to improve their working conditions and status, notably in respect to their recruitment, initial and in-service training, remuneration and career development possibilities as well as to allow teachers to fulfil their aspirations, social obligations, and ethical responsibilities.

34. In partnerships with school and community workers, libraries need to become a vital link in providing educational resources for all learners—pre-school through adulthood—in school and non-school settings. There is therefore, a need to recognize libraries as invaluable information resources.

35. Community associations, co-operatives, religious bodies, and other non-governmental organisations also play important roles in supporting and in providing basic education. Their experience, expertise, energy and direct relationships with various constituencies are valuable resources for identifying and meeting basic learning needs.

Their active involvement in partnerships for basic education should be promoted through policies and mechanisms that strengthen their capacities and recognize their autonomy.

2. Priority Action at Regional Level

36. Basic learning needs must be met through collaborative action within each country, but there are many forms of co-operation between countries with similar conditions and concerns that could, and do, assist in this endeavour. Regions have already developed plans, such as the Jakarta Plan of Action on Human Resources, adopted by ESCAP in 1988. By exchanging information and experience, pooling expertise, sharing facilities, and undertaking joint activities, several countries, working together, can increase their resource base and lower costs to their mutual benefit. Such arrangements are often set up among neighbouring countries (sub-regional), among all countries in a major geo-cultural region, or among countries sharing a common language or having cultural and commercial relations. Regional and international organisations often play an important role in facilitating such co-operation between countries. In the following discussions, all such arrangements are included in the term *regional*. In general, existing regional partnerships will need to be strengthened and provided with the resources necessary for their effective functioning in helping countries meet the basic learning needs of their populations.

2.1 Exchanging Information, Experience and Expertise

37. Various regional mechanisms, both inter-governmental and non-governmental, promote co-operation in education and training, health, agricultural development, research and information, communications, and in other fields relevant to meeting basic learning needs. Such mechanisms can be further developed in response to the evolving needs of their constituents. Among several possible examples are the four regional programmes established through UNESCO in the 1980s to support national efforts to achieve universal primary education and eliminate adult illiteracy:

- Major Project in the Field of Education in Latin America and the Caribbean;
- Regional Programme for the Eradication of Illiteracy in Africa;
- Asia-Pacific Programme of Education for All (APPEAL);
- Regional Programme for the Universalization and Renewal of Primary Education and the Eradication of Illiteracy in the Arab States by the Year 2000 (ARABUPEAL).

38. In addition to the technical and policy consultations organised in connection with these programmes, other existing mechanisms can be used for consulting on policy issues in basic education. The conferences of ministers of education organized by UNESCO and by several regional organisations, the regular sessions of the regional commissions of the United Nations, and certain trans-regional conferences organised by the Commonwealth Secretariat, CONFEMEN (standing conference of ministers of education of francophone countries), the Organisation of Economic Co-operation and Development (OECD), and the Islamic Educational, Scientific and Cultural Organisation (ISESCO), could be used for this purpose as needs arise. In addition, numerous conferences and meetings organised by non-governmental bodies provide opportunities for professionals to share information and views on technical and policy issues. The conveners of these various conferences and meetings may consider ways of extending participation, where appropriate, to include representatives of other constituencies engaged in meeting basic learning needs.

39. Full advantage should be taken of opportunities to share media messages or programmes that can be exchanged among countries or collaboratively developed, especially where language and cultural similarities extend beyond political boundaries.

2.2 Undertaking Joint Activities

40. There are many possible joint activities among countries in support of national efforts to implement action plans for

basic education. Joint activities should be designed to exploit economies of scale and the comparative advantages of participating countries. Six areas where this form of regional collaboration seems particularly appropriate are: *(i)* training of key personnel, such as planners, managers, teacher educators, researchers, etc.; *(ii)* efforts to improve information collection and analysis; *(iii)* research; *(iv)* production of educational materials; *(v)* use of communication media to meet basic learning needs; and *(vi)* management and use of distance education services. Here, too, there are several existing mechanisms that could be utilized to foster such activities, including UNESCO's International Institute of Educational Planning and its networks of trainees and research as well as IBE's information network and the UNESCO Institute for Education, the five networks for educational innovation operating under UNESCO's auspices, the research and review advisory groups (RRAGs) associated with the International Development Research Centre, the Commonwealth of Learning, the Asian Cultural Center for UNESCO, the participatory network established by the International Council for Adult Education, and the International Association for the Evaluation of Educational Achievement, which links major national research institutions in some 35 countries. Certain multilateral and bilateral development agencies that have accumulated valuable experience in one or more of these areas might be interested in participating in joint activities. The five United Nations regional commissions could provide further support to such regional collaboration, especially by mobilizing policymakers to take appropriate action.

3. Priority Action at World Level

41. The world community has a well-established record of co-operation in education and development. However, international funding for education stagnated during the early 1980s; at the same time, many countries have been handicapped by growing debt burdens and economic relationships that channel their financial and human resources to wealthier countries. Because concern about the

issues in basic education is shared by industrialized and developing countries alike, international co-operation can provide valuable support for national efforts and regional actions to implement the expanded vision of basic Education for All. Time, energy, and funding directed to basic education are perhaps the most profound investment in people and in the future of a country which can be made; there is a clear need and strong moral and economic argument for international solidarity to provide technical co-operation and financial assistance to countries that lack the resources to meet the basic learning needs of their populations.

3.1 Cooperation within the International Context

42. Meeting basic learning needs constitutes a common and universal human responsibility. The prospects for meeting basic learning needs around the world are determined in part by the dynamics of international relations and trade. With the current relaxation of tensions and the decreasing number of armed conflicts, there are now real possibilities to reduce the tremendous waste of military spending and shift those resources into socially useful areas, including basic education. The urgent task of meeting basic learning needs may require such a reallocation between sectors, and the world community and individual governments need to plan this conversion of resources for peaceful uses with courage and vision, and in a thoughtful and careful manner. Similarly, international measures to reduce or eliminate current imbalances in trade relations and to reduce debt burdens must be taken to enable many low-income countries to rebuild their own economies, releasing and retaining human and financial resources needed for development and for providing basic education to their populations. Structural adjustment policies should protect appropriate funding levels for education.

3.2 Enhancing National Capacities

43. International support should be provided, on request, to countries seeking to develop the national capacities needed

for planning and managing basic education programmes and services *(see Section 1.4)*. Ultimate responsibility rests within each nation to design and manage its own programmes to meet the learning needs of all its population. International support could include training and institutional development in data collection, analysis and research, technological innovation, and educational methodologies. Management information systems and other modern management methods could also be introduced, with an emphasis on low and middle level managers. These capabilities will be even more in demand to support quality improvements in primary education and to introduce innovative out-of-school programmes. In addition to direct support to countries and institutions, international assistance can also be usefully channelled to support the activities of international, regional and other inter-country structures that organize joint research, training and information exchanges. The latter should be based on, and supported by, existing institutions and programmes, if need be improved and strengthened, rather than on the establishment of new structures. Support will be especially valuable for technical cooperation among developing countries, among whom both circumstances and resources available to respond to circumstances are often similar.

3.3 Providing Sustained Long-term Support for National and Regional Actions

44. Meeting the basic learning needs of all people in all countries is obviously a long-term undertaking. This *Framework* provides guidelines for preparing national and subnational plans of action for the development of basic education through a long-term commitment of governments and their national partners to work together to reach the targets and achieve the objectives they set for themselves. International agencies and institutions, many of which are sponsors, co-sponsors, and associate sponsors of the World Conference on Education for All, should actively seek to plan together and sustain their long-term support for the kinds of national and regional actions outlined in the proceeding sections. In

particular, the core sponsors of the Education for All initiative (UNDP, USESCO, UNICEF, World Bank) affirm their commitments to supporting the priority areas for international action presented below and to making appropriate arrangements for meeting the objectives of Education for All, each acting within its mandate, special responsibilities, and decisions of its governing bodies. Given that UNESCO is the UN agency with a particular responsibility for education, it will give priority to implementing the *Framework for Action* and to facilitating provision of services needed for reinforced international co-ordination and co-operation.

45. Increased international funding is needed to help the less developed countries implement their own autonomous plans of action in line with the expanded vision of basic Education for All. Genuine partnerships characterized by co-operation and joint long-term commitments will accomplish more and provide the basis for a substantial increase in overall funding for this important sub-sector of education. Upon governments' request, multilateral and bilateral agencies should focus on supporting priority actions, particularly at the country level *(see Section I)*, in areas such as the following:

   (a) *The design or updating of national and subnational multisectoral plans of action* (see *Section I. 1)*, which will need to be elaborated very early in the 1990s. Both financial and technical assistance are needed by many developing countries, particularly in collecting and analyzing data, as well as in organising domestic consultations.

   (b) *National efforts and related inter-country co-operation to attain a satisfactory level of quality and relevance in primary education. (cf. Sections I. 3 and 2 above).* Experiences involving the participation of families, local communities, and non-governmental organisations in increasing the relevance and improving the quality of education could profitably be shared among countries.

(c) *The provision of universal primary education in the economically poorer countries.* International funding agencies should consider negotiating arrangements to provide long-term support, on a case-by-case basis, to help countries move toward universal primary education according to their timetable. The external agencies should examine current assistance practices in order to find ways of effectively assisting basic education programmes which do not require capital- and technology- intensive assistance, but often need longer-term budgetary support. In this context, greater attention should be given to criteria for development co-operation in education to include more than mere economic considerations.

(d) *Programmes designed to meet the basic learning needs of disadvantaged groups, out-of-school youth, and adults with little or no access to basic learning opportunities.* All partners can share their experience and expertise in designing and implementing innovative measures and activities, and focus their funding for basic education on specific categories and groups (*e.g.* women, the rural poor, the disabled) to improve significantly the learning opportunities and conditions available for them.

(e) *Education programmes for women and girls.* These programmes should be designed to eliminate the social and cultural barriers which have discouraged or even excluded women and girls from benefits of regular education programmes, as well as to promote equal opportunities in all aspects of their lives.

(f) *Education programmes for refugees.* The programmes run by such organisations as the United Nations High Commission for Refugees (UNHCR) and the United Nations Relief and Works Agency for Palestine (UNRWA) need more substantial and reliable long-term financial support for this recognized international responsibility. Where countries of refuge need international financial and technical assistance to cope with the basic needs of refugees, including their learning needs, the international community can help to share this burden through increased cooperation. The world community will also endeavour to ensure that people under occupation or displaced by war and other calamities continue to have access to basic education programmes that preserve their cultural identity.

(g) *Basic education programmes of all kinds in countries with high rates of illiteracy (as in sub-Saharan Africa) and with large illiterate populations (as in South Asia).* Substantial assistance will be needed to reduce significantly the world's large number of illiterate adults.

(h) *Capacity building for research and planning and the experimentation of small-scale innovations.* The success of Education for All actions will ultimately be determined by the capacity of each country to design and implement programs that reflect national conditions. A strengthened knowledge base nourished by research findings and the lessons of experiments and innovations as well as the availability of competent educational planners will be essential in this respect.

46. The coordination of external funding for education is an area of shared responsibility at country level, in which host governments need to take the lead to ensure the efficient use of resources in accordance with their priorities. Development funding agencies should explore innovative and more flexible modalities of co-operation in consultation with the governments and institutions with which they work and co-operate in regional initiatives, such as the Task Force of Donors to African Education. Other forums need to be developed in which funding agencies and developing countries can collaborate in the design of inter-country projects and discuss general issues relating to financial assistance.

3.4 Consultations on Policy Issues

47. Existing channels of communication and forums for consultation among the many partners involved in meeting

basic learning needs should be fully utilized in the 1990s to maintain and extend the international consensus underlying this *Framework for Action*. Some channels and forums, such as the biannual International Conference on Education, operate globally, while others focus on particular regions or groups of countries or categories of partners. Insofar as possible, organisers should seek to coordinate these consultations and share results.

48. Moreover, in order to maintain and expand the Education for All initiative, the international community will need to make appropriate arrangements, which will ensure co-operation among the interested agencies using the existing mechanisms insofar as possible: *(i)* to continue advocacy of basic Education for All, building on the momentum generated by the World Conference; *(ii)* to facilitate sharing information on the progress made in achieving basic education targets set by countries for themselves and on the resources and organisational requirements for successful initiatives; *(iii)* to encourage new partners to join this global endeavour; and *(iv)* to ensure that all partners are fully aware of the importance of maintaining strong support for basic education.

Indicative Phasing of Implementation for the 1990s

49. Each country, in determining its own intermediate goals and targets and in designing its plan of action for achieving them, will, in the process, establish a timetable to harmonize and schedule specific activities, Similarly, regional and international action will need to be scheduled to help countries meet their targets on time. The following general schedule suggests an indicative phasing during the 1990s; of course, certain phases may need to overlap and the dates indicated will need to be adopted to individual country and organisational contexts.

(i) Governments and organisations set specific targets and complete or update their plans of action to meet basic learning needs *(cf. Section 1.1)*; take measures to create a supportive policy environment (1.2); devise policies to improve the relevance, quality, equity and

efficiency of basic education services and programmes (1.3); design the means to adapt information and communication media to meet basic learning needs (1.5) and mobilize resources and establish operational partnerships (1.6). International partners assist countries, through direct support and through regional co-operation, to complete this preparatory stage. (1990-1991)

(ii) Development agencies establish policies and plans for the 1990s, in line with their commitments to sustained, long-term support for national and regional actions and increase their financial and technical assistance to basic education accordingly (3.3). All partners strengthen and use relevant existing mechanisms for consultation and co-operation and establish procedures for monitoring progress at regional and international levels. (1990-1993)

(iii) First stage of implementation of plans of action: national coordinating bodies monitor implementation and propose appropriate adjustments to plans. Regional and international supporting actions are carried out. (1990-1995)

(iv) Governments and organisations undertake mid-term evaluation of the implementation of their respective plans and adjust them as needed. Governments, organisations and development agencies undertake comprehensive policy reviews at regional and global levels. (1995-1996)

(v) Second stage of implementation of plans of action and of supporting action at regional and international levels. Development agencies adjust their plans as necessary and increase their assistance to basic education accordingly. (1996-2000)

(vi) Governments, organisations and development agencies evaluate achievements and undertake comprehensive policy review at regional and global levels. (2000-2001)

• • •